THE GOOD PRISON GUIDE

THE GOOD
PRISON GUIDE

Charlie Bronson

with Stephen Richards

Published by John Blake Publishing Ltd,
3 Bramber Court, 2 Bramber Road,
London W14 9PB, England

www.blake.co.uk

First published in paperback in 2007

ISBN: 978 1 84454 359 5

British Library Cataloguing-in-Publication Data:

A catalogue record for this book is available from the British Library.

Design by www.envydesign.co.uk

Printed in the UK by CPI Bookmarque, Croydon, CR0 4TD

5 7 9 10 8 6 4

Papers used by John Blake Publishing are natural, recyclable products
made from wood grown in sustainable forests. The manufacturing processes
conform to the environmental regulations of the country of origin.

Every attempt has been made to contact the relevant copyright-holders,
but some were unobtainable. We would be grateful if the appropriate
people could contact us.

I dedicate my book to my two angels, Sami and Saira
– without them I would have rotted in hell –
and to my loving brother John, whom I miss dearly.
Forgive me for not being with you at your final hour
of life, but the journey has to go on.

CONTENTS

FOREWORD

For anyone who has never been to prison and served time, understanding what prison is all about is well nigh impossible, but I will try to explain it to you. Remember when you were a child – maybe you played hide-and-seek – you looked for the best place to hide. Usually, the hiding place was a cramped space in a dark and dingy cupboard; that experience might have been the nearest you will ever come to understanding what being in prison is really about.

Let me tell you a little about prison segregation units, as they are where both Charlie Bronson and I spent most of our prison life. Charlie continues to experience these units whilst I have long since left them behind. Even so, the memory of them is branded deep within my mind.

I have been given the almost impossible job of having to describe the hell on earth these segregation units represent. I don't even think the imagination of horror writer Stephen King could impart the degradation, the pain and suffering these places create for mankind.

These places are 'extreme'; they are places where even the rodents and cockroaches only prowl around in a last desperate attempt to find food. Finding a cockroach in one of these places is like finding a long-lost friend; it is your only friend!

According to how dangerous you have been labelled, between two and ten screws await you when your cell is unlocked. Should you decide to fight them, then you can be certain that however many are there at the start, twice that amount will come running to the aid of their colleagues. And, as Charlie says, no matter how many times you land a punch on them, you will receive ten back for every one you throw.

You will find yourself stripped naked and forced into a piece of equipment called a 'body belt'. This is forcibly wrapped around your midriff and is fastened so tight that every breath becomes so painful that you wish your breathing would stop, but it can't ... it's what keeps you alive! The belts come in various sizes, but you can count on them wrapping you with one which is always a couple of sizes too small.

Then your hands are cuffed to each side of the body belt in a cuff that is attached to it. You're now trussed up and not able to defend yourself from the boots and fists that come flying your way.

In the days when the liquid cosh was around, you were forcibly injected with it; all that was needed was a simple authorisation from the MO (medical officer), so the following morning the doctor would come in and sign all these back-dated authorisations for the screws. In effect, then, you would have been forcibly injected without the prior authorisation of the doctor, but what doctor would defy the system and own up to this having happened – none!

You are then slung into a strip-cell that only has dirt on the floor and muck on the walls; your brain is drained and your body is weakened. Anyone without a strong mind could crack in such a place. That is how it was when I first met Charlie in Armley Prison in Leeds almost 30 years ago! Ever since, we have remained good friends and things have changed in some of the prisons ... but not all!

Currently, Charlie is in Wakefield Prison, in the Special Unit. He's totally isolated from mainstream and other high-security prisoners because he's considered double dangerous. These secure conditions enforced upon Charlie can vary in the degree of degradation and violence inflicted on him, depending on which prison he's in. Although the staff within certain prisons might be welcoming and understanding, as they seem to be where Charlie is currently housed, this doesn't mean that the conditions are acceptable. Being locked up on your own for 23 hours out of a 24-hour day cannot be considered humane.

In such an environment, your whole existence becomes regimented and controlled by regular events. You become used to the hour of day when you are given the free run of the exercise cage or yard. When the appointed time arrives, come rain or shine, you want your exercise ... it becomes a ritual. No matter whether the prison has a shortage of staff, no matter whether the Governor's wife has died ... you expect to be unlocked at the appointed time.

You expect to be let out of your cell at the appointed time for your weekly shower; you expect the library trolley to be on time; you time your day by your meals. And when any of these patterns is broken, you can become a very angry and disgruntled person. That's all you've got in your life. Nothing else matters; nothing else can matter. Everyone has forsaken you, or so it seems, and you're on your own, you have to stand up for your own rights. Many flounder by the wayside, but a few like Charlie and I grasped the nettle of solitary confinement. We bathed in all its gory glory, we filled our senses with the infusion of pain and we embraced the unremitting violence inflicted on us. We braved the coldness that winter brought and, in the summer, we stifled in the heat. We couldn't escape the elements.

These units are nothing but a punishment inflicted on those within by Prison Service HQ. They argue that segregation is not a punishment but merely a tool to stop dangerous prisoners mixing with their fellow cons. Isolation within the confines of a prison is legalised brainwashing. Isolation is sensory depravation at its best ... or worst. The doors are several feet thick ... or so it seems, they might as well be, as you can't hear anything going on beyond them. You've got two doors in your cell, one opens to another, and that's why you can't hear what's going on. This is why a cockroach can become your friend, a living thing. Never mind if there's life on Mars, just seeing another living thing in your cell can be just as awesome.

What alternatives are there for the prisoner in isolation, what can they spend their time doing? Recreation is limited. Education means studying in your cell on your own; you have to find the strength from within. Religion is no longer forced upon you, it's there if you want it. But that's it.

How do you go about challenging such a state of isolation? You can do it physically or legally. Years ago, we did it physically, but now we've got the European courts behind us, and some are doing it legally. That is what Charlie is starting to understand ... that the pen is mightier than the sword. Until the courts actually challenge and outlaw these isolation units and make them obsolete and illegal, then I know that someone somewhere will be suffering in one of these places.

To give you an idea of what it's like being in isolation, I will tell you about the time Charlie and I had a little mix up which was caused by the paranoia that such isolation creates in prisoners.

Charlie once sent me a letter to the effect that he believed me to be making fun of his life sentence. I have still got that letter, in which he wrote 'do not make fun of a life sentence'. Those were the words he used for one reason or another – I don't know why – but Charlie is Charlie. Of course, me being me, I blew my top completely!

I lost it, I really did, and, as a consequence of what I did out of temper, I could have been killed that day ... his letter flipped me. I actually went into Newcastle's East End and put my gloves on because I was just so wound up. It was a slagging letter and that was just part of it. I went to this boxing club, and you are talking about a lot of big lads there, you are talking about big bouncers. At my age, I shouldn't even have been in the ring.

I ended up with a face like a piece of raw liver, but I could not feel any pain, I was just blinded from the pain and I just wanted to battle on and on. I went round after round, one after the other.

And what brought me round was hearing this voice, it was Carlo's, one of my sons, and he was at the ringside crying. I was in a right state, and so were a few others, but the aggression kept me going, but I didn't know I was doing it.

That is how much respect I have for Charlie for what he's gone through and endured, but this one letter ... all my past just came flooding back in one big gush. For Charlie to say that I was laughing at his life sentence was something that had been misunderstood by him caused by the paranoia that being in isolation brings with it. I wouldn't laugh at somebody doing a *week* behind bars.

Since then, it has all been straightened out and Charlie gave me real big apology because he realised what had happened in this crazy mix up. And I did crack that day – I know for a fact I had, I had just flipped my lid. It was then that I realised that your past never leaves you, because I just became the animal I always was. It was as if I had gone back to being in the block. Maybe that shows you what isolation all about. Even as a professional isolationist, after many years of freedom, such a place can still come back to taunt and haunt you.

Charlie, stay sane.

Harry Marsden

INTRODUCTION

Let me start out by telling you that, contrary to public opinion, I have never killed anyone ... hard to believe, ain't it! The film director Michael Winner called me a murderer when he wrote about me in his *News of the World* column. The following week, after he was put straight on the matter, he apologised in the same column and withdrew his remarks ... apology accepted.

Why did Michael believe me to be a killer? Simple – public opinion. Another feature in a national newspaper by Chris House had me down as 'the man, killer and robber ...' It's an easy mistake to make, and a mistake that has caused me to lose public support for the hell I've been put through.

Why is it that a man like me who has served so long behind bars and has been branded the most dangerous con in the UK penal system is considered automatically to be a killer? Why am I mistakenly branded in such a way? I've never killed anyone in my life!

Propaganda perpetrated by HM Prison Service has caused me no end of trouble. Sneaky little stories leaked to the press by prison officers only sets out to cut you all off from me; it makes you turn your backs on the 'no good Bronson'. Well, this book, after you've read it, will cause you to

Bronson the Barbarian..

Death Wish star Bronson

EXCLUSIVE by CHRIS HOUSE

ONE of Britain's most-feared prisoners could soon be on the move again – after being switched between five jails in less than a year.

The man, killer and robber Michael Peterson, has a history of prison violence.

He now calls himself Charles Bronson, after the Death Wish movie star he idolises. In fact Peterson changed his name by deed poll, grew a moustache like his hero's – and insists fellow inmates address him as "Charlie".

Currently, Bronson, 39, is believed to be in Long Lartin prison, Worcestershire, after spells in Wandsworth, Lincoln, Parkhurst, Lincoln and Hull jails.

In Broadmoor, he is said to have caused thousands of pounds of damage stripping off roof

Prisoner Bronson – history of violence

tiles and ripping out plumbing

Other incidents he has been involved in include:

● Smashing up dining hall tables and chairs because the potatoes were cold.

● ... whg bu...ets of urine ov... prison o... cers. Sal ... an ...

the governor of Parkhurst: "He's not the easiest person to deal with.

"It's fair to say most prisons fear him because he can change the atmosphere."

He added: "But I believe he is trying to stay out of trouble. He needs help and support."

have grave concerns about the way HM Prison Service can get away with gross acts of violence against me with the full backing of HM Government's Home Office.

I do not stand without admitting my own failure as a convict and human being; I do not stand without admitting my own failure as a caring man; and I do not stand without admitting my own failure as an example for young people to look up to. But neither does HM Prison Service stand without being able to admit defeat when it comes to why they haven't been able to help me and why the prison population is steadily growing.

For those of you who have never cast eyes on the inside of a prison or even a police cell, this book should act as a deterrent. For those of you unfortunate enough to find yourselves lost and forlorn and pushed up against the wall of a prison cell, this book could be your saviour. For those of you already incarcerated in prison, then this book should help pass the time ... unless, of course, they've banned it! And then you're not to know what is within, but my thoughts are with all of those in such a situation.

Just about everyone on earth has or will be affected by some sort of crime at least once in his or her lifetime. You've all been hurt by crime, even if it's been indirectly. A member of your family, a close friend or a workmate can cause you to share their pain by virtue of the crime they have had perpetrated against them.

Whole communities can be affected by a sudden monstrous crime carried out against one of their own. Look at how Mary Bell, as a child, caused so much pain and suffering in her community when she murdered her peers. Look at how Brady and Hindley caused so much suffering. Look at how Sutcliffe caused so much blind panic amongst women. Look at how Fred and Rose West preyed on those too weak to defend themselves. Look at how the murder of Sarah Payne caused so much emotional turmoil. Look at how paedophilia causes us to want to kill or, at the very least, punish the perpetrators of evil. Crime affects all of us – you included – without you even necessarily being a victim of a crime?

Doesn't that tell you something? Doesn't that explain why we have prisons and why people like me should be locked up for ever and have the key to their cell thrown away? 'Bollocks' is what I say to that!

How can I make such a statement? How can I qualify what I mean without causing every good citizen to break out in a sweat? First, read this book and then let it soak in. I intend to show you that prisons are obsolete and that they do not act as a deterrent to crime, neither do they rehabilitate those within their walls ... mind you, it's a good way to keep hundreds of thousands of people employed, isn't it?

Think about how the economy of any Western country would falter if prisons ceased to exist, but also think about how many others would be employed in other ways. OK, we can't have paedophiles and child-killers walking the streets, we can't have evil killers walking the streets and we can't have any sort of criminal walking the streets. But what about when the day comes and they are legally free to walk the streets of your community amongst you and your children?

Well, that is happening right now; you might be living next-door to a paedophile or, as you walk along your local streets, you're bound to see someone with a shady past. What if these characters – anyone who has ever had a criminal record, say – were all rounded up and just slung behind bars! Do you know how many millions in this country would be imprisoned? Fucking loads! Bring back the prison 'hulks' is what they'd be screaming for!

Where would we imprison them all? I once read that if everyone on earth stood next to each other, then they would all fit on the Isle of Man. Maybe we could do the same with these criminals – stand them all on an island next to each other. We could drop food from a helicopter and keep sharks and piranha fish in a giant moat to seal the island off from all those other nice people in the world.

But, in reality, you know all of that just isn't possible and if you do believe what I say, then you need to get real. The public is out for revenge against anyone who has committed a crime against them ... and you can't blame them.

I mean, look at Tony Martin of the Bleak House murder. He suffered a sting by two burglars and he reacted in the way any person defending their property should be allowed to. Joe Public is out for blood – he wants revenge. And when he has exacted his revenge, he wants a further gallon of blood by wanting prisoners to suffer. What if it was your little Johnny who'd been shot at Bleak House?

Now look at it another way. What if it was your little Johnny who was doing time in the Grey Bar Hotel? Would you be pleased to see little Johnny beaten or even raped by another con? Would you give the prison officers a pat on the back for knocking some sense into your loved one? Would you congratulate the prison officers who allowed your little Johnny to tear some sheets up, make a noose out of them and hang himself?

You see, prisoners are just as much victims of crime as those they have wronged. When you're in prison you are a helpless victim, nothing you do or complain about will prevent some sort of malady creeping into your life. You cannot walk away from a situation because there is no place to walk to. You are in an enforced position of having to do as you are told or face the consequences.

What if you were living in a town with 74,000 other occupants, the size of the current prison population? You can't tell me that there wouldn't be some sort of crime committed against some individuals, yet in prison all these crimes against individuals are overlooked or brushed under the carpet. Police should be brought in to man the prisons and you should outlaw drug-users by pulling them out and putting them into drying-out institutions on an island somewhere where they can't get drugs.

The whole prison-system has gone tits up and needs an overhaul, just as the prison system was shaken up in the early 1800s when over 50 new prisons were built in England The same should happen now ... a shake-up! New systems need to be brought in; the old regime has to go.

The rehabilitative process in our so-called modern-day penal system is a complete failure. Until you know what the real deal is in prison then you cannot begin to understand how it is failing every citizen in this country. Forget the humiliation of prison, forget about the stigma of having your name in the newspapers, start to think about how a whole community has to start surviving the new-found agony of isolation and brutality of prison life.

The Good Prison Guide is about surviving in prison. Just as there are rules in every society, there are written and unwritten rules in any prison. Just as stable behaviour is expected of your peers out there in Civvy Street, so it is expected of prison inmates; even though we are in an unstable and volatile environment, we are expected to remain stable. One minute you can be standing waiting in the dinner queue, and the next minute someone has the top of their head sliced off with a steel dinner tray! In prison, that's normal and no one would bat an eyelid. Out in 'civilised' society where you are, it would involve trauma teams being sent out to help everyone get over the shock! In prison, when that happens, you are banged up in your cell.

What is and what is not acceptable behaviour? I define acceptable behaviour as that which is deemed acceptable by the majority. A tribe of cannibals finds it easy to indulge in the consumption of human flesh, but when those who are revolted by such acts outnumber the rest of the tribe, then it becomes unacceptable. But that doesn't mean it's wrong to eat human flesh. Look at those people who survived that plane crash; they survived for months by eating the flesh of their dead fellow travellers. Suddenly, the rules had changed, and suddenly the survival instinct kicked in and suddenly it was all right to do what was once considered taboo.

Just as the survivors of the plane crash broke the rules that control society, so the public breaks rules every day. So long as you see it as a means of survival, then you will do it; you will break the speed limit while driving your car if you're late for an appointment, and just as you are not perfect then it also applies to everyone else. Yet you want everyone else to be perfect and adhere to the rules. A speeding motorist doesn't care about others, yet if anyone was to go speeding along the road they live on ... see what I mean? There is not a person living who can say that they have never done or thought about doing something that breaks the rules of society.

The consequence of breaching these rules means someone wants retribution. In a modern society, the way to exact retribution is to have someone sit in judgment and/or mediate. Before the government came along and appointed judges it was up to the village elders or the tribal council to resolve such matters. Their decision was final – no appeals, no nothing.

In 1215, King John introduced the Magna Carta, paving the way as a sort of Bill of Rights for everyone. You had the right to remain silent, and it couldn't be held against you, but now that right has been changed. Now, if you remain silent and don't say anything that you later rely on in an open court, then it can harm your defence.

Courts were set up to dispense justice without fear or favour; equal rights for all. No matter who you were, there was a prison just for you. A nice warm dungeon, a homely little fortress beneath the ground or a nice big tower for the well-to-do. Whatever your station in life, there was some place exclusively to lock you up in. And if that wasn't enough, then they could have you breaking up rocks or pushing a giant grinding wheel around all day long.

Prisons were never designed to assert a rehabilitative influence; this came about when prison reformists meddled and tinkered with the inner machinations of prison life. In order for reform to work, you need commitment from those involved. The system is failing miserably!

Tell me this – how can someone be diagnosed as being mentally ill just because they are a paedophile or sex attacker? What about speeding motorists, drink-drivers, litter louts, burglars and the like? Why is it that people working within the professions have a soft spot for convicted paedophiles and rapists? Suddenly, these academics are all experts in how to treat a convicted sex attacker, but what about the lowly burglar who has been reduced to the status of a convicted crook?

You don't find many burglars in Broadmoor or Ashworth, I can tell you. The wards are full of sexual deviants, very few are like me. That is why prison cannot work; already, as a prisoner, you are discriminated against. You get out of prison and anyone can call you an ex-con, but dare to call someone a 'Paki' and you're in for it. 'Paki' used to be the shortened word for anyone from Pakistan, but it became bastardised by academics and was turned into something derogatory.

It's the same with the prison stigma; society has been brainwashed into thinking that ex-cons have a disease. The only difference between ex-cons and most of the population is that ex-cons have been caught and convicted! So why should they be discriminated against?

We've moved on from prisons being places of incarceration to being places of pain and suffering. In medieval times, such places could be handled by most who were thrown into them. A warm place to sleep and be shielded from the elements was often considered to be a sanctuary. You could even have your own servants at your beck and call as well as having your family stay with you. But look at prison now. You've got to be doing life just to qualify to have a budgie in your cell! Things have gone from bad to worse. Why shouldn't a prisoner be allowed conjugal visits or have a family house within the confines of a prison wall? They allowed it in this country hundreds of years ago. The charter for Human Rights states that a man is allowed to found (start) a family ... you cannot found a family from behind bars!

People are used to the home comforts of TV and video, dishwashers, mobile phones, video links, soft furnishings, Playstations, DVD players and the like. Take all of that away from them and sling them into a concrete cell and see how easy it is to break a man's resolve.

Modern man is supposed to have found himself, found his femininity, as the namby-pamby brigade would have you believe. Should that be the case then you will understand how such an austere place as Strangeways Prison can cause such an extreme state of mental turmoil. Yet people are expected to get through it all and come out as reformed characters after guarding their arses for two or three years or having to suck dick to feed their addictions in order to earn a £5 bag of smack.

Prisons are awash with pretenders, full of what I call 'charvas' and wannabes! But when they are alone in their cells and they've just had a 'Fuck off out of my life' letter from their missus, well ... that's when you can see what prison does to a man.

I am for making prisons obsolete ... easy for me to say, but I bet a lot of free people would say that, too. I know what a lot of others in the 'hang 'em' brigade would say, too – they say that you can't have lethal criminals walking the streets and that society needs protecting from them. This is true, people do need protecting from all these mentally ill people, and why can't they be regarded as mentally ill, I ask?

Perhaps not in my lifetime, but eventually, there will be fewer and fewer prisons with more and more centres for the therapeutic treatment of offenders. Offending, you see, is a state of mind ... an illness. Prisons are no answer to what is needed but, in the meantime, we have to tolerate such places and, while we have to, we may as well make them into better places.

I hope that this book goes some way to helping reform how prisons are run and how they are set out and how they treat people. Oh, I forgot to say that the cure for paedophiles is to hang them up by their balls for an hour and then see if the re-offend. Rapists would have the same punishment and on a second conviction would have surgical removal of their tackle ... without anaesthetic! And that is how it would go for all sexual attackers and the likes. They would be discriminated against in a positive way. And anyone who came out of the woodwork to save them would be equally as done against ... who can befriend a paedophile ... yuk!

By giving you an insight into prisons, I hope that you can prepare yourself for the day of your incarceration. Hey, it might never happen, but who knows what's around the next corner? Shit, as they say, happens. You'll be glad you read this book, you'll be glad that Bronco showed you the way ahead.

As for you old lags out there, you know the score and you know what lies ahead. You've endured it and been through it, you all deserve a winner's medal. Wear a T-shirt for me, will ya?

When you're behind bars, you have no control over your food, clothing or any of the details of your life. You live within a framework of strict supervision and control, whether you are banged up in a prison cell or working as a day-release prisoner.

The control is not reliant on prison walls or cell bars – it is regulated by the powers invested into the custodians of that particular system.

The real meaning of a con's punishment is that he or she is wholly subject to his or her custodians and can do only what they allow or direct. This is when you value the right citizens have to freedom from restraint, which is a precious right, and the loss of that right to freedom is a severe deprivation.

Just imagine you have been taken hostage and illegally held by your captors, and let's assume you suffer a grave injury. The courts would award you a massive payout. And this is true even if your captor treated you very nicely.

But when an offender is held in legal custody, he or she suffers a grave punishment, however free from punitive conditions their treatment might be. What about the prisoner who hardly gets any letters or visits compared to his peers? Isn't he being discriminated against? What about the prisoner who is forced to accept visits under what are called 'closed' conditions, in which he is placed behind a bulletproof screen and is not allowed even the minimum of human contact from his visitors? These are very distressing circumstances, the prisoner being wholly cut off from his family, friends and all familiar life. Their crime also affects their family. Prison has been described as 'a monastery of men unwilling to be monks.'

Prison does not just take a person's liberty from them; it also punishes on an unremitting scale without fear or favour.

GLOSSARY

No doubt, in the course of reading this book, you'll find some slang words that aren't in your everyday vocabulary and you'll wonder what they mean, particularly as I've built up quite a following around the world, and I don't want all my readers abroad to wonder what the hell I'm on about. It is a rough guide to prison terminology, which is sometimes used in the street but has probably originated from prison. Here's an example of a judge being bamboozled by slang:

Prosecuting barrister: 'M'lord, the defendant was masked up when he did the blag.'
Judge: 'What is a "blag"?'
Prosecuting barrister: 'A robbery, m'lord. The defendant had with him a sawn-off shooter.'
Judge: 'Sorry to stop you again, but what is a "sawn-off shooter"?'
Prosecuting barrister: 'A shotgun, m'lord. The defendant copped for being nicked.'
Judge: 'What does that mean, "copped for being nicked"?'
Prosecuting barrister: 'It means when he was caught, m'lord. The defendant's previous form was a nine-stretch for robbery.'

Judge: 'What does "stretch" mean?'

Prosecuting barrister: 'It means time served, m'lord. I have the evidence here, m'lord ... a blow-up doll.'

Judge: 'Was that the deluxe blow-up doll, or the super silk lips deluxe blow-up doll?'

Well, perhaps it didn't quite happen like that, but as I've asked for blow-up dolls when I've taken hostages in the past, I couldn't resist it.

Arse-bandit/shirt-lifter/ cacky-stabber/ backdoor burglar	Homosexual
Banged up/ behind the door	Locked in your cell
Baron	Prisoner dealing in illicit items and making profit from it
Beast/nonce	Sex case
Bible Moth	Prisoner who can't leave religion alone
Big Bird	A long prison sentence
Big House	Prison
Bird	Serving a sentence
Blade	Knife or cutting blade used in attack
Blag	Robbery
Blagger	Robber
Block/seg unit	Prison within prison
Boss	Friendly name given to prison officer
BoV	Board of Visitors
Box	Strongbox, impenetrable isolation cell
Brek	Breakfast
Brown	Heroin
Bruv	Term used to express closeness to a fellow prisoner
Burglars	Prison security team searching your cell
Burn	Tobacco
Cabbaged	Brain dead
Canister	Head
Canteen	Prison shop
Cat	Category of prison (A, B, C or D)

CDM	Cadbury's Dairy Milk
Centre	Main prison control room
Charva	a person of limited intelligence who always wears sports labels, swears a lot and drinks too much
Chib	Knife
Chivved up	Stabbed or cut up by a chiv
Chokey	Prison
Civvy	Civilian worker/manufactured cigarette
Clink	Prison, named after a prison called 'Clink'
Con	Convict
Cop for this	Have some of this (usually said to person on receiving end of punishment beating)
Copped	Caught
Crack/Craic/what's the crack?	The talk/What's going on?
Crack on	Hurry up
Crashed in	Beat up
Cutting	Relating to being slashed with a blade
Daddy	Alpha male prisoner
Dear John/Jane	A letter from your wife or girlfriend ending their relationship with you
Diamond Geezer	A real good man
Dirty Protest	Covering cell and yourself with your own excrement
Dis	Disrespect
Div(vy)	Stupid idiot
Doing time/bird	Serving a prison sentence
Double up	Two beds put into one cell that is designed for only one bed
Draw	Cannabis or tobacco
Dropsy	A gift from a soon-to-be-released prisoner
Duff	The pudding part of a meal. 'What's for duff?'
Dump/Pony	Having a crap
Frisk	A bit of fun/body search
Gaff	A place, such as a room or a house
Geezer	A man

Ghosted	Shipped out of a prison to another one very quickly
Grass	Informant
Grey Bar Hotel	Prison
Had it away	Escaped
HMP	Her Majesty's Prison/Her Majesty'sPleasure; an indeterminate sentence for young prisoners
Hooch	Home brew
Horsebox	Prison transport of a secure nature
HQ	Headquarters
HSPSCB	High Security Psychiatric Services Commissioning Board
Jail bird	Ex-Convict who returns to prison
Jam role	Parole
JR	Judicial Review
JR'd	Judges Remand
Judas hole/flap	Spy hole in cell door for checking on prisoners without opening the door
Judge in Chambers	Hearing in judge's chambers, sometimes resulting in bail being granted
KB'd	Knocked back for, refused something
Lag	Convict
Lemon	Nasty
Lifer	Convict serving life imprisonment
Liquid cosh	Injection of lardactyl, etc.
Make one	Escape
Meat wagon	Secure prison transport
Monster	Evil person/sex case
Mule	Person secreting drugs about their person and smuggling them into prison
MUFTI Squad	Prison officers trained to handle unruly prisoners or riots (Minimum Use of Force and Tactical Intervention)
Nash on	Hurry up
Nicked	Put on report for committing an offence against prison rules
Nonce	Sex case
Nutted off	Sectioned off under the Mental Health Act

'Now then'	A form of greeting
Old lag	Old convict
Old school	From the past with higher morals
One off	A convict suicide/what a screw says when one con leaves the wing
Ov	Where you are from
Pad	Prison cell
Pad mate	Cell-sharing prisoner
Paddy wagon	Secure prison transport
Patches/Stripes	Patches of bright yellow on a prisoner's clothing to signify he is a former escapee
Pegger	Smoker
Peter	Cell (outside of prison it meant a 'safe')
Plug	Hide something up your anus
POA	Prison Officers Association
Porridge	Serving time in prison
Puff	Cannabis
QE	Going Queen's Evidence against your co-accused at trial
Receptions	New prisoners entering prison regime
Recess	The place where the sluice is, usually showers, sink, toilets, etc.
Segregation Unit	(Seg Unit) prison within prison to keep you away from other prisoners
Served up	Cut with a blade or served up punishment from a fellow con
Screw	Prison officer – the crank machine, a form of useless labour, was introduced in the middle of the last century to make prison life tougher for those prisoners sentenced to hard labour. Male prisoners had to turn the handle 14,400 times a day, forcing four large cups or ladles through sand inside a drum. The number of revolutions was registered on the dial. The warder could make the task harder by tightening a screw, hence the slang word for prison warder
Shit and a shave/ shit and a brek	A short prison sentence

Shit up/dirty protest	The act of covering yourself and your cell in your own excrement in protest over something
SHSA	Special Hospitals Service Authority
Skin	Cigarette rolling paper
Skin up	Make a cigarette
Sky Pilot	Vicar/Priest, etc.
Silent protest	Not speaking a word
Slopping out	The action of emptying a cell pot out into the sluice (outdated)
Smack	Heroin
Smack-heads	Junkies addicted to heroin
Snout	Tobacco
Sorted	Something's been accomplished
Spin/turnover	Have your cell searched by prison security
SSU	Special Secure Unit
Stitched up	Not being given your full quota of something
Strip cells	Cells in which you were naked
SVO	Special Visiting Order
Sweet	Happy
Tailor-made	Any branded cigarette
The Ones	Ground floor cells
The Twos	Cells on the first floor landing
Toe-to-toe	Fight each other with fists
Top (guy) man	Good person
Topped himself/herself	Suicide
Turnkey	Prison officer
Two and a brek	Means two days and a morning left until release, etc.
Twos up	Share your cigarette with me
Unlock	Cell door opening to let convict out
UFF	Ulster Freedom Fighter
VO	Visiting Order
Wing	A block full of cells
Wrapped up	Tied up or taken care of
YP	Young Prisoners
YOI	Young Offenders Institute

CHARLIE BRONSON – PROFILE

The following is a list of the prisons Charlie has visited so far; some visits to the same establishment have not been listed to save duplication.

1969   Risley Remand Centre; two months for criminal damage.

1969   Risley; banned from driving for life (hit-and-run). First of six separate visits. Unknown period.

1970   Werrington House Detention Centre; three months.

1971   Risley; suspended sentence (smash-and-grab).
        Unknown period.

1974   Risley Remand; normal wing.

1974   Walton; normal wing, seven years for robbery.

1974   Strangeways; block (dungeons).

1974   Wakefield; block (dungeons).

1975   Wandsworth; block (dungeons).

1975   Hull; block (dungeons).

1975/76   Armley; block (dungeons).

1976   Wakefield; block (dungeons).

1976   Wandsworth; block (dungeons).

1976   Parkhurst; Special Unit (three days en route).

1976   Pentonville; Seg Unit.

1976/77   Wandsworth; block (dungeons).

1977   Winchester; block.

1977   Walton; block (dungeons).

1977   Wandsworth; block (dungeons).

1978   Parkhurst; certified insane.

1978   Camp Hill; seg block (one day), awaiting transfer to Rampton.

1978   Parkhurst; straight from Camp Hill.

1978   Oxford; reception area and straight back to van.

1978   Rampton; block (dungeons).

1979   Broadmoor; block (dungeons).

1981   Park Lane (Ashworth) Hospital, Liverpool; moved, three
           years added for various assaults

1984   Park Lane; normal wing.

1985   Risley, remand wing.

1985   Walton; certified sane.

1985   Armley; block (dungeons).

1985   Walton; block (dungeons).

1985   Albany; block (dungeons).

1985   Parkhurst

1986   Wormwood Scrubs; block (dungeons).

1986   Wandsworth; block (dungeons).

1986   Parkhurst; Special Unit.

1986   Winchester; block (dungeons).

1986   Wormwood Scrubs; block (dungeons).

1986   Parkhurst; block (dungeons).

1986   Wandsworth; block (dungeons).

1986   Parkhurst; normal wing.

1986   Wandsworth; block (dungeons).

1986   Albany; block (dungeons).

1986   Winchester; block (dungeons).

1986   Wandsworth; block (dungeons).

1987   Gartree; block (dungeons).

1987   Leicester; block (dungeons).

1987   Gartree; block (dungeons).Released 30 October 1987 from Category 'A' from the block at Gartree.

1988   Luton Police Station; arrested 7 January for suspected weapons offences and assault.

1988   Brixton on remand.

1988   Leicester; remand, block (dungeon).

1988   Brixton; remand, cage (Special Unit), 17 June 1988 received seven years' imprisonment for robbery.

1988   Wandsworth; normal wing.

1988   Strangeways; block (dungeons).

1988   Full Sutton; normal wing.

1988   Norwich; Seg Unit.

1988   Durham; cage (Special Unit).

1988   Full Sutton; normal wing.

1988   Armley; block (dungeons).

1989   Full Sutton; normal wing.

1989	Long Lartin; normal wing.
1989	Bristol; block (dungeons).
1989	Winson Green; block (dungeons).
1989	Winchester; block (dungeons).
1989	Wandsworth; block (dungeons).
1989	Albany; block (dungeons).
1989	Parkhurst; Special Unit.
1989	Albany; block (dungeons).
1989	Gartree; normal wing.
1990	Durham; block (dungeons).
1990	Parkhurst; block (dungeons).
1990	Frankland; normal wing.
1990	Albany; block (dungeons).
1990	Parkhurst; special unit.
1990	Wandsworth; block (dungeons).
1990	Full Sutton; normal wing.
1991	Parkhurst; normal wing.
1991	Wandsworth; block (dungeons).
1991	Albany; block (dungeons).
1991	Leicester; block (dungeons) for just one day.
1991	Hull; block (dungeons).
1992	Lincoln; special unit.
1992	Albany
1992	Parkhurst
1992	Wandsworth
1992	Wormwood Scrubs

1992	November; released, free for 55 days, arrested on conspiracy to rob a bank, possession of a firearm and grievous bodily harm. Remanded for a short time in January 1993 and released a few weeks later.
1993	Woodhill; remanded for conspiracy to rob and related offences.
1993	Winson Green.
1993	Belmarsh.
1993	Bristol.
1993	Wandsworth.
1993	Belmarsh.
1993	Bullingdon.
1993	Belmarsh.
1993	Bullingdon.
1993	Belmarsh.
1993	Wakefield; cage.
1993	Frankland.
1993	Hull; Special Unit.
1994	Leicester.
1994	Wakefield; cage.
1994	Bullingdon; block (dungeons).
1994	Leicester; block (dungeons).
1994	Wakefield; cage.
1994	Strangeways; block (dungeons).
1994	Walton; block (dungeons).
1994	Highdown; block (dungeons).
1994	Belmarsh; Special Unit.
1994	Lincoln; block (dungeons).

1994   Wormwood Scrubs; block (dungeons).

1994   Wandsworth; block (dungeons).

1994   Winson Green; block (dungeons).

1994   Lincoln; block (dungeons).

1994   Bullingdon; block (dungeons).

1994   Wandsworth; block (dungeons).

1994   Bullingdon; block (dungeons).

1994   Full Sutton; block (dungeons).

1995   Strangeways.

1995   Frankland; block (dungeons).

1995   Armley; block (dungeons).

1995   Frankland; block (dungeons).

1995   Highdown; block (dungeons).

1995   Winson Green; block (dungeons).

1995   Lincoln; block (dungeons).

1995   Frankland; block (dungeons).

1995   Winson Green; block (dungeons).

1995   Belmarsh; block (dungeons).

1996   Full Sutton; block (dungeons).

1996   Walton; block (dungeons).

1996   Bullingdon; block (dungeons).

1996   Belmarsh; block (dungeons).

1996   Wakefield; cage.

1996   Bullingdon; block (dungeons).

1997   Walton.

1997   Durham; block (dungeons).

1997   Full Sutton; block (dungeons).

1997	Belmarsh; block (dungeons).
1997	Wakefield; cage.
1997	Belmarsh; block (dungeons).
1997	Wakefield; cage.
1997	Belmarsh; block (dungeons), sentenced to further 7 years (reduced to 5 on appeal) for Belmarsh siege.
1997	Wakefield; cage.
1998	Woodhill; CSC (Close Supervision Centre).
1998	Hull; special unit.
1999	Whitemoor; block (special CSC cell).
1999/ 2000	Woodhill; 'A' Wing solitary, no privileges. Luton Crown Court, jailed for life for Hull siege, and not eligible for parole until 2010.
2000	Whitemoor.
2000	Woodhill, new Seg Unit with cages.
2001	Wakefield.
2001	Whitemoor.
2001	Frankland; block.
2001	Durham; Special Unit, the cage.
2002	Wakefield; special cages.
2002	Woodhill; Special Unit
2002	Wakefield; special cages.
2002	Full Sutton; high-security Seg Unit.
2003	Whitemoor.
2003/ 2007	Wakefield special cages.

CHILDHOOD AND UPBRINGING

Charlie Bronson is the middle of three brothers; his older brother died at his home in Australia at 9.10am on 3 March 2001 in the arms of his dear wife, Fliss, after his long and brave battle against cancer of the brain. His younger brother Mark spent some time in the Royal Navy. There is no family history of mental disorder.

Charles Bronson was born Michael Gordon Peterson in Luton, Bedfordshire. No problems with the pregnancy and neo-natal period. He was nocturnally enuretic until ten years old, was also scared of the dark and had occasional nightmares and night terrors. He is described as having a bad temper from an early age. He is also described as being shy, sensitive and a loner. Suggestions from reports mention that the family doctor saw him in childhood because of these behavioural traits.

His early schooling was unremarkable, but from 12 years of age he began stealing and was expelled at least twice. As a youngster he got into many fights, because he felt that other boys were looking at him. He ran away from home twice in his early teens and finally left home, following an argument with his father, to live with his grandmother in Cheshire.

Charlie left school with no qualifications and then worked briefly in a supermarket, as a labourer and, for three years, as a painter and decorator.

MARITAL HISTORY

Charlie is heterosexual. He first had sexual intercourse in his teens and married in 1970 at the age of 19 years, his son being born the same year. The marriage was unsuccessful and other reports mention Charlie's heavy drinking. The couple finally divorced in 1976 and Charlie has had no contact with his ex-wife since then.

Although Charlie had numerous sexual encounters, he found close relationships difficult. He said that he found close physical contact unpleasant and did not like 'cuddling or people holding me, so I can't have a relationship. I am not like other people.'

1968 – convicted of criminal damage and was sent to Risley Remand Centre for two months.

1969 – convicted of a hit-and-run charge and banned from driving for life and spent time in Risley Remand Centre.

January 1970 – convicted of criminal damage to cars and placed on probation for a year.

March 1970 – convicted of taking and driving away.

February 1971 – convicted of burglary and criminal damage and sentenced to three months in a detention centre.

June 1972 – convicted of criminal damage. Earlier reports say that he broke a beer glass in a pub as he thought people were talking about him.

December 1972 – found guilty of criminal damage to a shop window. A report in 1978 says that he told psychiatrists that he was upset about his marriage but other accounts have said that this was simply a 'smash-and-grab raid'.

1974 – convicted of robbery, aggravated burglary, assault with intent to rob, illegal possession of firearms and carrying a firearm. He was sentenced to seven years' imprisonment.

August 1974 – assaulted someone he believed had cheated him at cards, followed him home and attacking him. In the same month, he entered a sub-post office with a shotgun and threatened an assistant behind the counter. Later in the month, he robbed a petrol station and beat up the attendant. All of the offences occurred in the same month and were carried out with the same group of associates. He has told psychiatrists on previous occasions that he felt people were talking about him and that he was under physical threat.

December 1975 – given an additional nine months' imprisonment after assaulting another prisoner with a jug in Hull Prison.

1978 – in Parkhurst Prison he was having problems with another prisoner whom he believed to be an informant and he attacked this man with a broken bottle. This was the most serious incident in a term of imprisonment that had been marked by very difficult behaviour, including repeated assaults on prison officers. He was declared insane and transferred to Rampton Special Hospital in November 1978, by which time he had lost 600 days' remission for thirty-seven offences against prison discipline.

1978 – transferred to Broadmoor Special Hospital and carried out a succession of rooftop protests causing an estimated £500,000 worth of damage.

1981 – transferred to Park Lane Special Hospital and had three years added on for various assaults.

1985 – he was sentenced to three years for GBH, having attacked another patient in Park Lane Special Hospital with a broken coffee jar. He said that this was because the man had made a pass at him and had written him 'filthy letters'. He said, 'I cut him. That was out of order, I should have just chinned him.'

1985 – carried out a rooftop protest at Walton Prison for which another year was added on.

October 1987 – released from Gartree as a Category 'A' prisoner. Survived sixty-seven days of freedom.

November 1987 – seven weeks after his release, he was arrested for armed robbery on a jeweller's shop and remanded.

January 1988 – sentenced to seven years' imprisonment for the robbery charges.

1990 – took an assistant governor of Frankland Prison hostage.

November 1992 – released from Wormwood Scrubs as a Category 'A' prisoner and survived fifty-five days of freedom.

2 January 1993 – re-arrested for conspiracy to rob, possession of a firearm and grievous bodily harm.

February 1993 – fined £600 for the GBH and acquitted of the other charges. Eighteen days later, he was re-arrested on shotgun and conspiracy to rob charges.

March 1993 – arrested on suspicion of conspiracy to rob a bank and possession of firearm and remanded to Woodhill Prison.

March 1993 – at Woodhill Prison he took prison librarian Andy Love hostage.

September 1993 – found guilty of intent to rob and possession of shotgun, not guilty of conspiracy to rob, sentenced to eight years.

1994 – took prison governor Adrian Wallace hostage at Hull Prison.

April 1994 – was charged with false imprisonment, threats to kill, ABH and two counts of criminal damage resulting from the Hull siege and received a further seven-year prison sentence.

1995 – went on an eighteen-day hunger-strike at High Down Prison in protest at constant moves and solitary confinement.

1996 – momentarily took a doctor hostage at Winson Green Prison but was attacked by up to sixty prison officers and the doctor was released without harm.

1996 – took two Iraqis and another prisoner hostage in Belmarsh Prison.

October 1996 – took a lawyer hostage in Bullingdon Prison; this was brushed off as a senseless, half-hearted action and he was not charged.

1997 – sentenced to further seven years (reduced to five on appeal) for Belmarsh siege.

August 1998 – took prison teacher Phil Danielson hostage for forty-four hours in Hull Prison.

February 1999 – went on a forty-day hunger-strike when they took his artwork away from him at Whitemoor Prison.

February 2000 – jailed at Luton Crown Court for life for the Hull siege, and is not eligible for parole until 2010.

July 2000 – moved to Whitemoor after being stormed by sixty MUFTI Squad officers at Woodhill Prison.

Further attacks on prison staff, fellow inmates, rooftop protests and prison sieges has resulted in Charlie spending a total of twenty-six years in solitary confinement out of thirty years served since 1974.

PSYCHIATRIC HISTORY

From an early age, Charlie reports that he had a quick temper. He also had a history of intermittent heavy drinking, although he was never dependent upon alcohol. A referral to his general practitioner as a child because of his shy personality did not result in any further assessment or treatment.

His involvement with psychiatrists began during his prison sentence of 1974–78. His difficult behaviour in prison, including assaults on officers and other inmates, meant that he spent no time on normal locations and was assessed by various psychiatrists and treated with neuroleptic medication. The consensus of the various reports is that Charlie had a paranoid and hostile personality. In addition, it seems that he has suffered a psychotic breakdown on at least one occasion, although this does not amount to schizophrenia.

Charlie's difficult behaviour continued after his transfer to Rampton Special Hospital in November 1978. He attempted to strangle a paedophile sexual offender, in the hope that he would be convicted, given a life sentence and returned to prison. He was transferred to Broadmoor Special Hospital in October 1979 and further incidents followed, including self-harm with a knife, attacking another patient, rooftop protests and attempts to escape from the intensive care block.

He was transferred to Park Lane Special Hospital in June 1984 and made good progress, being given ground parole before his attack on a fellow patient seven months later. He was discharged by a Tribunal on 23 September 1985, on the grounds that he was not suffering from a mental disorder within the meaning of the Mental Health Act 1983.

Since then, Charlie has not had any psychiatric treatment, although he has spent most of his time in prison and has never been on normal location. He has spent most of his time in segregation units and has had short spells on C Wing at Parkhurst and the Lincoln Special Unit. He said that he was sent away from the Special Unit at Lincoln after he had hit a governor because he was 'taking liberties and lying to me'.

Charlie said that he refused to have any contact with prison doctors because of an experience in Armley Prison in 1985. He said that he had been hurt in a brawl with officers following a rooftop protest and was lying naked on the floor, in a body belt, covered in blood. The doctor came and stood over him and asked him if he had any injuries. Since that time he has refused to speak to prison doctors and is abusive to them. He has no objection to doctors from outside prison.

MENTAL STATE AT INTERVIEW

Charlie has a very intense manner and reported anxiety attacks when he was in crowds or queues. He said that he would become tense and break out in a sweat, although he did not think that people were looking at him. He said that he was a loner and simply could not cope with large numbers of people, especially following his long experience of segregation units, where he spent most of his time locked up in a single cell. Because of his anxiety in crowds, Charlie did not think he could cope on normal location within prison.

He has respect 'for people who are straight with me, whoever they are'. He could not stand being lied to or people 'taking liberties'.

He said that he had a quick temper and would sometimes 'do mad things'. 'Straight away, afterwards, I know I shouldn't have done it and I feel embarrassed. For example, when they take you out of the cell, you would just be walking past a table and then you might pick it up and throw it across the room, just on impulse. Then they are all around you, looking at you.' He believed that he was 'probably going to die on one of these blocks'. He believed he was 'too damaged for normal location'.

Charlie said he had been suffering from head pains and blackouts that had started in 1975. He said he had been working out on a punch bag in the gym when he had lost his vision for a few seconds and then woke up on the floor of the gym. He said his last blackout had been about nine weeks ago in Winson Green Prison. Before the episode, he had developed pains in the right side of his head, which had lasted for about two hours. He then fell unconscious and found that he had wet himself when he came round.

In total, he had had about three episodes of blackouts since the first one in 1976 but had only wet himself on one occasion and had never bitten his tongue. As he spent almost all his time alone, there were no other accounts of these blackouts, so it was impossible to know whether or not he had had convulsions. He had feared that he was developing a brain tumour but accepted that this could not be so; otherwise he would have died by now.

Charlie was correctly oriented in time, place and person. He was articulate and appeared to be of at least average intelligence.

'YOU'RE NICKED!'

Many people have written to me over the years, and all sorts of questions have been asked but, you know, no one has asked me why I'm violent. Don't you find that rather odd? What it tells me is that people accept violence and bad behaviour. I mean, if a star behaves badly then they put it down to artistic temperament. But I can tell you that violence is nothing more than a basic instinct; look at the amount of attention and glorification given over to violence. Go and look on my mate Julian Davies's website –www.unlicensed2000.com – and then tell me that you or others aren't impressed by pure brutal force.

Look at those celebrities in today's society who have faced imprisonment; mostly it's because of childish acts or just wanton lust. A breakdown of society's values occurs in everyone ... not just me.

For anyone hitting the prison system for the first time, it must be a daunting prospect, if not a frightening one. Me, well, I'm already in the system and can survive. For those mere mortals on the street arriving in the prison queue for the first time, it can tear their lives apart. But can you imagine being famous (or infamous) with the trappings of everyday wealth that you and I can only dream of and then facing the prospect of going to prison? Not just losing your dignity, but losing your minders, your assistants, your luxuries and losing your entourage of followers!

For those of you who don't know what happens to someone charged with committing a crime, I'll explain how it works. That way you will understand the indignity these stars suffer.

After you've been arrested for an offence, you are taken to the local cop shop. You stand before a policeman – the desk sergeant. He asks you to empty your pockets, and that means everything you have on your person, not just your pockets. So if you've got a gram of cocaine down your sock then that also comes into the equation.

Once you're booked in, the desk sergeant will ask you if you want anyone informed of your arrest. Now if you're a really big star then you've got a joey (runaround) who you can call to sort things out for you. But obviously you're not going to want to inform the *News of the World* about your arrest, are you? This offer of informing anyone of your arrest is in addition to your legal right to have your solicitor called.

After the formalities are completed, the desk sergeant asks you to sign your property sheet and you are given a copy of PACE (Police and Criminal Evidence Act); don't throw this away 'cos you'll need something to read while in the cell!

Now let's assume you've been arrested while wearing your 24-carat gold ring with diamond-encrusted inlay. This item is simply listed as 'gold-coloured ring'! You can swear blind that it's valued at £10k, but they won't wear it. In the property bag it goes! And if you smoke fags, then these also go in the prop bag. So behave yourself and be nice to the desk sergeant, 'cos later you are going to have to ask for one to be passed into your cell.

Once you've been formally charged, the desk sergeant will ask you if you've anything to say. Here's where you keep your trap shut. OK, you can deny the offence, but don't admit to anything – keep quiet! You'll have plenty of time to deny the charge in court.

Did you know that your right to silence has now been reduced to nothing more than a token gesture? Since the days of the Magna Carta, you have had a right to silence, but this has been stripped away from the statute books and replaced with a more incriminating piece of wording, which goes something like this: 'You do not need to say anything, you have the right to remain silent. But if you remain silent and then, later, rely on something that hasn't been said and use it in your defence at court, then this can be taken to mean ...' What that means is that you can't stand there with nothing to say and then at court come up with an alibi to explain away why you were doing whatever it was you were doing without it being inferred that you had time to construct such an alibi ... clever bunch of bastards, these Law Lords!

So if you have a cast-iron alibi, then you had better declare it there and then, and that shows you've not invented it. If you were in the local barmaid's arms at 2.20am when the crime was committed, then say so; don't leave it to the court date 'cos they'll only think you've paid her for the alibi.

After the desk sergeant is through with you, then – if, and only if, you have been charged with an offence – you are taken into a nice little room to have you fingerprints, photo and DNA swab taken. Yeah, you thought it was all over and that you were going to be taken to your nice little cosy cell, but the fun is only just beginning!

After your mug shot, you have your prints taken. Now if it's one of those ultra-modern cop shops then you simply have to press your fingers on the glass and the rest is done by magic. But if it's an outdated prehistoric cop shop, then your prints will be taken in the old manual way, with ink and roller ... messy.

Then comes the DNA swab ... open wide! A sample of your saliva is taken for the DNA cross-referencing, so if you were involved in some sort of crime years and years and ago and they have DNA evidence from that time, then you are bang to rights if you were involved then and it turns out that the DNA they have on file is yours. This is how they catch rapists years and years after they've committed an offence. Some young girl might have been raped way back in the 1970s, and they've got traces of the rapist's sperm from her underwear. Back then they didn't have the know-how about DNA, but they've since analysed the sperm and now have the DNA profile to hand. Then, thirty years later, Joe Bloggs comes along and commits a minor misdemeanour of sorts, but he still has his DNA swab taken ... and BINGO! His DNA matches that of the rapist's of some thirty years earlier. What can he say? He's nicked!

Technically, you do not need to give a DNA sample; it's in contravention of your human rights. But all that will happen is that the police will apply to the courts and they will grant them permission to take it from you forcibly. What about all these innocent men who willingly give their DNA samples during door-to-door enquiries when the police are trying to catch local rapists. Technically, after the DNA has been cross-referenced, the police are supposed to destroy their databank of DNA given on a voluntary basis ... this does not happen, believe me. If you have ever had your DNA sample taken and then, later, were found 'not guilty' at court, you would think that your DNA sample would be destroyed ... bollocks!

After the DNA swab, and when the nice policeman or civilian (as the case may be) has finished with you, you are taken to your place of abode. Before entering the cell while in police custody, you are asked to remove your belt, tie and shoes ... no, they are not going to give you a pipe and slippers. This is in case you want to hang yourself. Why they ask you to take off your shoes when they are slip-ons beats me; maybe you are going to beat yourself to death. As well as all of this being degrading, it is for your own safety. I mean when you see how many people have died, statistics don't lie. That's all you become, a number.

Once stripped of your potential means of suicide, you are free to go into the cell. Don't expect the Savoy or the Ritz. A wooden bench and steel toilet (without toilet roll) is all you will find. It might be night-time, you could be tired and want to sleep, so ask for a blanket and pillow. Before using these, check for last night's leftovers. Very rarely are you given clean blankets and pillows. Personally, I'd rather sleep without them.

Whether you are male or female, the same applies. But if you are a female, then a female custody officer should process you.

Every time a police officer visits your cell, this is entered into the 'Custody Record'; you are entitled to a copy of your custody record for up to twelve months after you were locked up in that stinking cell. This can show who the officer was who entered your cell, important evidence if you later claim that you suffered any form of violence while in custody.

You are now in the system and under the rules of PACE. There are custody time limits; they cannot hold you in there forever without first seeking the permission of the court to extend these time limits. Preferably, if the charge is minor then you can be let out under your own control, bailed to appear before the court or to come back at a later date to the police station.

However, should you have been arrested on terrorism charges, they may as well throw the key away. Nearly all of your rights are gone. You can disappear into the hands of MI5 and never be seen again.

Should the police want to interview you, then you can have your solicitor present, but if it is a very serious charge then the police do not have to inform your solicitor for some time, as this might hamper their investigations.

Should your charge be minor, then your solicitor will tear himself out of bed in the early hours of the morning and make his way to the police station you're being held in. Do not expect your solicitor to hurry along, unless you're a cash-paying client or a really big name.

Once at the station, the police will tell them what the charge is and what they want to ask you. You sit there in the interview room and are cautioned under PACE. Unless you are cautioned, then what you say cannot be introduced as evidence, but try telling that to the court if you've just admitted killing someone without being under caution ... they'll still use it against you.

The chances are that you've been lifted on a minor charge, fighting in a restaurant or something similar. Pushing someone can be classed as an assault; you've had one too many and pushed them away from you when they asked for your autograph. This is a situation many celebrities find themselves in ... God help me when I get released!

So there you are in the interview room, tense and worried. Your solicitor is sitting beside you and should be taking copious notes at a furious pace. You should have had a private meeting with your solicitor prior to the interview. This interview can take place within sight of the police, but it should be out of earshot from them. If not, make it known that you want a private meeting in a room.

Your solicitor will tell you what your rights are; you can remain silent or you can issue a statement via them or you can answer questions that are put to you. The interview then commences in a room that looks like a recording studio; the wall has special acoustic padding on it. Don't worry – this isn't so that when the police beat you up no one can hear it! That happens in the cell when they wrap you up in the mattress (this is so the bruises don't show). An audiotape is placed in a machine, the police officers present name everyone in the room and then the questions commence.

Once the interview is over, the police officer doing the interviewing will say, 'Interview terminated at ...' and he will say the time. What happens to the audiotape/s? They are sent to the CPS (Crown Prosecution Service) who will make a decision on whether charges should be brought, because at this stage you might not yet have even been charged.

Should you be charged, then you are entitled to a copy of the audiotape. It can make good listening on days when you are depressed, if only to see how much you've incriminated yourself.

Right, the interview is over and charges have either been brought against you or you're bailed and you await the outcome of the CPS decision. You can be bailed for four weeks or even longer and conditions might be attached to the bail, such as staying away from witnesses, remaining at a certain address, and so on.

Should the police believe that you might interfere with witnesses, commit further offences or abscond, then they can oppose bail. That will result in you being brought before the court and the charges being read out to the court and the reasons for the prosecution wanting to have you remanded. Don't worry, all is not lost. Your solicitor can object to these accusations and apply for bail. The court might grant bail, but with conditions. These conditions may require you to report to the local police station once a day at a given time. Conditions of bail are so variable that I cannot even begin to list all the permutations; the main thing is that you get bail.

The minute you walk out of the court and into the fresh air, you feel reborn, the air hits your face, everything seems unreal and what you've just gone through seems a nightmare. Unless you are a seasoned criminal veteran, you will relish your freedom and this is when the thought of being locked up becomes a far more daunting prospect than the night of drunken bravado that got you in the fix.

So you've done your best to keep it out of the newspapers, you've been whisked out of court in a disguise, but come Sunday your face is splashed all over the front page. How come? I'll tell you how ... the police do not subscribe to the Data Protection Act and the press pays handsomely for this information ... be warned!

What now? Let's say you've been charged and face the prospect of appearing in court. Are you pleading guilty or are you fighting the case? Should you be fighting the case and eventually be found guilty, then the sentence will be more severe than if you first entered a guilty plea. The court usually deduct 20 per cent from the sentence if you plead guilty; obviously, if you walk free and are acquitted then there is no sentence and nothing to add on ... only you can decide on your course of action. I mean, look at UK TV presenter John Lesley ... he walked, but at what price?

On the other hand, let's say you've been found guilty. At this stage, you are usually let out on bail unless, of course, you happen to be OJ Simpson and then you might not be released! Probation reports will be requested by the judge before you are sentenced; these can take up to four weeks.

Probation are a law unto themselves; unless you show remorse at what you've done and accept that your offending behaviour was your fault, then the report is going to go against you. The rest is in the lap of the gods and also depends on whether the judge is sympathetic to your plight.

The day of sentencing arrives and you haven't yet left the country to go and live in Cuba; you are either walking into court under your own steam or you are shipped in from prison from the remand wing.

You are standing in the dock, trying to look your meekest, giving all those fancy Masonic signs to the judge in the hope that he's a sympathetic fellow Lodge member and you've got that lucky four-leaf clover in your pocket while standing with your legs crossed ... yes, it all worked – you are sent to prison!

Celebrity or no celebrity, you are prison fodder; you are at your most vulnerable. You've seen all those films about prisons and prisoners getting done by arse bandits and you've even seen *Scum* on video starring Ray Winstone! My advice is, befriend the hardest (and straightest) con on the wing and look after him by sending his family some nice gifts; get your minder and stay out of trouble or you'll get smacked. Do your time the easy way and don't play the 'I'm a Celebrity Get Me out of Here' tune!

When you think that paedophiles like Jonathan King can survive in prison, then that might make you feel a little easier in yourself. For the likes of him, there is no hiding place; you just have to surround yourself with prison queens. Look at Gary Glitter – he's not gay, he had no one inside ... he had to stay behind his cell door. No one likes paedophiles, but most cons can tolerate the queens; they can be a laugh, but don't bend down to pick the soap up in the shower.

When you enter into the prison system, you go through what is called 'reception'. You've been unloaded from the prison van that picked you up from the court, you're probably part of a larger group of convicts who have been collected from other courts along the way or just part of a group that has been collected from the court where you were convicted.

You would have been picked up between 4.00pm and 5.00pm, and dumped off at the nearest allocation prison, possibly ending up sitting in a holding area full of cells; there could be up to twenty of you in each of the holding cells. During the course of this 'reception' period, you will be given a meal of sorts and a mug of prison swill tea. Cells are opening and closing like there was no tomorrow; cons disappear and your holding group gets smaller. Where are the cons going and what's happening to them?

You are called next. They take you from the cell and you are given a brief interview by a Reception Prison Officer. He asks your date of birth, which court you've come from and your sentence. He's not asking you this so he can be nice, he's asking so he can confirm he's got the right prisoner in front of him ... it's his job. Oh, and they ask you your religion as well. This is so that if you are a Muslim or Jew and so on, then you can be given the right sort of food to comply with your religious requirements. I have known cons to give their religion as Judaism, even if they aren't Jewish, just so they get better grub while behind bars.

After all your details are confirmed and you've given them your autograph, you will be moved on to the stores part of the reception area, where you will be served up prison clothing and other items for use during your sentence.

You are now the new boy on the block, the new starter, the new inmate. Don't expect to be throwing your weight about, there's always somebody bigger, stronger and more violent than you in these places.

You're now on your own and you'll have to grow up quickly otherwise you could go into a state of deep depression. Just remember – nothing is for ever, even the Ripper will escape his incarceration one day ... when he's dead! This whole process of isolation alienates you from everything; you've no friends or family to see you through it.

At such a time, you really need as much moral support as you can get, but don't expect it. These places are cold, heartless institutions designed to break the will of the strongest man. I should know, they've been trying to break my will for the last thirty years. OK, the sky pilot will call at your door and briefly ask if he can be of help.

'Yeah, let me out of here.'

But he cannot really do much, unless he offers you a drink of wine. Should you be of the Muslim faith then, eventually, you will get to see the Imam. Should you be a bible moth then this will be up your street, but I'm not into these sky pilots; they preach but don't carry out what they say. But if it helps, go and cry on to them and they might let you have a phone call.

Then there's the probation service. Everyone prison has a resident officer; again, as much use as a chocolate fireguard. They only want you to come to terms with your offending behaviour; they want you to change your ways. How the fuck can you change your ways? You're probably a man and are serving time for a manly act. However, should you be a woman, then you've got it tough ... the courts do not act leniently towards women. Being a woman is more than likely to mean you are going to go to prison for your offence, whereas a man might walk from court.

You might, if you're lucky, be given a set of prison rules. Yeah, they've even got 'em inside of prison, too! You will have to weigh up how slack the prison wing is, how far you can push the rules without getting nicked. Believe me, you can get nicked and put on report for the stupidest of things.

Years ago, you were nicked for the most basic of rule infractions. Now you can plead ignorance. You can grow your hair as long as you want. You can wear some of your own clothes (after making an application or coming through reception with them). You can probably wear your own trainers, but you must have a pair of shoes or footwear to go into your civilian clothing box; I don't know why, but you do. So if you know you're going to prison when you go to court, take an extra pair of trainers in with you so you've got something for your property box.

Then you'll be given a bed pack. The bed pack is needed 'cos your cell will just have a bare bed and mattress. Some prisons have bed packs already prepared for you in the cell, but this is rare. I don't have to go through any of that routine; I get whisked straight into my special little cell ... usually full of cardboard furniture. Once over, after getting out of bed in the morning, you used to have to make up your own bed pack every morning and lay it out at the bottom of your bed, all neat and tidy. Nowadays, you can leave the bed as messy as you want.

By the time you've gone through all of this routine of being on the induction conveyor belt, it will be late and the prison may well be shut down for the night. When I say 'shut down', I mean everyone is banged up due to their association coming to an end and the majority of screws like to get away for a few pints of their own special swill.

You might get the chance to be seen by the prison doctor, or if not on that first night then it will be the next day. The doctor will ask if you're taking any prescribed medication or if you are an addict or if you have any outstanding hospital appointments for medical conditions. The visit is swift and then you are paraded back to your cell. These doctors are nothing more than vets, that's my personal opinion. I refuse to see prison doctors due to the way they are up the arses of the Prison Service. I even recall when Dr Harold Shipman first got sentenced, he had all the cons and prison officers queuing up for his advice! Now doesn't that tell you something about prison doctors? I mean, if the cons would rather see a convicted serial killer over and above a prison doctor ...

You will also be entitled to what is called 'canteen' or the prison shop. You'll be allocated about £2.50, but you don't get to handle the hard cash. You are then called for by the canteen staff (they could be prison screws or civvies. You can spend your cash on tobacco products, extra food rations, toiletries other than prison-issue items, and so on.

Never leave these possessions on show; guard them with your life. A half-ounce of tobacco is prison currency; I've seen people get cut up over that amount. Don't try to buy friends with these rations; you'll get loads of peggers (smokers) coming on to you on the exercise yard for a smoke, until you fathom out who is who ... leave it out.

Eventually you'll get to see an Allocation Officer. It is their job to decide what category of security to assign you to. There are five levels (not officially) of security category; corresponding to the level of security risk you are deemed to present to the authorities. Doctors (not Harold Shipman, he's dead) who have been caught drink-driving for the umpteenth time will be allocated Category 'D' status, as will bankers (mortgage fraud) solicitors (misappropriation of clients' funds) and the likes of George Best, and so on.

Category 'D' status is the lowest security risk that can be allocated to you, which means that an open prison awaits you. Should you be lucky enough to fall into the 'D' status but are serving a short sentence, then don't expect to moved instantly. As long as you are within that allocation prison then you are handled as a prisoner of medium security status and have to comply with the rules of that prison. Eventually, if you are category 'D', you will be moved to an open prison. This is what happened to George Best when he was in for drink-driving offences; they offered him a place on the prison football team and he turned them down.

Category 'C' security level means a semi-open prison environment is on the cards for you; you've got to be serving four years or less for this and, of course, have no previous record of absconding from prison or custody. This semi-open environment is alien to me; I only know of closed high-security conditions; so if you get such a category allocated to you, savour it. Mind you, these conditions mean you've still got a 20ft wall topped with razor wire and bottomed out on the free side with ankle breakers! Don't be fooled into thinking that you can step over a 3ft wall, and you're probably going to be banged up in a locked cell, so what's semi-open about it?

Category 'B' status means you are probably serving over four years and have a reason to escape. These prisons are the likes of HMP Frankland; you tend to get more of a relaxed regime in these environments due to the prisoners being 'time served' tradesmen – robbers, burglars and the like. The petty criminals are harder to find in this grouping. Although some celebrities have been given long prison sentences, they usually find themselves steered away from such places for fear that they'll be nonced (sexually assaulted) or attacked. The big boys in these places don't like to be upstaged! Should you find yourself in such a place, then show respect to all around you ... you just don't know who's who.

Category 'A' status means you're nearly the créme de la créme of the criminal underworld. Prisons like HMP Full Sutton are going to be the places for you while on your tour of the prison system.

Category 'AA' status does not officially exist, but that's when you get the likes of Bob Maudsley, Reg Wilson and me being locked away from the rest of the cons, even from those classed as Category 'A'. Should you find yourself in such circumstances, then you can kiss your arse goodbye.

Category '?' – this category is hard to define; you're probably a spy or a war criminal. There has been talk about the war criminal Slobodan Milosevic being sent to an English prison and he would fall into this category. He would probably be sent to a secret location like HMP Hull in the old 'special unit' or to HMP Parkhurst in the protected witness suite. But a mainstream venue like HMP Belmarsh is also an option due to its high security.

Right ... you're now in the system and starting to settle down. You've seen all the dodgy-looking characters who have assessed you and you're ready to meet your fellow inmates. There are right and wrong ways to do things behind bars. Some first-timers try to make out that they've done time before, but you soon get caught out. Just admit it if it is your first time behind bars; don't ruffle any feathers.

One of the big problems in *all* prisons is the drug problem, and it isn't that there's not enough of it about ... you'll have the drug barons swooping down on you like flies swarming around shit. They'll be offering you anything you want in the line of drugs, smack, crack, cocaine, happy baccy and even brown (heroin).

The laws behind bars allow for what is called 'mandatory drug testing'. That means if they request you to give a urine sample, you cannot run off and hide, you've got to do it. Me, I personally refuse these tests 'cos they can't give me any more time on top. But for you, you have to comply or you'll lose time. The reason I don't piss for them is that I am religiously against all drugs; they are taking the piss by even asking, and it is an insult to my integrity. But you must comply ... or lose time.

When they brought the mandatory tests in it changed the whole drug culture behind bars. Screws were happy to turn a blind eye to those smoking cannabis; it calmed people down and that was what was needed behind bars. They didn't want hyperactive cons running around, but mandatory drug testing brought about exactly the opposite of what it was supposed to stop!

Why? I'll tell you why, because cannabis stays in your system for up to twenty-eight days. Crack is not oil-based like cannabis and therefore doesn't stay in your urine for too long, you piss it out within a day or so! Should a prison officer be able to tip the wink and warn the cons of an impending drugs test, then they can cool it down a bit and pass the test, but any con on cannabis doesn't stand a cat in hell's chance.

Meddling politicians, this is what they do, and then when prisoners kick off due to not being able to get their fix, it is the prisoner officers that get the backlash. Mind you, some prison officers deserve a whiplash, never mind the backlash!

So if someone does offer you some 'puff' (cannabis), then you're not just letting yourself down, you're also letting your family down. Testing positive for drugs behind bars goes against you; it can upset parole plans, reclassification of your security category and make them come down hard on you whenever they want.

You'll be wanting some contact with your family, and you are entitled to what is called a 'reception visit' (RVO – Reception Visiting Order). Everything in these allocation prisons is done by application. You practically can't even have a shit without putting in an application. Different prisons have different methods of putting in applications. Some prisons have a wing officer who stands with his board in the morning; you go up to him and make an application for this, that and the other. Make sure you know where to go to make these applications, otherwise you'll miss out on the daily applications and have to wait until the following day. Me, I've got a manservant who very kindly comes to my door to take my applications.

There used to be three ways to get a message to someone – letter, telephone and tell a woman. Prison has many more methods than this, but that is for you to find out. You can be in your cell and you might hear the faint pulse tone of a mobile phone; don't ask me how they get hold of them behind bars, but they do. In the unlikely event that you haven't been able to secrete one of these up your arse, then you'll have to get sorted for the wing phone. Each, if not all, prison wings have a telephone for use by the cons; it is controlled by the centre or wing office. They can knock it off whenever they want, or put it on. All calls can be monitored, so don't swear your life away in these telephone calls.

You used to be able to buy a BT Phonecard from the canteen, but now most prisons are changing over to the PIN system. You get issued with a PIN number and this can be credited on a weekly basis up to a certain amount. All of the numbers you call are also stored; you cannot now just ring any old number. Once, cons used to be able to call any number they wanted and this led to an outcry when witnesses were being threatened by cons ... you get my drift.

The less security risk you represent to the prison service means you

THE GOOD PRISON GUIDE

will eventually become a lower security category and things like using the phone at set times aren't as strict, you can relax; but in a tougher prison, then you have to handle all the shit they can throw at you. This is why many prisoners crack up, including me ... I lose my rag over the pettiness of things and broken promises. 'Yes, Charlie, you can use the phone at six o'clock ...' Six o'clock arrives and no phone! No wonder I crack up.

When you're behind your door, time goes by quickly. But when you're in an open environment, I've heard from many prisoners, time drags on. How you do your time is up to you, but always try to do it the easy way ... not the Bronson way! Don't try to beat my record.

A–Z OF PRISONS

Welcome to my world. It's a journey through the penal system. This chapter covers all of the prisons and special hospitals I've been in over the last thirty years.

I want you to strap yourself in and come with me on the ride of a lifetime. It will open up your mind and blow a hole clean through your soul.

This journey is on the very edge of the razor ... if you slip, you are dead! The hole is bottomless, black and empty.

Your sweat turns to ice
Your blood to treacle
Your tears to fire

There are no rainbows in hell
The stars are grey
The sky is crimson
The grass is concrete
The walls are stone
The glass is razor wire
Face it ... you're caged!

There can be no escape from your mind
How do you escape from yourself?
The eyes are mirrors
The mirror is just a reflection
It's you

The journey sucks you in
The reality blows you out
There are no brakes
You can only crash
And die

Dead men do breathe
Dead men can talk
Prisons are full of stiffs
Dead – rotting meat
Eyes of marbles
Faces of stone
Heartless
Soulless

Psychos full of hate
Full of bitterness
Full of nightmares

Like a canary in a cage
A bear in a box
A tiger in the zoo

They're all dead inside
Lost souls
Nothing to wake up for
Forever sleeping
Forever dreaming

Dreaming to roam the land
Grass and trees
Lakes and rivers
Flowers and butterflies
Companionship
Love – and freedom

This is a book on a lifetime of prison madness. If you have read my books you already know I've been certified insane. But who has the right to say who's mad?

What is normal? Is a psychiatrist normal? They say they are madder than the lunatics.

If you stuff your face with shit
You become shit

If you jump in a sewer
You smell of shit

If you spend your life talking with madness
You become mad

Did you know there is a high rate of suicide and nervous breakdowns among psychiatrists? Alcoholism, too! They are fucking insane ... take it from me!

The lunatics are taking over
The asylums are exploding
Mad men are the genius!

Look back in time
Go right back in history

Some of the Greats were a bit strange. Were they insane? Just because they are not normal don't make them insane!

Is an Eskimo mad living in ice?
Is a headhunter a psychopath?
Is Saddam Hussein insane?
Who the fuck are we to say!
Is my journey insane?
Am I insane?

I'll leave that for you to decide
Is my art insane?
Is my poetry insane?
Is my philosophy insane?
I say I am just on the edge.

Licking the honey from the razor's edge
It's dangerous
It's a serious gamble
Crossing a road is a risk
Drinking tap water is a risk
Catching a plane, a train, a taxi
It's all a risk.

A swim in the sea could be your last!
That shark could be waiting for you
There could be a mad axeman behind that tree
Just waiting, watching, wanting your head!

It's life ... Fate ... Meant to be!
You can't change it, nobody can!

Nowadays they fly planes into skyscrapers!
They strap bombs to their bodies
They push bombs in prams with babies on top
They release gas in the air
Germ warfare!

Is all that insane?
What journey are they on?

Yours?
Mine?
Theirs?
Whose?
Why?
What for?

Fuck it ...!
It's all mad to me!

I'll stick to my own journey.
'It's safer'

Welcome to my world of prisons.

Keep kicking
Till the angels come.

HM PRISON ALBANY

This image is an extract from The Millennium Map™ © getmapping.com plc

LOCATION:	Newport, Isle of Wight – get there by ferry or hovercraft.
CAPACITY:	400 beds.
CATEGORY AT PRESENT:	Closed 'B' – Male (mainly sex offenders).
OPENED:	1963 as a prison for Category 'C' males and in 1970 became a dispersal prison.
HISTORY:	Dubbed 'The Island' because of its location, was closed down in 1983 when prisoners wrecked the place.

This jail is right next-door to Parkhurst Prison on the beautiful Isle of Wight. You can get to the island from the mainland by ferry or hovercraft. Albany was the first maximum secure dispersal prison with electronic doors, and it was influenced by the Lord Mountbatten report in the early 1970s that was brought about because of the many prison escapes.

I actually first landed here in the mid-1980s and from day one I felt the 'atmosphere' – shit. It is a very claustrophobic place with tiny square cells and little space to do anything in. The whole place reeked of despair. It had seen its share of riots, shit-ups, violence and hardships.

But nobody had ever escaped from here, which is probably why it had this imposing atmosphere about it. But it had one saving grace – lovely fish and chips on a Friday. I mean it, their fish and chips were as good as any in the country. And it had a bloody good canteen that sold a good selection of cakes and fruit. And you could order 'meat'.

Each wing had its kitchen area, so you could cook up a nice meal. It also had a great gym.

Sammy McCarthy (ex-British featherweight boxing champ) was the gym orderly. Sammy copped eighteen years for a blag with East End gangster Harry Batt. Harry was an old pal of mine, one of the best.

Once, Sammy was cleaning up in the gym, whistling away, when all of sudden a loud-mouthed con got very argumentative; he was actually abusive to Sammy. Now this guy was maybe 14st. Sammy was just an old man, still a flyweight. 'Excuse me,' Sammy said, 'Could you please calm down and treat the gym a bit nicer?'

'Fuck off you little ...' That is all he managed to get out. Sammy had let one fly – BANG – the loudmouth was out cold.

That is Sammy – a total gentleman. And one of the nicest cons I have ever met. A wonderful man!

There was a con in Albany, a gay chap we called 'Mary'. He was harmless, but I must say, he did look like a bird. A lot like that Una Stubbs who used to act in *'Til Death Do Us Part*.

Anyway, Mary worked in the tailor shop and some con was bullying him, but it turned out Mary was no walkover. The con ended up dead with a pair of scissors through his chest.

It was also here that my next-door neighbour hung himself. I could actually smell shit. I thought it strange. He had topped himself by tying the sheets around his neck, tying the other end to the bars and jumping.

It's fact, people who hang themselves always shit themselves. The bowels and bladder just empty automatically when the muscles relax.

This may sound insane – death also has a smell to it. Don't ask me to explain that because I can't. But death lingers on in the air we breathe. It is a very strange smell, and would you fucking believe it, this con that hanged himself actually owed me four Mars bars. We had had a bet on the football, and I won, not that I'm saying he topped himself to get out of paying me.

Albany did have a nice big field which we used to run round on weekends. And in the summertime, the Island, as we called it, was the place to be. We were all tanned and looked liked we'd just spent the week in Tenerife. Do you know that if you got sunburn then the prison authorities classed it as being self-inflicted and they didn't have to give you anything for it? Kind-hearted bastards! But despite the sunbathing, it was still a bad jail to be in, nobody seemed to be happy, so I wasn't surprised to learn that it had been torn apart by the cons in 1983.

When I was there, Jennifer Rush's 'The Power of Love' was number one in the pop charts. Fuck me, you may well ask, how can I remember that? Easy – I smashed the TV set because of it! During the song, cons were making too much noise and it upset me. Could that girl sing! What a voice ...what a song. One of my all-time greats.

My time at Albany came to an end when I was in the kitchen; I hit a Rastafarian with a wok a dozen times over the crust. I caved his big, fat, ugly head in, the thieving bastard. He was a cell thief. He had to have some!

I actually wanted to cut his fingers off but my pal, Big Albert, said, 'No, Chas.' So I thought, fuck it, I'll just cave in his canister!

I am giving Albany 1/10, and that's only for the fish and chips.

HM PRISON ARMLEY

This image is an extract from The Millennium Map™ © getmapping.com plc

LOCATION:	Armley, Leeds.
CAPACITY:	1,250 beds.
CATEGORY AT PRESENT:	Dispersal and Remand – Males.
OPENED:	1847 and only had a capacity of just over 300.
HISTORY:	Has had extra wings added to it over time and now acts as an allocation prison, sending prisoners received from the local courts to more permanent accommodation. Although this prison is officially titled 'Leeds Prison', it has become commonly known as 'Armley Prison'.

This prison was originally designed on the 'modern penitentiary principle' of four radial wings. Firstly, it was a local prison catering for those around the West Riding area of Yorkshire. It played a role in judicial executions from 1864 to 1961 when ninety-four (including one female con) were executed within the prison. In 1864, the first double execution took place outside of the prison walls, which was to be the only public execution. The execution took place with up to 100,000 sightseers looking on as James Sargisson and Joseph Myers met their deaths and were left to hang for the time limit of one hour before being cut down and buried within the confines of the prison.

The most famous prisoner to be housed at Armley Prison was Charlie Peace (1832–1879), an infamous Victorian criminal. In 1879, Peace was executed by hanging in Armley Prison. A violent blagger of his time, Peace was serving time for robbery, murdering a copper and the attempted murder of another copper. By time Peace was nineteen years old he was already on his way to becoming a hardened career criminal, just like me!

At one time in Peace's career, he actually moved to Hull and opened a café but he still continued burgling and would always carry his piece (revolver). In one incident, a copper trying to arrest Peace was shot and killed; in the mélèe, Peace escaped. Would you believe, though, that two other men (totally innocent) were arrested for the murder! Two local villains, brothers John and William Habron, were arrested for the crime. William was convicted and sentenced to death but fortunately reprieved and later pardoned.

Charlie Peace shot and killed another man in a love triangle and then escaped capture when he hid out in London for over two years where he continued with his burglaries. Eventually, Peace was caught committing a burglary; he gave a moody (false) name, but was grassed up by his mistress who thought she'd collect the reward money. Police travelled from Yorkshire to Newgate Prison, where Peace was held, and correctly identified him.

Peace stood trial at the Old Bailey in November 1878, and on the charges of burglary and attempted murder he was sentenced to life in prison. But it doesn't end there. There was the slight problem of another murder he had to answer for. The love triangle killing of a Mr Dyson saw Peace being shipped to Sheffield, where he was charged with murder on 18 January 1879 and, at his subsequent trial, it took the jury ten minutes to find him guilty; he was sentenced to hang. This was a celebrated case and caught the imagination of the public.

While Peace was in the condemned cell, he confessed to the murder of the policeman he had killed during the bungled burglary and, as a consequence, William Habron was given a pardon.

The date for hanging Peace was set for Tuesday, 25 February 1879, and it was to be a private affair, although four newspaper reporters were present. The following day, a large piece appeared in the press, and even Madame Tussaud's Wax Museum had the execution scene on show.

The only woman to hanged at Armley Prison was Emily Swann. This was a double hanging; alongside her was John Gallagher, 30, her lover. Both were hanged on 29 December 1903 for the murder of Swann's husband, William.

For those wishing to collect data about Armley, I can tell you that the last double hanging at Armley was Thomas Riley and John Roberts on the 29 April 1932. Soon after this, double hangings stopped because of the time it took. Not out of concern for the condemned!

The last hanging to take place at Armley was that of Zsiga Pankotia, 31, a Hungarian national, on 29 June 1961. The executioner was Harry Allen.

And then I landed there a few years later.

I landed here back in 1975 for the first time and it started from the second I got off the van – eyeballing, pushing, shoving and verbal. Nothing seemed to have changed since the last hanging.

A gauntlet of gruesome-looking types met me, and led me all the way to the bowels of hell. Shining tunic buttons, polished boots and pudding-bowl haircuts ... what a neat bunch of bastards they were. Nowadays, half of them look like tramps. Back then, it was a pleasure to take a beating from such a smartly turned out bunch of screws when fighting them.

Their block was down under B Wing. It was like an old castle dungeon and, in fact, the place was built like a fortress.

This place wasn't just put together with bricks and mortar, but big slabs of Yorkshire stone. It was cold and made you shiver to the bone; no heating, one blanket and a smelly mattress added the finishing touches to the décor. I can imagine what the condemned felt like while waiting to be executed. In fact, execution was preferable to this.

There was no window (glass or plastic), just cold wind blowing in through a hole where a window used to be with the stink of despair rushing in with it.

The place was infested with vermin – rats, mice and screws. They served my meals cold. The reason for my being sent to Armley was over some assaults on screws in another jail. Hence the reception committee. They were waiting for me! That's how it works in jail. If you attack a screw, you attack them all. You attack their system. So they love it when you arrive.

And Armley was the tough jail of the North; it also had the highest suicide rate of YPs (young prisoners). Armley jail saw three young prisoners take their own lives by hanging, all within the space of five months, from May to October 1988, and then a further two hangings in the beginning of 1989 – both were YPs.

I knew my stay here would be a crazy time, so I gave it my best shot ... that's where I ripped my door off and wrecked their precious little block. It was truly worth the drubbing I got for it. I remember that I was making my way through the cell door. A fellow con, Dave Anslow, was also making his way through his door. I managed to get through my metal door; then they had to close those cells down and we both ended up in 'strip cells'.

They had to call in reinforcements and a score of screws, some with dogs; they were all right outside our cell doors waiting for us – our plan, obviously, never worked.

Armley is run with an iron fist. Some screws put a pair of steel-capped boots on and look as if they feel they're entitled to kick the shit out of you.

Another gauntlet awaited me after the roof job in Walton Prison. Once more, I felt their punishment in 1985 so I write from the painful truth – Armley is a hellhole and, for a young lad, it's probably terrifying.

Believe me, it was awesome. It even amazed me, and that's saying something because nothing amazes me.

In fighting them, I was black and blue. As if that wasn't enough, they left me in the box; I was stripped off like a Christmas turkey. What a way to treat a guest! Especially in Her Majesty's house of correction. Disgusting!

The doctor came to see me; I spat a mouthful of blood all over him. 'Fuck off, you vet!' My lawyer at the time was Ted Saxon. He came to see me. What a joke. They took his pen off him and give him a tiny pen an inch long!

They told him, 'It's in case he stabs you.' Ted told them I would never do that to him. But that is how they like to work. They seem to get a kick out of intimidating people but it doesn't work on everybody.

You might recall the 'Free George Davies' campaign in the 1970s. A big campaign to get George out of jail for a robbery he did not do. It took years to prove it. In the end, the campaign won.

You might recall the Headingley cricket pitch incident in which the cricket pitch was dug up at the famous Yorkshire cricket ground as a protest to speed up the freeing of George. It was Chapman who copped for it, a diamond of a geezer. He came into Armley on remand over that. I met him there. What a smashing chap he was.

Another top chap I met in Armley was Harry Marsden, a Newcastle armed robber; he was about ten years my senior. Only a small chap, jet-black hair, with deep-set eyes, what a fighter. Harry had the heart of a lion.

He just steamed into those Leeds screws like skittles. Sadly, Harry suffered some serious physical opposition and spent years in isolation, but he won in the end. He made it home and made a decent life. I'm still in touch with Harry to this very day.

The guy beat cancer, too. I told you he was a winner. Harry reminds me a lot of Frank Fraser, a gentleman, but fuck with him and you are crippled! He got out of prison and, eventually, after more trouble, he turned his life around and became a boxing coach in the amateur ranks. He even opened his own boxing club and made me Life President of it.

Armley bent and smashed a lot of good people ... it broke men into mice. Paul (Sykesy) Syke's arms got broken; Paul fought for the British Heavyweight title against John L Gardner. Sadly, he lost. Dominick Noonan's arm also got broken and Joe Uradits received serious injuries all as a result of fighting with screws.

I recall John Massey – he was moved to Armley Prison after he beat a prison doctor up; it was what the man had coming to him. After he arrived at Armley, he had a really hard time. Later, John had the last laugh – he escaped!

I will add this; all of those suicides in Armley in the 1970s and 1980s, 90 per cent were youngsters! They were terrified! Driven to despair! I would say to all those bad screws from that era, hang your heads in

```
T SPOTLIGHTS      *
MACAROON BAR      *                0.33
GREETING CARD     *                1.48
GREETINGS CARD    *                1.98
BOOK                               4.00  **
CHICKEN S/WICH                     1.68

TOTAL                             10.53
Visa Debit SALE                   10.53
  AID        A0000000031010
  NUMBER     : xxxxxxxxxxxx1332    ICC
  PAN SEQ NO : 01
  AUTH CODE  : 304576
  MERCHANT   : 46273752
  START : 04/08 EXPIRY : 05/11
  Cardholder PIN Verified
CHANGE DUE                         0.00
```

CLUBCARD STATEMENT

```
CLUBCARD NUMBER 63400402406775993*
POINTS THIS VISIT                   10
TOTAL UP TO 14/08/08               210
TOTAL INCLUDES :
  GREEN CLUBCARD POINTS              0
```

CHOOSE HOW TO SPEND YOUR VOUCHERS;
IN-STORE, ONLINE OR WITH CLUBCARD DEALS

Clubcard Points up until 27th July
have been converted to Vouchers
and will arrive by 31st August

15/08/08 21:52 2737 015 1240 2

shame, as you lot were responsible for that and you lot will have to face that in your last breath on the planet. This really is a hanging prison.

But like all jails, there were decent screws and some characters, like Roger Outram. He was a screw when I met him there and then he worked up to become Governor in Belmarsh Prison.

When he was a screw, he was a tough guy, a big fella, hard as nails. A typical Yorkshireman. Loves a pint. Loves a fight. But he was a fair man, never a bully. I have known him stand toe-to-toe with a con and shake hands afterwards. He never needed nine fellow screws to back him up. And he turned out a decent governor, too! Men like that, I can respect. But the ten who jumped on my head and those who bully YPs to the point that they hang themselves, I fucking despise the maggots.

Some maggots even bring in drugs for cons. A screw from Armley Prison was jailed for two-and-a-half years after he admitted attempting to supply heroin to an inmate. I'm dead against drugs, and this reinforces what I have already said about screws supplying cons with drugs.

At Leeds Crown Court, Martin Wood, 42, was convicted when the court heard how police drug squad officers stopped him as he arrived for work at Armley Prison, Leeds, in January 2003.

The undercover police searched Wood's car and found 2.93gms of heroin wrapped in cellophane and hidden down his underpants.

Would you believe that Wood told the coppers that he thought it was cannabis he was bringing into the prison for a man called Dickinson in E Wing.

Armley, I believe, has all changed now, but it is still Armley to me. Always will be. Belsen is Belsen. Colditz is Colditz. Alcatraz is Alcatraz. And Armley is Armley.

A bit of paint or a new wing doesn't take away the ghosts of the past. Why kid yourself?

I am giving Armley 1/10. That is for the cell door I ripped off that cons said couldn't be done. Stick to your Yorkshire Puddings. Leave the door game to me.

ASHWORTH SPECIAL SECURE HOSPITAL

This image is an extract from The Millennium Map™ © getmapping.com plc

LOCATION: Maghull, Liverpool.

CAPACITY: 436 beds. Ashworth High Security Hospital today consists of two sites – Ashworth East and Ashworth North. Ashworth East has six refurbished wards, two newly built wards and the Wordsworth Ward, a new sixteen-bedded ward. Ashworth's female patients are located on the East Site, as well as a large number of mentally ill men. A high wire wall provides physical security. Ashworth North has seventeen wards with a total capacity of approximately 370 patients.

CATEGORY AT PRESENT: Special High-Security Hospital.

OPENED: In 1878, it was sold to the overseers of the Liverpool Workhouse – Liverpool Select Vestry, who used the large house as a convalescent home for children from Liverpool workhouses. Eventually, in 1911, construction began on a new hospital to be used as an epileptic colony.

HISTORY: In 1914, the 'Lunacy Board of Control' bought the whole estate, including a large unfinished hospital. Before it could be pressed into use as a State institution, however, the hospital was taken over for the treatment of shell-shocked soldiers from the Great War.

In 1920, the Ministry of Pensions took the hospital over and it was not until 1933 that the hospital became a State institution.

In 1948, the hospital became part of the new National Health Service and, in 1959, the Ministry of Health took over responsibility for running the Special Hospitals.

In the 1970s, further enlargement came when the decision was taken to build a fourth Special Hospital to relieve overcrowding at Broadmoor. There was still land available from the original estate in Maghull and 50 acres of land were made available for the new Park Lane Hospital.

In 1974, Park Lane opened in stages up to 1984. Unlike Moss Side Hospital, a high-security wall, completely separating it from the rest of the site, surrounded it. Moss Side and Park Lane shared some facilities but operated as independent hospitals.

In 1990, one of the first acts of the new Special Hospitals Service Authority (SHSA) was to merge the two hospitals.

On 19 February 1990, the new hospital, Ashworth, was born. The old Moss Side Hospital became known as Ashworth South and East, and Park Lane was renamed Ashworth North. Ashworth South, the original Moss Side Hospital, closed in 1995. I have also spent time in Moss Side, making me unique in that I've been in all the best lunatic hospitals.

In March 1991, the hospital was severely criticised in a *Cutting Edge* television programme, alleging widespread abuse of mentally ill patients by staff at Ashworth.

A public inquiry was chaired by Sir Louis Blom-Cooper QC, which put forward ninety recommendations. There was a call for wholesale culture change at Ashworth. This led to a further reorganisation of the hospital and much work to try to change the culture of the institution.

In April 1996, the hospital became a 'Special Hospital Authority' when the High-Security Psychiatric Services Commissioning Board (HSPSCB) succeeded the SHSA.

The capacity of 520 beds was gradually reduced. As one of the three Special High-Security Hospitals (Ashworth, Park Lane and Broadmoor), Ashworth receives patients from the North of England, Wales, the West Midlands and North-West London.

Approximately 80 per cent of patients have been convicted of a criminal offence, most of whom are subject to restriction orders. The average length of stay is eight years – a small number of patients will never be ready to leave and will spend the rest of their lives at Ashworth.

I landed in the cuckoo's nest in 1984. It was about the time of Michael Jackson's 'Thriller'. And, boy, was it an eye-opener. Ashworth was originally Park Lane Asylum. There was a swimming pool (over-heated), a gym and a big shop to buy clothes and food. Visits were brilliant.

The lunatics were smoking cigars there and eating chocolate cake. Talk about spoiling us. TV in cells ... sorry, 'rooms'.

And the screws ... sorry, 'nurses', some of the women were like Page 3 birds. But there is always a downside to such a place – too many nutters for my liking.

Let's not forget, it is a top-security asylum. It is like the *Big Brother* house, but 100 times bigger and more secure.

I only survived there for six months. I ripped open a lunatic's face with a sauce bottle. The nutter bled all over the new gym kit I had on. You would have thought he could have bled away from me and not over me.

But I will tell you now, it was here that I realised that the psychiatrists are definitely madder than us lot. Remember, they work with madness day in and day out, year after year. It has got to rub off on them. And believe me, it does. They are all fucking mad.

I am giving Ashworth 8/10, simply as it was a comfortable stay. Break out the Cadbury's Dairy Milk.

HM PRISON BELMARSH

This image is an extract from The Millennium Map™ © getmapping.com plc

LOCATION:	Thamesmead, London.
CAPACITY:	850 beds.
CATEGORY AT PRESENT:	Dispersal, Remand and Category 'A' – Male.
OPENED:	1991 and only had a capacity of just over 300.
HISTORY:	A prison mainly for prisoners considered to be high risk or likely to want to escape. A special wing houses seventy prisoners convicted of mainly sex offences.

Oh yeah ... one of my favourites is Hellmarsh! I had some lovely stays here. My first spell was in their SSU (Special Secure Unit). By 1993, it was a maximum secure unit and was the most secure unit in Europe.

The prison housed mostly terrorists and top-class blaggers, some spies, serial killers and little old me.

I was there over a 'bank' and a few other minor charges – innocent, of course!

Sadly, the Governor at this time was a little fat fellow who smoked a pipe. I told him straight, 'Fuck off before I ram the pipe down your neck.' It is always best to make it clear how you feel – clears the air.

I had a few old pals there at the time – Rocky Lee, Pete Pesato, Rab Harper and Del Croxen. All good armed robbers. They were on the wing part of the unit. They kept me in the seg block on my own. But I was sweet, and the block screws were diamonds. A right good bunch.

The food was shit, though, but I could buy tins of fish and fruit from the canteen. So I was well sorted. I also trained hard. All day long, press-ups, sit-ups and I ran on the yard.

It was here that Del Croxen died in his cell. He was only in his 30s. A great man.

I was allowed out of the block to go to a service in the prison chapel with the lads, which I thanked the Governor for. I said a little piece for Del in respect. It's an old saying of mine. I am not sure who wrote it, I am not even sure if it is right, as I may have changed it over the years:

> 'We the willing – led by the unknown – have been doing the
> impossible for so long – with so little – are we now qualified
> to do anything at all?'

I don't know why I chose to say that, but, it felt right. To me, it says it all. And I hope Del would have approved.

Peter Pesato also read a piece, and it was a lovely service, sad and respectful.

I first met Del in Wandsworth; it was Frankie Fraser who introduced us. I would have loved to be on a robbery with Del, as he was a good blagger.

It was around this time the IRA lads upset me. The day we had Del's service, that night I could hear them playing their rebel songs and throwing out burning paper and singing. They were always throwing out burning paper! I felt it was disrespectful to Del, and I made it known. It stopped.

But it was too late for me. It played on my mind, as I am a very sensitive man. So it set me off on one of my mad spells. I wanted the door off.

It was on my second stay there that they gave me a break and put me up on the Cat 'A' wing. It was there I knocked out a con and stuffed him inside the industrial washing machine. He had it coming, one disrespectful slag. Playing his music until all hours. Shouting his mouth off, he was only a drug mug. I told him to slow up, but he got lemon, so – BANG – out cold he went!

I would have put him in the incinerator outside, fucking low-life rat. Fortunately for him, a pal stopped me turning on the machine. He vanished soon after that and it was all peaceful again.

That was until the Iraqi hijackers turned up. I wrapped 'em up, costing me another seven years. Seven fucking years I get over the Iraqis, and the armed forces get medals! I told you this journey is insane.

Belmarsh is a good jail, with some good screws in it, but the food is shit. The cells are good, with nice windows, an iron bed and good showers, too. Visits are reasonable, considering it's mostly remands in the prison, and on a good day the screws give you extra time.

My visits were always in the seg block. And the screws even made my visitors tea, and were polite to them.

Old Lord Longford – Frank to me – would visit me every month here. Frank's visited me for years, all over the country; he put me in his two books, *Prisoner or Patient* and *The Longford Diaries*.

Sadly, he is no longer with us. I loved the old boy. He always made me laugh. He had some good morals, but he got a bad name over his fight for the now dead Myra Hindley. I told him straight, 'She is a fucking monster.'

And how do you tell an old man to clean his shoes? He was twice my age, and lived a full life. I am nobody to tell anybody how to live his or her life, plus he was a lord. So let us be respectful. I couldn't say 'Bollocks', could I?

Apart from my couple of slip-ups, I was good there. But it still cost me seven years. My slip-ups are costly.

I am giving Belmarsh 10/10, simply because I was happy there and they treated me well.

HM PRISON BRISTOL

This image is an extract from The Millennium Map™ © getmapping.com plc

LOCATION:	Cambridge Road, Bristol.
CAPACITY:	400 beds.
CATEGORY AT PRESENT:	Local – Convicted, Remands and Long-Term – Male.
OPENED:	1882.
HISTORY:	Originally opened to house prisoners from the Bristol locality. It dates back to medieval times, and was the workplace of that famous executioner, old Albert Pierrepoint (1874–1922, from Bradford, Yorkshire). He managed to do his duty at 109 executions ... how many were innocent? There are ghosts in that place. Take it from me; in fact, take it from the screws! They have seen them. It is a spooky old place. In 1990, it had a prisoners' uprising.

I have landed here three times, once in the eighties and twice in the nineties. Each time, fuck all had changed. Bear in mind I am always destined for the seg block. I recall that it was on my first stay at Bristol that I got kicked in the nuts; I ended up on a dirty protest. Not really my scene. These dirty protests are called 'shit-ups' for obvious reasons! For those of you with a limited imagination, let me tell you what a shit-up is – you spread your faeces on the walls of your cell, over yourself, over every surface.

These shit-ups are not a pretty site and often cause screws to run out of your cell retching their guts up in disgust at the sight and smell of it all ... you can't do anything but have a smile on your face at the sight of this.

But in acts of desperation, we all have to do what we need to do. Most people outside can't relate to a shit-up, but it can work, believe it or not. So if you're ever in the position of having to carry one out, then at least you have an idea of what it's all about.

I covered the four walls and the door with shit. I even smeared it on myself. Why? Simple – I was fucking sick and tired of the system fucking me about. But all in all, Bristol is a strange old jail.

From the exercise yard, in the seg unit, you can see some houses over the wall (a loft window). A rare sight in any jail, if not a security weak link.

Anyway, one day, I was walking around the caged yard and I saw something move up in that window. I pretended not to look, but I saw it – a naked woman! Whether she was flashing at me or it was an accident, I don't know, but, God, I saw it!

Well, I am only human. Flesh and blood. A young man. How do you think I reacted? I shouted up, 'Stick your body closer to the window!'

I dropped my trousers and shouted, 'Hey, look at this for a two pounder!' In no time, the screws were on me and back inside I went. Fucking spoilsports.

This is one of the really old-style jails that has got a lot of character to it, and some of the 'old school' screws are there. They are the best screws you can get, so much better than the new breed of screws.

I am giving Bristol 5/10. They do a really nice drop of porridge, too, and they do a lovely bowl of soup.

THE GOOD PRISON GUIDE

HM PRISON BRIXTON

This image is an extract from The Millennium Map™ © getmapping.com plc

LOCATION:	Brixton, London.
CAPACITY:	825 beds.
CATEGORY AT PRESENT:	Category 'B' – Male.
OPENED:	1821, a real old piece of overcrowded madness.
HISTORY:	The land was bought in the early 1800s and a 'House of Correction', as it was known back then, was built. Originally designed to house just over 150 men, it did, in fact, house three times this amount, so nothing much has changed there since then. Eventually became a prison for females, then a military prison and eventually reverted back to an all-male prison, which it remains to this day.

Do you realise, it is 16 years since I was last here? Hey, doesn't time fly when you're having fun?

It was 1988 I was there, held on 'D' Unit, which was maximum secure. There were only twelve of us on there. All of us were remanded and all looking at 'Big Bird' if found guilty; I am talking big-time porridge, enough to fill up a swimming pool.

On this unit, all this time, were Charlie McGuire, cop killer; Ronnie Easterbrook, armed robber; Valerio Veicci, armed robber; Finbar McCullen, IRA; Liam McCotton, IRA; Mickey Reilly, armed robber; Tommy Hole, armed robber; Wayne Hurren, armed robber; John Boyle, American Mafia drug king; Denis Wheeler, drug king; and Vick Dark, armed robber – which, including me, makes the dirty dozen! Do you get the picture? It was serious stuff.

Out of all of these guys, only two won their trial and went free – John Boyle and Finbar McCullen. The rest of us got bird. Some were lifed off, with recommendations for thirty years.

Poor Charlie McGuire has since died, passed away in his cell. And Valerio Viccei got extradited back to Italy to finish off his twenty-year sentence. He got some jam role (parole) and got shot dead by a trigger-happy copper. Tommy Hole was shot and killed in a bar-room hit. It's a bloody dangerous game this! Here today ... shot tomorrow. And blown away into orbit.

This unit is small. It has two special cages. Guess who was in one? Yeah, yours truly. I always seem to end up in a cage for some reason, and that is fate. Destiny!

Like some apes get caught and put in a zoo, that is the story of my life. But we did OK in there. We could spend £50 a week in the canteen ... if you had £50, that is. (Some don't have 50p.) Me, I have always got a few bob stashed away for a rainy day.

Well, I don't smoke, or fuck with drugs; I have no vices in jail so I'm sweet. And I have got some good pals, who look out for me. As I look after them. It's a family thing, see. We all think as one. That is how it works. Should you have the unfortunate piece of bad luck to end up behind bars in the clink then remember to have a good support team behind you. Prison isn't a place to go it alone, even for the likes of me ... remember that.

I don't take a penny off my blood family. In fact, I don't even like to bring them into my world of criminality, because they are all honest, you see. They don't understand my way of life, as I do not understand theirs. My mother is my angel. So I keep it at that. But my pals are my true brothers. My real family.

So, Brixton 'D' Unit. It was here I crashed in Liam McCotton's canister. No hard feelings. He is a top guy. I admire the way he took it. I also got a screw's nose and twisted it! (Only for a laugh.) Not that I would do it in a nasty way. But he was sticking his nose into things that did not concern him. So in these sorts of situations you need to twist a nose or two just to show that it is bang out of order.

I remember, one day, I was upset over the food being cold. So I picked up the tea urn and poured it all over the food waiting to be served out to us on the hot plate. We all got fish and chips that night as a treat. Another day, I picked up the office desk above my head. I am not sure why I did that. To be truthful, I am not sure why I do a lot of things.

It was there I fixed a pigeon's wing. I found it in the yard, it was shivering and cold, and its wing was not right. I wrapped it in my shirt and brought it back to my cage. I washed it in some shampoo and dried it. Brushed it with my brush. And set about healing it. I fed it bread and milk. And I sort of made a bit of a splint with a plastic spoon and strapped it around its body.

After a week of this, I thought, 'Yeah, it is time!' I took it out on the yard and threw it up in the air, it would either fly or crash. It flew round the corner of the unit. I swear it looked down at me and smiled at me, I swear it did. I don't really know how I did it, but I did. I was right proud of that. Because of that, I knew what the Bird Man of Alcatraz got out of healing birds.

It was later that two IRA lads escaped with a gun, and Brixton stopped taking Cat 'A' prisoners. And it was then that Belmarsh that took all the 'A' prisoners. A shame, really, as Brixton was a good old jail.

This was a dirty old place, mind you, infested with vermin, maggots, rats and roaches ... and screws. But I liked Brixton. I got on well. And I think the screws were a half-decent lot. They sort of let us get on with it. Well, they had little choice because we would have demolished the place. It was on this very unit, years before, where Stan Thompson escaped with Big Ron Moody and Gerald Taite. They all got clean away.

Taite made it back to Ireland. Big Ron never did get caught but he later got shot dead in a pub gangland hit, and Stan just drifted back in.

But it was a lovely escape from such a secure unit. They dug through three cell walls and made it out.

I am giving Brixton 7/10. Yeah, it is worth that just for the memories. I have never been back since; sad, really.

BROADMOOR SPECIAL SECURE HOSPITAL

This image is an extract from The Millennium Map™ ✧ getmapping.com plc

LOCATION:	Crowthorne, Berkshire.
CAPACITY:	404 beds.
CATEGORY AT PRESENT:	Special Secure Hospital – Male and Female.
OPENED:	1863.
HISTORY:	Broadmoor Hospital was originally named Broadmoor Criminal Lunatic Asylum. The first patients to arrive there were ninety-five women in 1863; male patients arrived the following year. The asylum had been built following the Criminal Lunatics Act of 1860; it's uncertain why Crowthorne was chosen as the site. The Mental Health Act of 1959, which came into operation

**in 1960, changed the name to Broadmoor Hospital
making it into a Special Hospital for psychiatric
patients of dangerous, violent or criminal propensities;
its role was to treat these patients.**

In 1979, the prison van pulled up in this asylum – I was inside it. This
is the 'Big House' of all the institutions in the UK. Don't let anybody tell
you different. If they do, then send them to me. Because I am telling you,
this is the daddy of them all.

For 141 years, this giant of a place has stood on the hill in
Crowthorne village, Berkshire. The old austere, Victorian red brick with
beautiful carvings give it an air of authority, so splendidly built in its
magnificent countryside setting.

Sounds romantic, eh? Well, it is hell on earth! And I became their
number one devil. For five long, hard years, I lived under this asylum
roof. Oops ... tell a lie ... three times I was actually on the roof.

Broadmoor was a place of sheer amazement and electrifying incidents,
some horrifying scenes, and even murders and plenty of near-murders.

Sometimes, the murders are a blessing. As it is an escape from hell.

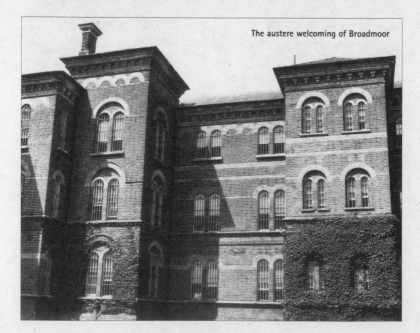

The austere welcoming of Broadmoor

KILLER ON THE ROOF

The-ripping protest at Broadmoor 'raw deal'

CONVICTED killer Reggie Peterson was camping out on the roof at Broadmoor yesterday.

He took a rest in the sunshine after an orgy of

Another one where they got it all wrong! As you know,
I'm not a convicted killer and they got my name wrong, too!

To survive a murderous attack from a lunatic, one has to live that nightmare for ever.

There was the mad, fat lunatic who had a knife stabbed into his ear, it penetrated his brain. Cabbaged, or in his case, double cabbaged, as he wasn't the full bottle of lager to start with. Or what about the lunatic who got raped with a broken bottle by a psychosexual madman. Not nice. But what do you expect? Fruitcake and coffee? Or the religious freak who stabbed the Jew in the neck with a pair of scissors. Why a Jew? Who knows? Ask him why!

Broadmoor has got stories that would turn your hair white overnight. And for once, I will say that those screws – er ... nurses – have got their jobs cut out. They have got to have eyes in the back of their nut. Because at any time, anything can happen. There is no place like it on earth. If so, tell me where. It is hell on earth.

It makes Parkhurst seem like a Wendy House. Ask Sutcliffe, the Ripper. He walks around bumping into things. One eye ripped out, the other one almost. Sad, really ... should have been both!

And what about the time David Francis was taken hostage by Bob Maudsley and John Cheeseman. Guess what? They cut his bollocks off and caved his skull in. All in a day's work, I guess.

That is Broadmoor in a nutshell. Dangerous. You can't afford to drift off to sleep in the day room ... or you may not wake up again.

The food was excellent, but it is a quarter-of-a-century since I ate there. I am sort of only in the past. Not in the future or the present. So it could be like Butlin's now. But I doubt it.

How can it change with mad axemen walking about? Serial rapists and child sex killers.

That evil bastard Erskine is there, too ... who? That evil slag who killed and raped all those old people in London. Some were old men. How can it be safe with monsters like him prowling about? I bet the old lunatic hasn't dared have a shower since he has been there.

But I must say, there were some lovely old mad men there, too. Old boys who had spent forty years there. Some who had sat in the death cell waiting to be hanged, only to be reprieved and sent to Broadmoor. I met them all there. The good, bad and crazy mad! But think about all the pain and misery, all the violence and madness.

I am giving Broadmoor 10/10. Why? Simply as it is the Number One Mad House on this planet. And I gave five years of my life to Broadmoor and I am proud of that.

And not forgetting the beautiful grounds and flowers and trees. And all the lovely Berkshire countryside, even though I only saw that from up on the roof.

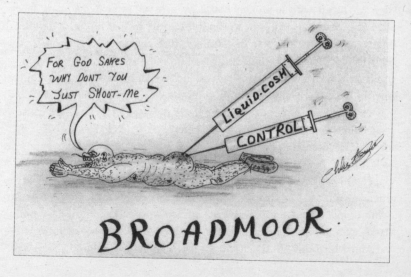

HM PRISON BULLINGDON

This image is an extract from The Millennium Map™ © getmapping.com plc

LOCATION:	Bicester, Oxfordshire.
CAPACITY:	900 beds.
CATEGORY AT PRESENT:	Dispersal, Local and Remand – Male.
OPENED:	1992.
HISTORY:	One of the so-called 'new breeds' of prisons. Now also acts as a training prison.

I landed here for the first time in 1993, I was only held in the seg block while one of my many trials went on at Luton Crown Court on 6 September 1993, with Patrick Felix, my co-accused. We were up for robbery.

And I have got to say, it was a nice stay at Bullingdon! Clean and humane. As you can see by the aerial shot, it's a nice, neat and compact place – no messy wings spread about the place making it look like an octopus ready to take off.

The food was good, and lots of it. And I can't think of even one bad thing. Only I fucked it up.

I went on a legal visit and wrapped my lawyer up; I tied him up and barricaded the visiting room!

It was just one of those insane days. Like a train out of control, no brakes. It has got to crash. But it was not the jail. It was me.

I am giving HM Prison Bullingdon 9/10. Why should I blame Bullingdon for my own madness? Even my lawyer sacked me! It is bloody terrible not to be wanted. When a lawyer sacks you, you are in trouble.

· PRISON · PROPERTY ·

BULLINGDON·

HM PRISON CAMP HILL

This image is an extract from The Millennium Map™ ⊕ getmapping.com plc

LOCATION:	Newport, Isle of Wight – get there by ferry or hovercraft.
CAPACITY:	550 beds.
CATEGORY AT PRESENT:	'C' Training Prison – Male.
OPENED:	1912 by Winston Churchill, the Home Secretary of the day.
HISTORY:	This prison was originally a Detention Centre, adjoining HM Prison Parkhurst. Eventually it became a Borstal, then back to a prison, then a Borstal again, and then a corrective training regime kicked in, but was soon slung out and it became what it is today, a Category 'C' prison.

This is the one of three jails on the Island. It is directly at the back of Parkhurst Prison. Unlike Parkhurst and Albany, it is not a jail for long-term prisoners, but their seg block was being used to take us at times of trouble. I was one they took. It was in the mid-1970s just before I was 'nutted off' and sent to Rampton Asylum.

The van drove me out of Parkhurst; I was in a straightjacket and ankle straps with half-a-dozen screws on top of me. But I still managed to bite one on the leg.

Once in Camp Hill Prison seg unit, they took it out on me and left me in their strip cell. Strangely, the next day I was moved back to Parkhurst the same way I had left it. That was the only time I landed in Camp Hill.

So, it is really impossible for me to give the place a run-down, as the bastards never even gave me a cup of tea, and my breakfast was thrown on to the floor. So much for hospitality!

The bunch who thought they were hard men for taking it out on me while I was defenceless can look back on that and praise themselves for being 'real' men.

I am giving HM Prison Camp Hill 2/10, and that is only for getting rid of me the next day – they were probably scared in case I bashed any of them. I am not a nasty, embittered, evil man, but good fucking riddance to Camp Hill.

HM PRISON DURHAM

This image is an extract from The Millennium Map™ © getmapping.com plc

LOCATION:	Old Elvet, Durham City.
CAPACITY:	1,000 male and 120 female beds.
CATEGORY AT PRESENT:	Dispersal, 'B' local, Close Supervision Centre – Male and Female (High-Security for those females serving 4 years+).
OPENED:	1819 during the reign of King William and the same year Queen Victoria was born – this place is old!
HISTORY:	Talk about a history! You can see Durham Cathedral from its exercise yard. You used to be able to hear the mixture of chatter, banter and brass bands coming from Durham Miners' Gala when it was on. The big clock in the town centre would rattle off the hours, every hour.

In 1810, Durham Prison's construction started at Elvet when the prison was designed to replace the jail in the Great North Gate. The simple reason for this was to help alleviate serious traffic congestion. A pledge of £2,000 towards the construction was made by Bishop Shute Barrington.

On the 31 July 1809, Sir Henry Vane Tempest laid the foundation stone. The second architect to take over died during the construction, the former architect being dismissed. Finally, Ignatius Bonomi completed the construction. Durham Prison, when it opened in 1819, had 600 cells.

Not surprisingly, Durham was a hanging prison and, in total, 92 men and 2 women were executed by being hanged at Durham between 1800 and 1958. Only 14 of these executions were public. Prior to the prison opening and up to 1816, hangings took place in the grounds of what is now the nearby Dryburn Hospital.

Fast-forward in time, and the moonlight glints off the razor-sharp knife that Laurena holds in her hand. She steps closer to the bed, where her husband sleeps unsuspectingly. Slowly and deliberately, she pulls the covers away from his naked, unprotected body ... exposing his penis. He lies still, not knowing the damage about to be inflicted upon his body. She raises the knife and brings it down ...

It was the story that shocked the world. Overnight, John Wayne Bobbitt was the man everyone was talking about, but who no one wanted to be. It was a story that sent fear into the hearts and groins of men everywhere. That was a modern-day crime, but there was an original Laurena Bobbitt.

The last person to be hanged at the old Dryburn hanging site was Ann Crampton. She had also been found guilty of cutting off her husband's penis while he slept. She suspected him of having an affair. On 25 August 1814, Ann was executed. At this time, society was male dominated; cutting off his John Thomas was the equivalent of destroying his manhood.

In 1816, a new courthouse was built and this included a new style of gallows known as 'drop style'. The gallows were erected on the steps outside the new courthouse, which was right next to the prison. The first execution to take place outside the courthouse was when John Grieg was hanged on 17 August 1816 for the murder of Elizabeth Stonehouse.

The last public execution outside the courthouse took place on 16 March 1865 when Matthew Atkinson was executed for the murder of his wife at Spen, near Winlaton, Tyne and Wear. When the trapdoor bolt was drawn, Atkinson dropped downwards and the rope broke. They got him on the second attempt.

After the Act of 1868, all executions had to take place within the prison walls. The abolition of public hangings resulted in the gallows being set up in one of the prison yards; this was set over a brick-lined pit. This was replaced when an 'execution shed' was built.

The first of these executions in Durham Prison's grounds was a double hanging that took place on 22 March 1869, when John Donlan, 37, and John McConville, 23, were executed for unrelated murders.

Although Rose West is housed in Durham Prison's 'She' wing, she was not the earliest of prolific female serial killers. This distinction falls to the mass murderer Mary Ann Cotton (1833–73); her count of 15 killings – although some twenty people connected with her died mysteriously over a period of twenty years – remained unrivalled until the 1980s.

After a series of mystery deaths, bodies were exhumed and it was found that arsenic was the cause of these deaths. After a short trial, Mary was found guilty on one specimen charge of murder.

On 24 March 1873, Mary's body fell the 18in drop when the trapdoor was released. It is reported that she began to struggle violently for three minutes before dying an agonising death. Her ghost is still supposed to haunt her old home in Newcastle-upon-Tyne. After this, the 'long drop' method was used for hanging executions, which was a relief to all those watching.

There was even a triple hanging on 5 January 1874, when three murderers were convicted of unrelated crimes: Charles Dawson, Edward Gough and William Thompson. This was all to do with saving money.

On 2 August 1875, Elizabeth Pearson, 28 – the second of only two women ever to be executed at Durham Prison – was hanged after being found guilty of poisoning her uncle in the hope that she would be left something in his will. The hanging was a triple execution; all three were simultaneously launched into oblivion. Alongside Mary were two male murderers. Both executed women are buried next to each other.

The last person to be executed at Durham Prison was dispatched with on 17 December 1958. The execution was carried out on Brian Chandler, 20, for the murder of an 83-year-old woman, whom he had robbed.

In the 1900s, Durham retained a permanent gallows; it was one of only a handful of prisons to do so. At that time, the execution block was on the ground floor of one of the wings near, it is said, to D Wing.

Remember, when executions took place, they needed to allow room beneath the gallows for the body to drop; therefore, the gallows were usually on an upper or raised floor. In this case, the body of the condemned fell into a basement area below the trap in Durham Prison. The execution block still remains to this day, but the adjoining execution chamber and the trap doors have long been removed and the drop pit covered over. The room is still there, but is better off being used for its current purpose ... storage!

The prison has a special 'She' wing that was opened in 1974 for females serving four years or over; this is H Wing and housed the likes of Myra Hindley, and currently houses Rose West. At its height, the prison held 1,700 prisoners.

Would you believe that this prison was successful in attaining the 1998 Butler Trust Award for 'Outstanding Contribution to the Quality of Prisoner Care'? I hear they now mix nonces with ordinary cons; strange way of working, isn't it?

This place fascinated me. It is built in such a beautiful, picturesque place, by the river and cathedral, all so very heavenly, but behind its walls it is hell.

I first landed here in the mid 1970s and I've been back to this prison, the second most northerly in England, several times. In fact, quite recently, I was caged there for eight months in their special secure unit on G Wing. But for me, I am kept in a special cage. Total isolation. They had two wings (G and I) for special cases like me, each holding nine prisoners.

Durham Prison is a very old jail, over 200 years old, but it is a strange place as it's one of the few jails that caters for male and female cons, all segregated, of course.

The infamous, now deceased, Myra Hindley spent many years on their female wing. As I've already mentioned, Rose 'Dog' West is on the wing. It seems that old Rose is trying out the lesbian scene; I was told by one screw that the search team found a huge vibrator in Rose's cell. I asked how huge.

'Awesome, Charlie.'

'How fucking awesome?' I asked. When he told me, I could not believe it.

'Inhuman.'

She is just a sicko. A sexually perverted monster. Mind you, four women prisoners committed suicide in the space of a nine-month period here in 2002. Doesn't that tell you something about the regime? An 'open' verdict was given by the Coroner's Court in September 2003 for one of the four suicides, during which time the female population at the prison increased by 150 per cent.

Some women cons actually have affairs with women screws. I recall an incident when a female con fell for a woman warder. Sharon Miller, 45, had fallen for the warder while on remand at Gloucester's Eastwood Park Jail.

It all got lemon, though; the two became lovers after Francesca Westcott left the prison service, but she called off their six-year affair late in 2001. Miller just couldn't take it and she began to bombard her with telephone calls and even assaulted her. Eventually, Miller travelled to Bigyn Road in Llanelli from her home in Somerset armed with gallons of petrol. Two houses had petrol poured through their letterboxes and two families had lucky escapes. These dykes, they just go mad! Miller got ten years.

Durham is run by the militant POA (Prison Officers' Association) union. They have a stronghold up there (always have had) and I have always felt that the governors up there are too respectful of the POA. So they're never really bold enough to make on-the-spot decisions. That is my own personal opinion based on my time spent there.

I remember a young con hanged himself there in the eighties and I pulled one of the many different grades of prisoner governor at my cell door as he was doing his morning rounds.

I asked him, 'Can we organise a bit of a whip round for some flowers? If all the cons in the jail put in 50p each, we could have a nice few bob and give it to the lad's family.' The bastards never wanted to know. I believe it was the screws who were against it. If it was, then they are fucking scumbags.

They also had some of the most bigoted screws in the country; they hate blacks, and despise Cockneys or any southerners. So if you are unfortunate enough to fall into one of these categories, be warned!

They seem to be very tight-knit lot up there and very jealous of anybody who's done well for themselves. The jail is mostly full of junkies or burglars, or out-and-out thugs.

These are a hard breed of men – love a drink, love a fight. A lot of violence up that way. Even the prison officers get involved in fights on the pub and club scene in the town centre, which is predominantly frequented by the many students who attend the university and its many annexes.

There is no real organised crime to speak of up there (more the spur-of-the-moment or drunken-stupor crime), more pot luck. They have a serious drug problem; the jail is full of drug crime, a lot of smackheads, mugging people for their next fix. They brought in special sniffer dogs and random drug-testing on cons. All that did was make cons drop the soft drug of cannabis (that stays in the system for twenty-eight days) and move on to drugs like smack that can be washed out of the urinary system within twenty-four hours.

Food? They do a lovely curry up there and there are some top screws. There is a brilliant dentist there, a woman! She also does Frankland High-Security Jail, too.

A good education department. But the jail reeks of despair. Something very eerie about Durham, probably all the ghosts of the condemned cons they hanged there. Big crows sat on the wall looking at us as we walk around the yards. I always said, 'I bet they are cons who were hanged and have come back to haunt the place.'

Many screws have had them crows shit on them as they fly over. But I have never known a con being hit by them. So I could be right. Spirits ... back as birds.

Every hour, you will hear the bells of the Cathedral, and on a Sunday it is bloody murder with those church bells! Clang, clang, clang! One evening a week they do it, too. I am sure it is just to wind us cons up. I have been told that you can go up into the Cathedral's tower and look down on the exercise yard of the prison ... any ex-cons nostalgic enough might go and do it, but not me.

Near to the prison there is a fish and chip shop, near the wall; on some nights, we could smell the aroma drifting over the wall. That winds me up, too, because I love fish and chips. You can also hear the drunks on their pub-crawls every Friday and Saturday night.

I actually changed my name from 'Bronson' to 'Ahmed' up in Durham by deed poll. I did it out of respect for my wife's late father.

The cage they kept me in up there is a 12ft by 8ft cell with a steel cage door behind the solid steel door. So in the cell there are two doors keeping me locked in. They also have a cage on my window. My furniture is made up of compressed cardboard; even the chair is made from this horrible stuff, and you can see your furniture fall to bits before your very eyes and around your very body! You can be sitting on your chair one minute writing a letter and suddenly, the next minute, the chair buckles beneath you and you're on the floor. Well, I am 16st.

I am fed through a flap in the lower part of the door; I am let out just once a day for only one hour's fresh air in the yard. I will be searched and metal detected. There will never be less than eight screws escorting me; electronic cameras follow my every move.

The other 23 hours a day, I will be caged up alone. My visits (social and legal) are through the door. Now you see why Durham Prison is hell on earth for me.

When I went to the dentist, ten screws took me over there and some were accompanying me with dogs; I was double-cuffed, and that was even while I was in the dentist's chair.

The female dentist, I could see, felt embarrassed. But that's Bronson's life. This is how I live inside, under extreme daily security.

My sadness is the effect it has on my wife and daughter. Not being able to cuddle them. Touching their fingers through the cage wire like I am a fucking beast in a zoo. It is torture to see it; it kills me inside to do it. But it rips their hearts up to see me in such inhumane conditions.

I will give HM Prison Durham 1/10. Well, I could have given it nil. The 1 is for Tony the art teacher who helped me a lot. And Kath the lady who worked on the censoring of my mail, she was lovely. A wonderful human being. Always got a smile and a kind word. I bet she was a smasher in her youth. She is still a looker in her fifties, and her heart is in the right place!

HM PRISON FRANKLAND

This image is an extract from The Millennium Map™ © getmapping.com plc

LOCATION:	Brasside, Durham.
CAPACITY:	670 beds.
CATEGORY AT PRESENT:	High Security and Category 'A' wing.
OPENED:	1980, albeit on a temporary basis to relieve over-crowding in mainstream prisons due to POA industrial action, which resulted in the Army having to be brought in to man the prison for a period of four months. After the POA failed in their action over Continuous Duty Credits, the prisoners housed there on temporary basis were returned to mainstream prisons. The prison proper opened officially in 1983 after building work was completed.

HISTORY: Originally, the prison was earmarked to become a dispersal prison, but is now a high-security establishment.

This is most northerly maximum-secure jail you can go to in England; it is well past Scotch Corner, and on the outskirts of Durham city.

I first landed up there in 1990. Since then, I have been back there many times. It's crazy! So much for helping me to maintain ties with my family, who are hundreds of miles away from the place. I may as well be on the moon. It's bloody ridiculous for families to travel so far.

In fact, it is disgusting. You imagine a mother with children travelling all that way just for an hour's visit. Then all the way back home again. It is a bloody crime on it's own to put so much stress on loved ones.

Adding it all up, I must have spent a good part of my thirty years inside up north. It is a wonder I don't talk like them ... but I divvent let that gan te me 'ed, like!

It was on my second stay up there; I was out on the yard with 200 other cons when I lost the plot! (Not like me, is it?)

I was chatting away to Kenny Noye and Vick Dark when I just flipped. I ran across the yard and hit this geezer in a black suit, and put him on my shoulder and ran off with him.

I wanted to smash my way into a wing office and take control. Would you believe, I did not even know who he was. Obviously he had to be an official, either a governor, or a doctor, or a teacher, or maybe a member of the Board of Visitors. Maybe even a Home Office rat. It turned out to be Mr Masserick, the Deputy Governor. Oh well ... that's life.

Frankland Prison holds some right dangerous fuckers and it often explodes with violence. It is a very claustrophobic jail and has a serious drug problem. So you can imagine the backlash. I once went in the shower only to 'almost' step on a syringe. It terrified me. If I had stepped on it, I could have been infected with AIDS or hepatitis C, or whatever the junkies had, TB or whatever. It was a serious health hazard.

And it was a joke to some to slip acid tabs into cons' drinks and then watch them go crazy. Personally, I couldn't see what the fun was. They are sick bastards to do that. You get the pricks outside doing it in pubs and clubs. God help them if they ever did it to me. I swear I would kill the slags, I just know I would flip out. Those drugs are evil. Always will be to me.

Frankland's got a good gym but, sadly, I got banned from it, as I was about to cave the gym screw's head in. So I did all my workouts in the yard and in my cell. I really don't need their silly gyms. Read my book *Solitary Fitness* and you will see why.

The place had a great canteen. We could buy proper food to cook. And it had the best field out of the entire maximum-secure jails. Only one con has actually escaped from the jail itself – Frank Quinn. He slipped out in the laundry van. Others have got away from hospital escorts.

It was built in the 1970s and has seen it all – riots, arsons, rapes, stabbings, cuttings. To my knowledge, there have been no murders. That has to be a miracle.

Old Harold Shipman was up there, but they moved him in 2003 to Wakefield for an eye operation or something.

I met some smashing lads up there and they remain strong pals today. It is amazing just how many southerners actually get sent up there. I am sure it is a conspiracy to destroy all contacts and to fuck up our family life. Prisons are not happy with just locking us up, they want to punish our loved ones as well.

My old mate Ronnie Abrahms (the Screaming Skull) died up there. He had served over thirty years, all to die in a cell. He was a top legend, was our Skull. A complete one-off. There will never be another like him. I miss old Ron. It was also here that I got the news that Ronnie Kray had died. That was a bloody sad day for me, as Ron was the best friend I ever had.

I remember strangling a con in the TV room; it was fortunate for him that a pal of mine intervened. The fat piece of shit was forever farting. He only had to move and he'd let rip. We were all watching a football match, Spurs v Newcastle. So the northerners outnumbered us southerners 5-1, but it was all in good fun. And I had the fat piece of shit sitting next to me.

After the twentieth fart, I got sick of it and I just blew up. And before I knew it, I was on him, strangling him. His eyes bulged, his lips were starting to turn blue and he was about to leave this planet. As I say, a decent lad helped bring some sanity to it all. But the frightening fact is, out of a room full of cons, all sat there watching me kill a man for farting. Only one guy helped stop it. Now that is what you call insanity.

I could have killed him, and left him dead, and we would have all carried on cheering our teams on. That is prison life in a nutshell. It is just another day for us. We are all deep in the madness. You have to be mad to survive.

Frankland, to me, is a powder keg, but a very lively jail to be in. Just take this one piece of advice – stay clear of the drug scene. Because if you enter into that, your whole life will end in misery. Please believe it, as I have seen it time and time again.

I am giving HM Prison Frankland 7/10, only because of its electrifying atmosphere.

FRANKLAND.

HM PRISON FULL SUTTON

This image is an extract from The Millennium Map™ © getmapping.com plc

LOCATION: Full Sutton, York.

CAPACITY: 600 beds.

CATEGORY AT PRESENT: High–Security, Category 'A' and Remand – Male.

OPENED: 1987.

HISTORY: Always to be intended as a max-secure unit and now is under the remit of the Directorate of High–Security Prisons, a law unto themselves. Very sneakily, they also made the place into an assessment centre for sex offenders.

First, I'll start by saying that the prison is not normally a remand prison, but it has held people there on remand. One of the most famous remand prisoners held there for over a year from 2001–02 was John Sayers from Newcastle's Geordie Mafia. A great guy, and he walked free from a £22m murder trial held in Leeds.

This place opened up in the late 1980s. I first landed there in 1988. It is a real nasty maximum-secure jail. Considering it has only been around for seventeen years, it has seen it all. Several riots, murders, arson, suicides, cuttings, stabbings, assaults on screws. And some of those were down to me. I even grabbed an official hostage there.

I spent a great Christmas up there with Freddie Foreman and Eddie Richardson. And with proper booze, too. Some bent screws ... £50 a bottle of vodka. He must have made a fortune out of us lot! I squeezed three bottles myself, but that was my lot. I am not into making screws rich. Greedy pig ... 50 quid a bottle!

But I have got to say, Full Sutton was a bloody good jail then. We had it all – gym, field, cooking, good visits. The cons run that place, big time.

The screws just unlocked our doors and let us out. I tried to electrocute a con there ... he was a smackhead. He owed my pal 200 quid and he had no intention of paying up. It was more his attitude. Arrogant, 19st of shit.

So, when he was in the bath, I plugged in the electric floor polisher and slung it in the bath. It somehow bounced off his head and fell outwards! So I ran and tried again but by this time he was up and running. He ran all the way to his cell and banged himself up.

I was gutted! I went to his door later and spilt a load of petrol through the crack. Comes in handy that lawnmower on the works. You should have heard the rat screaming; he didn't half go up. But the spoilsport screws came running to save him with fire hoses.

And did you know that it was a con who invented a valve in the early 1990s that is now integrally built into cell doors? This valve allows a fire hose to be connected to the door from the outside landing and have the water aimed around the room while the hose sits in this multidirectional valve. It was invented to overcome those prisoners who barricaded themselves into their cells and set fire to contents. I bet they never thought about cons setting fire to those inside the cells when this invention was made.

I was there when Mickey Jameson topped himself. He got life in the 1970s along with Jimmy Anderson for killing four people in East London. Sad day that.

I had a riot of my own there. I went bananas in the hall, I wrecked it. Two Scouse brothers started me off, but they legged it and left me to face the screws. I really blew it that day. But what's new? I did one screw with a table leg and another with a broom. Such is life ... I got worse later. It's evil.

I went back there four or five times; each stay ended in violence. But I still enjoyed my time there. Even in the seg unit, the food was good, and you could get a shower every day. There are times if I cannot get access to a shower then I'll have a strip wash in my cell. My workouts cause me to sweat, and there's nothing worse than the smell of a sweaty body.

There was also a good canteen there. You can buy cakes and bags of fruit and nuts and other goodies. But I have not been back for a few years.

Old Billy Wilson was my old buddy there; Bill was in his sixties, and an ex-fighter, a big proud man, serving life. He had one of those silver tashes and his cell walls were covered with boxing photos of the greats – Marciano, Louis, Dempsey and so on.

FULL-SUTTON.

Bill always wanted to shape up; sadly, he was a bit paunchy. I would sit in his cell and listen to all his old times; I'd heard them 100 times over. He was such a man of pride that he even fucked off medical treatment. He had cancer of the kidneys ... bollocks to the lot! Old Bill died. He never did get to work out his dream, but I won't say what his dream was as it was told to me in private. A man's dream is personal, see. But it was a lovely dream that kept him going for years inside, only to be wiped away by cancer. I really loved that old git.

Full Sutton, for such a modern jail, holds a lot of misery. A lot of the violence was down to drugs. There must be a lot of AIDS in that place, as they use dirty needles. Plus there are a lot of young lads paying their debts off by getting their arses shagged or sucking dick! It is tragic, but it is life for a smackhead. You can't help them, they used to help themselves, but it is sad to see it. Mums and dads sending them in presents, all to be sold for smack.

People ask why do I hate drugs so much? Well, I will tell you. In the 1970s, in the asylum, I was forced to take drugs by injection. They held me down and pumped into me with a syringe full of psychotropic shit. That is why!

And I despise drug addicts because they are weak, dangerous people, so that is why places like Full Sutton breed desperate people.

I am giving HM Prison Full Sutton 4/10. But I did kick ass, didn't I?

HM PRISON GARTREE

This image is an extract from The Millennium Map™ © getmapping.com plc

LOCATION: Market Harborough, Leicester.

CAPACITY: 350 beds.

CATEGORY AT PRESENT: Category 'B' – Male.

OPENED: 1966.

HISTORY: Became a dispersal prison and then later became a Category 'B' prison for long-term cons (5 years+). Now leans towards a therapeutic regime with prison psychologists and counsellors. But why close down Parkhurst Prison's centre, which was run by the renowned Dr Bob Johnson?

Fuck me; I had some fun and games in this gaff. I first hit here in the mid-1980s and again in the '90s.

Gartree was built about the same time as Albany Prison; it was one of the dispersers for High-Risk Category 'A' inmates.

Well, that was until December 1987 when Johnny Kendal and Siddy Draper flew out in a helicopter, hijacked by Andy Russell. What a fucking classic that was. First and last chopper escape in England. Now I have said that, there'll probably be another one next week.

Gartree is a modern jail, a two-tier, flat-roofed building housing A, B, C and D Wings. It had a great gym and a good football pitch with a proper running track. We could cook our own meals.

It all sounds nice, but Gartree was a powder keg, and it often blew up. What the prison HQ failed to accept is that they couldn't expect to put so many high-risk prisoners under one roof and hope to keep the peace.

Face facts – if you put IRA with UFF, they kick off and they did just that in Gartree. Not just with the Irish but with everybody. And the end result was riots, violence and destruction. That place really was a war zone.

I remember Michael Hickey spent three months up on the roof, the longest ever prison roof protest in the UK. He was one of the Bridgewater Four, later to win his appeal. And he did those three months in the winter. A right achievement, amazing.

Con killer Fred 'Butcher' Lowe stabbed a sex case to death; he put forty holes in him. The blood ran like a river. Fred was laughing as he did it. The laugh of a madman.

The cop killer Freddie Sewell almost broke out but got caught on the fence. He spent two years in isolation after that.

The daddy of the prizefighters Roy 'Pretty Boy' Shaw, who wrecked the fucking place.

The monster Ian Brady went insane there in his isolation cell in the hospital wing; he began to eat and drink his own body waste.

A con cut his dick off, as he wanted to be a woman; another con cooked some budgies in a pie. There were hangings, cut-throats and overdoses.

The IRA cons were pissed up every weekend with hooch; the Jocks were slashing each other; the Afros were smoking their dope; the smackheads were junking it up; the faggots were pumping arse.

It was a crazy jail. Many cons lost the plot and got nutted off and were sent to Broadmoor.

There were hostage sieges and hunger-strikes. It really was a powder keg.

I come out of my cell one day and went berserk; it was on A Wing. Most of the cons ran and banged themselves up. I chinned three screws and kicked one down the stairs, then smashed the whole wing up.

I left there with a bad head, I can tell you, but Gartree for me was a real test of your sanity. You were pushed to your limits. And I enjoyed it!

I am giving HM Gartree 7/10 for the simple reason, I love a challenge.

HM PRISON HIGH DOWN

This image is an extract from The Millennium Map™ © getmapping.com plc

LOCATION: Sutton, Surrey.

CAPACITY: 700 beds.

CATEGORY AT PRESENT: Local and Category 'A' – Male.

OPENED: 1992 at a cost of £91m.

HISTORY: Anyone recall the infamous mental hospital of Banstead? This place is built on that site. Most of the buildings proved to be unsuitable, so this new prison was built. On part of the site, another prison was constructed – HM Prison Downview.

This is quite a modern jail, built on the same design as HM Prison Bullingdon and around the same time. I landed in High Down seg unit in the mid '90s and again in the late '90s.

Both times I was held in their seg unit. The first time I only lasted a week when I gave the Governor a right-hander and tried to stab his eye out with my toothbrush. I was having an off day. Not like me!

But I have got to say now, the food there was brilliant, and plenty of it. And the cells had toilets and sinks, with nice windows and a lovely bed!

It really was a decent, humane place and the screws were as good as gold. Unfortunately, the Governor I served up was an ex-screw in Wandsworth some years back, I remember him well. He set me off on a bad spell.

While I was there, a con hanged himself. But he was a multiple rapist, so no tears then. He should have hanged himself by his bollocks and let me in to kick the dog to death! I shouldn't really say dog, as dogs are lovely animals.

I will give HM Prison High Down 7/10. It is hard to give a jail points when you see so little of it. If I had made it up on the wing, then maybe I would have given it a 10 out of 10. Who can tell?

HM PRISON HULL

This image is an extract from The Millennium Map™ © getmapping.com plc

LOCATION:	Hedon Road, Hull.
CAPACITY:	700 beds.
CATEGORY AT PRESENT:	Local and Category 'B', Remand and Young Offenders – Male.
OPENED:	1870.
HISTORY:	What this prison hasn't been in its time in relation to detaining prisoners is hardly worth mentioning. It was originally used to house male and female prisoners, then acted as a military prison, then as a depot for civil defence, then as a Borstal, then a max–secure unit and then it hit a brick wall! A riot broke out on 31 August 1976 and continued for three days.

The conclusions of the inquiry that followed the riot shows the causes as the culmination of a series of disturbances throughout the dispersal system, dating back to the roof-top demonstrations of 1972. This was the most serious incident involving loss of control, since the Dartmoor mutiny before the Second World War. A total of 60 per cent of the prison population were involved in the riot, and the damage to the prison was estimated at £750,000. Hull Prison was out of use for about a year and staff morale, supposedly, suffered a setback. What a shame! Although the riot went on for a number of days, no prisoners escaped and staff and prisoners alike sustained no serious injury.

By the time the Hull Board of Visitors had finished their disciplinary hearings, they had removed almost ninety years of prisoners' remission. They did this without allowing any of the prisoners to be legally represented, they refused to allow defendants to cross-examine prosecution witnesses and the prisoners were rarely allowed to call witnesses in support of their defence. Understandably, the prisoners complained to the courts. This is where prisoners' rights began to change for the better.

In 1986, the prison changed its status and housed Category 'B' inmates, apart from having a special unit for the likes of me, but it closed in 1999. The unit is sometimes used to house supergrasses ready to attend court to give evidence.

Until the Hull Riot in 1976, this was the number-one dispersal jail in England. Anyone who was anyone was here. Top faces such as Great Train Robber Charlie Wilson; the IRA Old Bailey bombers Roy Walsh, Martin Brady and Billy Armstrong; the Balcome Street Mob; the mass killer Archibald Hall; some of the Kray henchmen; Frank Fraser; Roy Shaw ... oh, and me!

I first hit Hull in 1974. From my cell window in the seg block I could actually see the Humber Bridge being constructed. The docks were opposite the jail.

That lovely sea air, the smell of fish, those squawking seagulls. On a windy night, the smell of beer and fish and chips and laughter would drift into my cell.

Hull was without a doubt a fucking good jail. But like all the top-secure jails, it had its fair share of trouble. I once witnessed such a violent attack on a con, it actually made me feel sick. The poor sod's face was on the shower floor. I have never seen such a ferocious attack, ever. It was like being in a fucking slaughterhouse; that con's face was just ripped to pieces. Now if that wasn't enough, he then got sliced down the back; blood just pissed out.

Another time, I witnessed a guy's head caved in with a gym bar; and I witnessed a dumb bell smashed into a con's head. It really was a violent jail.

It was there I cut up John Gallagher, and later, when he was released, he killed four people. The slag even made a statement against me!

I also grabbed two hostages in Hull, the first being Governor Wallace. I got an extra seven years for this piece of shit. Then I nabbed Phil Danielson, a civilian teacher. For this siege I got a life sentence. Incidentally, it was the longest siege in the history of the UK penal system in which a hostage had been taken.

In another incident at Hull Prison, I also got on the roof. Without a doubt, the greatest sight! There are a load of flats just over the wall of Hedon Road, and in some of these flats there are women of the night.

You should hear the things they shouted at me – 'Get 'em off,' 'Show us your dick,' and 'Give it a pull for us.' What a foul-mouthed load of tarts ... I couldn't believe it. After all, I was only a youngster.

It was here in 1975 I last saw my son, Michael, as a child. He was three years old. His mum walked out of my life and I never saw him again until he was 25 years old. Some twenty-two years had passed us by. It is really the only regret of my life. Apart from that, I really don't give a fuck.

It was also in Hull I won my first ever Koestler Award for art. I have now won a total of eleven and have retired as the first con ever to win eleven of these awards. The race was on between my old mate James Crosbie of Scotland and me to see who would be the first to reach ten Koestlers; he ended up on nine and I exceeded the magic number. James was once considered the most dangerous man in the Scottish penal system; he was a great blagger and got away with plenty of big money.

Over the years, I have been back to Hull no less than eight times. Each time, I seem to end up in trouble. I have even demolished their unit. I have chinned a total of nine screws there. I have shit up three Governors. Once, I left Hull in a wheelchair, strapped up in a body belt and ankle straps and wheeled to the van.

I have been injected there many times, and I've also been beaten. But

I just love the place. It is a unique jail. A total one-off. The food is brilliant; well, it was on the unit. Proper fish, big pieces of it, nice fresh salads, even the porridge was made with milk. They make a treacle tart in Hull like no tart I have ever had – it was beautiful.

Hull was also the only jail in the UK with a boxing ring; it was great. Floyd Patterson once came to the jail and put on a show. But with the crowd running the prisons nowadays, they stopped all that. But it fucking worked, that ring was brilliant, we all enjoyed it. We would have bets on fights. I won all mine ... bets and fights.

Back in those days, the gym screws were a good bunch, they just let us slog it out, as long as we weren't using blades and table legs. But today, you're lucky to get a punch bag with these fucking imbeciles; they can't see how a ring can help youngsters relieve their frustrations. That's why I've got so much respect for people like Harry Marsden who has taken countless youngsters off the drug scene and helped put them back on the straight and narrow because of his boxing club.

Yeah, I had some great times in Hull. A lot of bad, too! I once cut a con's arse with a Stanley blade right across the cheeks. He opened up like a tomato! After that, he never nicked out of anybody's cell again. The fat rat couldn't sit down for a month; fifty-eight stitches he had. His arse must have looked like a mailbag.

It was also there that I scored my first and last hat-trick on the soccer pitch. I admit, I'm far from a good player. I'm more of a goal-maker, I'm a runner. I will run all day long. But the match, I just had the hot buzz. I just knew it was on. Bang. Bang. Bang. All good goals.

You don't forget days like that and it must have been taped, as Hull was full of Big Brother CCTV.

Plenty of memories. Awesome memories. But Hull jail ended up costing me a life sentence.

I will give HM Prison Hull 9/10, simply because it is just a big part of my life. I learned so much from being in there, such as: never bend down in the shower to pick the soap up; never sit in the front row of the TV room; never walk into another man's cell without tapping the door.

Believe me, three good tips there.

HM PRISON KINGSTON

This image is an extract from The Millennium Map™ © getmapping.com plc

LOCATION: Milton Road, Portsmouth.

CAPACITY: 200 beds.

CATEGORY AT PRESENT: Category 'B' Lifers – Male.

OPENED: 1877.

HISTORY: First used to accommodate criminals from the Portsmouth area up until pre–World War II when it was used to detain those likely to cause political trouble or on suspicion of spying. Taken over, after this, by the Royal Navy, it became a Naval Detention base. After a short spell of not being used for anything, it became a centre for Recall Borstal Boys

and remained so for just over twenty years until 1969. It then became a Category 'B' prison solely for life-sentence prisoners who had committed a domestic murder, the only prison to cater for this sort of prisoner. Now, though, the prison takes all sorts of lifers regardless of who they have killed ... you just can't get a decent class of murderer any more these days!

Now this place looks like an old fort, it is an all-lifers' jail. Most of the 200 cons it holds are old men who have served years and years.

I was on my way to Albany on the Island in the '80s when the van broke down, and a police van arrived and took me to Kingston Prison to be held until an escort could be arranged.

Once in the jail, I was put in their seg unit that was only about a four-cell capacity, and unused. A screw told me, 'We rarely have need to use it,' as most of the cons are old and institutionalised. It seemed they were happy, mugs of Horlicks and bags of seed for their budgies. They gave me dinner; it was bloody lovely, one of the nicest prison meals I have ever had.

I had just eaten it and my door crashed in; it was the Albany screws. 'Ready, Bronson.'

I was gutted. I could have spent a cosy six months in this little castle, it just felt so peaceful. Even the screws were so laid back and relaxed. I noticed that most of the screws wore shoes and not boots. They really seemed a decent bunch. There was no intimidation – or eyeball stares – it was such a shame I was just passing through. But in reality, it is better not to stay in a graveyard. Because that is basically all it is. 'Dead men breathing.'

I will give HM Prison Kingston 7/10, just for the good dinner and laid-back screws.

HM PRISON LEICESTER

This image is an extract from The Millennium Map™ © getmapping.com plc

LOCATION:	Welford Road, Leicester.
CAPACITY:	300 beds.
CATEGORY AT PRESENT:	Local Prison and Remands – Male.
OPENED:	1825.
HISTORY:	Since 1825 right up until 1990, building work has seen the prison expand from being a very large gatehouse to a prison with a visitors' centre and administrative offices.

This is in Welford Road, in the centre of Leicester, with Filbert Street, the Premiership football ground, close by. On match days you can hear them cheering.

Looking at the prison is like looking at an old castle; in fact, it *is* a castle. This is quite a unique jail as it is just one big long wing; take a look at the aerial photo. And the wing is cut into sections; one end is for remands, the middle is for the convicted, the bottom end is the seg unit, and the next bit is the protection wing. Then on the other end is the SSU – Special Security Unit.

Then there is the hospital wing, kitchen and workshops. That's Leicester, a very cramped jail.

I first went there in the 1980s. Unfortunately, all my stays in Leicester have been short, and always in the seg unit, so I have not been up on the wing. But I have been up on the roof, so I have seen more than most.

Apart from the SSU section, Leicester is just a local jail. The unit part was brought in for the Great Train Robbers, the Kray firm and the Richardson gang. Since then, many infamous cons have spent time on there – Harry Roberts (cop-shooter), Billy Skingle, Joey Martin, Freddie Foreman, Reg Kray, Harry Johnson, Angel Face Probyn, John Kendall, Steve Waterman, John McVicar ... then all the IRA lads, the drug barons and the spies. They have all been on there, some for years, others for months.

I was always kept in the seg unit under a ten-guard unlock – at least ten screws outside my cell door before it can be unlocked.

I was, in fact, the only con ever to have a police ID parade in their seg unit. And guess what? The witnesses never picked me out. Too fucking scared to, I bet! I swear to God, if they had of done so I would have attacked them there and then, I was just in the mood for a war.

I ended up ripping a door off there – well, I was bored, and a man needs to occupy his mind!

The food there was swill. I was always hungry there. But the screws were not a bad bunch.

I recall about 1986/87 when female screws started to work in men's jails. It really was a big thing in those days to see a 'screwess'. Especially in the morning when you unlocked to slop out your pot. It was embarrassing. What man wants to walk past a woman with a pot full of shit? Now you know why a lot of us used to crap in a paper and throw it out of the window.

Anyway, there was a gorgeous screwess and it turned out she was a sex change. It blew me away. I keep telling you, those screws are a funny breed.

I will give HM Prison Leicester 5/10, only because I enjoyed my stays there. I am not sure they enjoyed me, though, but let's not get personal.

HM PRISON LINCOLN

This image is an extract from The Millennium Map™ © getmapping.com plc

LOCATION:	Greetwell Road, Lincoln.
CAPACITY:	450 beds.
CATEGORY AT PRESENT:	Local Prison and Remands – Male.
OPENED:	1872.
HISTORY:	A Victorian prison that continued the tradition of a prison being in Lincoln since medieval times. A vast refurbishment project has seen the prison transformed into a more manageable place.

I hit Lincoln Prison on about ten occasions in the 1970s, '80s and '90s.

Each time I was allocated to their seg block, apart from 1991, when I hit their SSU. There were only four of us in there – Tony Steel, Joe Purkiss, Paul Flint and me.

Tony was only eighteen years old when he came in; he is forty now, and has never been out.

Paul is a strong lad; he once almost kicked his way out of a moving van.

As for Joe, he is just a big fat slob, but we all love Joe, not got a big brain but a big heart.

The unit was small, comprising about eight cells, a small yard, a workshop and a multi-gym. Our visits were held in a small room on the unit.

A con in there called Kelly – he left before I got there – had taken a hostage in another jail; he was a dangerous fucker. He was also as bent as a nine-bob note, a raving poof. He used to have his 'fella' visit him and they got caught on the visit giving each other blow-jobs. Could you make this shit up? Doesn't it blow your heads? It does mine.

The Governor on the unit was Mr Pratt – by name and nature. Sadly, I gave him a knuckle sandwich. BANG! So my time on this unit was short.

I recall once in their seg unit I was out on the yard for my one-hour exercise period which was in a caged-off fenced yard outside the kitchen and below the A Wing cons. Anyway, a pal of mine, Patch, walked into the kitchen, and shouted to me through the locked gate, 'Hi, Chas. Need anything?'

I said, 'Yeah, I am starving!'

Five minutes passed. A slab of cheese came flying through the gate and hit the fence. It was about half the size of a football. Then a big loaf of bread comes hurtling my way and crash, it hit the fence. But I am on the other side of the fence.

'How the fuck am I going to get it, Patch?' I ask.

'Leave it to me, Chas,' he says.

Five minutes passed and Patch was let out of the gate. He had a broom. The screw said to him, 'Be quick.'

Patch pretended to sweep up and he shot over and picked up the goodies and then slung them over the 18ft fence. What a genius he was.

I ate half of it. Then it was time to come in. The six screws who'd come to get me looked puzzled, but they never even tried to take it off me!

Lincoln had some first-class screws, proper characters, like Big Mick Freeber. He was a diamond. He used to go and get me a load of chips from the kitchen. And on visits he used to give me an extra half-an-hour.

There was also old Jack Spencer. He was the only screw in thirty years who ever opened my door alone. At times, he shouldn't have done. He has even sat in my cell with a mug of tea.

One Christmas, my door opened, it was about 8.00pm. He was there, alone, with a cake. He must be retired now. But I will always admire that man, a true gentleman. And he knew how to treat people; I always gave him respect. Screws like him are really so few, and he was no soft touch, a hard man, but he had a streak of kindness in him. Like the time I was in a body belt. It was too small, and really uncomfortable. It was causing me breathing problems; it cut into my mid section. I weighed 16st and they had restrained me in a small belt, as usual!

Jack made them take it off and get a bigger size. Most screws would have just left me in pain.

Lincoln's not a big jail but it is compact, it is a very old jail, but the sort that I love best. It has got character. And a lot of ghosts, too!

I really do have some nice memories of the place, and to think that I was bashed up there several times.

I will give HM Prison Lincoln 8/10. See, I am not bitter.

HM PRISON LONG LARTIN

This image is an extract from The Millennium Map™ © getmapping.com plc

LOCATION:	South Littleton, Worcestershire.
CAPACITY:	600 beds.
CATEGORY AT PRESENT:	Category 'A' and 'B' High–Security – Male.
OPENED:	1971.
HISTORY:	Originally was a Category 'C' prison, then sexed up into a high–security status for those serving four years to life. Predominantly for long-term prisoners.

I landed here in the late 1980s and again in the '90s. It is one of our maximum-secure jails, built in the sticks of Worcestershire.

A Governor I have a lot of respect for – and that's rare, coming from me – Mr Whitty was, perhaps, the fairest man in authority I have ever met, and, boy, did he give me a break.

I totally fell off the edge at Lartin in one morning of madness. I wrecked A Wing, I attacked three screws, scalded four others and seriously assaulted three cons with an iron bar.

Everybody, including me, thought it was all over for me, and that I would be nutted off again. But, somehow, Mr Whitty stood by me and helped me over this period of blackness. And I mean he helped me so much that I have never forgotten him. And for the first time in my life, I actually felt guilty for my actions, as I felt I had let Mr Whitty down.

Yeah, it is a fact. Don't ask me to explain it, I am not a psychologist, I just know this time was a very difficult period for me to work out. There I was, fucked-up completely, attacking people, destroying everybody in sight and, after it all stopped, I felt bad over it!

Normally, I would say, 'Good.' But this time, it was me who felt bad. The cons I hurt were scum anyway, sex offenders. So fuck them.

But the screw I attacked had done nothing to me and the damage I did was just senseless. I actually deserved all I got.

No sooner had I got all that behind me, I was off again on another load of destruction. Long Lartin really only saw the bad side of me and the truth is, it was a bloody good jail.

If I had to pinpoint it and try to explain it, I would say maybe I had fucked up and all the time in solitary I had spent had messed me up.

And when I hit Lartin, I just couldn't cope with the openness of it all. It was a big open space with massive fields all round it, even though it was maximum-secure; it was all new to me. I was used to a 10ft square concrete coffin, not all this.

Two of my pals died in Lartin. Eddie Watkins took a drug overdose and left a note behind. Ed had got life over shooting a Customs officer dead. And Barry Rondeau cut his throat and bled to death. Barry was serving life, too; he stabbed a guy at a football match. These fellow cons were two of my best pals. I think that nearly pushed me over the edge. Death affects us all differently.

But Long Lartin had seen some violent incidents over the years. Fred Lowe killed his second con there.

There was one con stabbed to death in the kitchen, another was punched to death in the TV room and another kicked to death down some stairs.

It was there that George Ince got cut (slashed with a blade) down the field. He got cut for his playing about with Dolly Kray (Charlie Kray's wife). But fair play to George, he kept his mouth shut as he did when a shotgun was put down his trousers in later years. He may have played about with someone's wife but he was a solid, staunch guy. For that you have to admire him.

Then there was the time Alec Sears, Andy Russell and a few of the chaps almost escaped. But the makeshift ladder snapped when they were captured in the grounds, and Alec got his head smashed open by the screws. The whole jail erupted in an orgy of violence. Alec later died in a car smash in Spain.

I remember when Chapman, the Barnsley Beast, got it in the recess. He was hit with everything – sticks, lead pipes, boots, fists. Hell ... he survived and fought back. It makes you cringe at what his poor victims had to go through with that monster.

The longest serving Category 'A' inmate in Lartin was John Straffen. Read Kate Kray's book *Lifers* and you will see why he has served fifty years; it is a great pity they never topped him! The animal killed three little girls.

Lartin is full of men who have served 20, 30, even 40 years. But they all seem to walk about like it is a hotel and they're happy. Maybe it is down to institutionalisation, or is it just insanity?

I walked into a cell one day. There was a youngster, twenty-two years old, sucking a black con's dick and another con was riding his butt. It just about sums it all up in a nutshell. Sick! The lad was only serving a six-year sentence; he had fallen into the hole of no return. Drugs, vice and madness!

One day, I was on a visit, and I looked over at the table next to mine; that lad was on a visit with his parents. It was that day that I realised what a jail can do to people.

They are sad, sick and evil places. And my advice to any youngster would be: 'Behave and get out fast and don't come back.' Or just stay out of trouble.

I will give HM Prison Long Lartin 7/10. It does a lovely beef curry.

HM PRISON NORWICH

This image is an extract from The Millennium Map™ © getmapping.com plc

LOCATION:	Norwich, Norfolk.
CAPACITY:	750 beds.
CATEGORY AT PRESENT:	Local Prison, Remands and YOI (Young Offenders Institute) – Male.
OPENED:	1887.
HISTORY:	A bit of history to this one. Although the prison opened in 1887 with only two wings, a further two wings were added in 1996 to accommodate Category 'C' prisoners. The YOI part of the prison is not attached to the adult male prison, it is on an adjacent site.

I was only here for two weeks and spent that time in their seg block in the 1980s.

I must say now, it was a smashing couple of weeks; the cell was clean and spacious. The food was excellent. It always is good in these little jails. And the population at the time I was there was not a quarter of that of some of the big jails. Since my stay, the prison has opened Category 'C' units and a detox wing for smackheads as well as its own Health Care Unit.

Norwich is an old jail but well preserved. It is quite laid-back. Even the screws were a decent bunch. They just went about their jobs how thay were supposed to, humanely.

I said to one old screw, 'Hey, guv, if I even get sentenced to hang, I will ask to be hanged in your jail.'

He asked, 'Why?'

I told him because it would be nice to go with a bit of humanity and no bitterness. He looked puzzled. But I fucking meant it.

It was a stress-free fortnight for me. I even slept like a baby and awoke happy. Do you know, I actually felt guilty; it is surely a crime to be so happy in jail.

I will give HM Prison Norwich 9/10. Maybe it was too nice. It could kill you with kindness. Not a nice end.

HM PRISON OXFORD

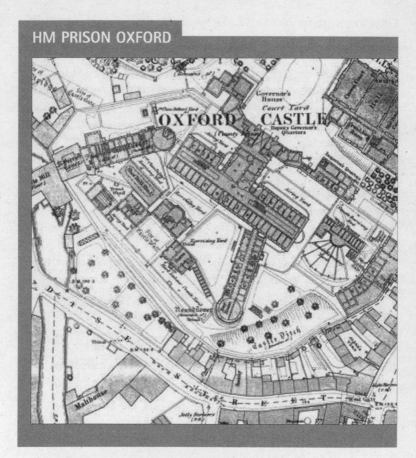

LOCATION:	Nearby to the County Hall on New Road, Oxford.
CAPACITY:	Nil.
CATEGORY AT PRESENT:	Leisure.
OPENED:	1166.
HISTORY:	Oxford Castle ceased to be a prison in 1996 and over the next few years will be redeveloped in a partnership between heritage and commercial uses. Since 1166, there has been a prison on the castle site, and in 1236 the Chancellor of the University was authorised to use the Castle 'gaol' for 'rebellious scholars'.

There was a separate wing, B Wing, for female prisoners, now destroyed. There were, in the early days, separate exercise yards for different classes of prisoners. At this time, it was common to be thrown into clink for owing money; remind me never to get a loan. The Debtors' Yard was adjacent to the Debtors' Tower. Except for the Governor's House in the centre of the main exercise yards, most of the large buildings remain, although altered inside. The Castle Mill was demolished in the 1930s.

The prison building that stands today is the result of major rebuilding in the late eighteenth and early nineteenth centuries which saw a house of correction, internal courtyards and new wings added, all of which were surrounded by a castellated wall.

The last public hanging to take place at Oxford Prison was in 1863, but the hanging cell became a place for private executions away from the public eye where executions were held until the 1950s.

In 1884, hard labour was introduced in the form of stone breaking. A contract was pursued to supply the local Highways Board.

In 1848, as if all the previous building work wasn't enough, a Governor's house was built, which was placed safely outside the prison walls.

Most of the inmates were local to Oxford, and so were the prison staff. Towards the end of the 1980s, the hospital wing began to fill up with psychiatric cases, changing the prison population from almost exclusively normal villains and crooks. I should know, because I was one of them.

The deluxe cells were those overlooking the exercise yard; you would have a view looking out over New Road, and level with the Nuffield tower.

The death knell for the prison rang when European Council standards were brought in and an overhaul of the British Penal System in terms of sanitation systems and wash areas would mean extra costs for all of the prisons.

After the prison closed, the local council took advantage of this empty shell that is testimony to human suffering and rented out the prison buildings to film and television companies.

Many drama series were shot there, including *Bad Girls*, *Inspector Morse* and *The Bill*. Big screen movies like *101 Dalmatians*, *The Spy Game* and *Lucky Break* generated extra cash to help fill the council coffers. Considering that fees started at £3,000 for a day's use, the Council pulled in over £500,000 from more than fifty productions.

And now, jumping on the cash bandwagon are the developers. Personally, I would have turned the place into 'Bronco's', a fitness centre and self-incarceration unit for those willing to pay.

I landed here back in December 1978; the van drove in and within five minutes of walking into reception, I chinned a screw. BANG!

I was jumped on and put in a body belt and carried back to the van, and off we went.

This had to be a world record! But I must add, we were only stopping off at Oxford for dinner. I was in transit heading for Rampton Asylum.

I was accompanied at the time by Parkhurst screws; they actually thought the whole thing was funny. What was funny? I actually had the Oxford screw's tooth embedded in my fist. But the other funny thing was, I couldn't be nicked for it, simply as I had been certified mad and was on my way to the asylum.

Who said you can't beat the system? This proves that you can.

I will give HM Prison Oxford a 5/10, just for the memory.

HM PRISON PARKHURST

This image is an extract from The Millennium Map™ © getmapping.com plc

LOCATION:	Newport, Isle of Wight – get there by ferry or hovercraft.
CAPACITY:	450 beds.
CATEGORY AT PRESENT:	'B' and Protected Witness Unit – Male.
OPENED:	1838.
HISTORY:	Although the prison first opened in 1805, it was designed as a Military Hospital. Something called 'The Parkhurst Prison Act' came into force in 1838 and the rest is history ... just about. Back in those days, they kept prisoners in what they called 'hulks'.

The forerunner to the punishment of being detained in a hulk was 'deportation to the colonies and Australia'. This was clearly a form of social vengeance. Banishment was the new punishment, to be sent away from your own shores was becoming popular and replaced penal servitude.

After the feudal system broke up, the wandering, jobless and lower-class-filled slums added to the already full prisons. From 1596 to 1776, deporting these unwanted social outcasts to the colonies relieved pressure on prisons. Transportation to colonies ended in 1776.

Just before the ending of transportation, Captain James Cook discovered Australia in 1770. You lucky Aussies! The plan was to have convicts tame the new land, and 135,000 deportees were sent there between 1787–1875. The conditions in these ships were worse than the conditions in the jails.

The problem of increased prisoner loads stretched England's facilities from 1776–1875. The (final) solution was to use the old 'hulks' or unusable transport ships. This represented an immediate solution to the overcrowding problem, and the hulks could be berthed in rivers and harbours.

Within these hulks there was no segregation, both young and old, male and female, criminals and miscreants were thrown together.

These great stinking hulks were moored off the coasts of England or moored in harbour under the ever-watchful eye of the turnkeys. One such hulk was called the 'York' and was moored close by at Portsmouth; they sent the first lot of boys from there to Parkhurst. What a relief this must have been for them to be released from the stinking hulk to a lovely cell. The hulk system of incarcerating prisoners continued until 1858, over eighty years!

The only time the prison swayed from being a male-only members club was when women were permitted to be prisoners from 1863 to 1869. After that short run it returned to male members only.

The maximum-security use of the prison was developed in 1968, just in time for the Kray gang when the prison became a secure dispersal institution.

The Protected Witness (Supergrass) Unit was opened in 1997.

Without a doubt, this is one of our most famous jails ... or is it infamous? Whatever, it is a jail that holds many a horrific story.

I first landed here back in 1976; I was a young man of twenty-four years of age. As the ferry left Portsmouth Dock, I felt I was going far away from England.

Around this time, Rod Stewart had a hit record in the charts – 'I Am Sailing'. Every time I hear that song, I can think back to that first journey over to the Isle of Wight.

For me, Parkhurst Prison was the hardest, toughest, cruellest jail in Britain. It holds the record for the most murders in any jail in the UK.

I was there for three of those murders – Johnny Patton killed McGhee on C Wing; Dougie Wakefield killed Brian Peak on C Unit; and Rogers killed Rocky Hart in the main kitchen.

McGhee copped it in the back with a 7in chib in the dinner queue. As he lay dead on the floor, cons just stepped over him as if he was a bag of spuds. Nobody sees anything in Parkhurst.

Brian Peak had his lot in his cell as he was painting a picture of a beautiful country landscape. Dougie strangled him with a bootlace, and then set about making a lot of holes in his body.

Rocky Hart got stabbed through the neck and back in an argument over a pork chop.

All three killers had killed before. All got a further life sentence. Only one has been released, and that was Johnny Patton ... he left prison some years later in a body bag. He hanged himself.

Parkhurst, for me, was an exciting jail, as there was always something going on – parties, hooch, escape plots and violence. Hey, making hooch ... now that is a favourite pastime of many a good friend of mine. I can't recall how many cell parties we've had behind bars. When we couldn't get booze smuggled in, then we'd have to drink some of the prison hooch we'd brew in our illicit stills.

One of the best drinks I've tasted was made from orange peel, fruit cocktail and water. All of this was heated in a prison sink and kept warm with prison-issue blankets; well, they do come in handy for something.

Then comes the hard part, keeping it away from the screws, 'cos some of the thieving bastards will drink it ... it has happened to us before in Parkhurst! You then hide it away for between five and seven days, then extra sugar is added and it is kept warm for three more days. Skim the head off and get it down your neck ... lovely.

Now, if you've got access to yeast, then you're gonna have a real good party in a few days' time! Yeehaaaa!

When yeast is added to crushed fruit, it starts consuming the natural sugars in the flesh of the fruit. This process carries on until all the sugar has disappeared and then the yeast will die. The resulting beverage (with a bit more love) could be the perfect Beaujolais, if you used grapes.

Should you have access to barley, hops and yeast, then you can make beers and lagers. To get bitter on tap, you need to get the yeast to fall to the bottom of the fermentation container and have a warmer temperature. Hey, I sound like a right alco, but it's only 'cos I've had thirty years' practice.

To make lager, you need to get the yeast to float on the top of the fermenting container (not aluminium, as alcohol reacts badly with aluminium) and have slightly colder storage conditions. The sugar that is fermented comes from the barley. Hops are added for their flavour and to prevent the growth of certain bacteria, which might cause the beer to go off.

The daddy of hooch is the spirit. Before I can go any further, you have to know how a spirit is made. When a spirit is created in a proper distillery, an already fermented drink is treated to increase its percentage of alcohol. You are increasing the alcoholic proof.

Only once have I had real spirit hooch, and that was just like drinking whisky. But when times are hard you just have to resort to the simplest methods of making hooch. We'd grab a plastic bucket, throw in some raisins, sugar, water and yeast and leave it under the bed. We'd keep an eye on it and so long as we didn't get our cell spun over by the burglars, we'd have a party the following week.

We've even had the boys pick dandelions on the sports field and make dandelion wine. One of the funniest places we've brewed hooch is in the inside of a football in a prison gym. The fuel can for the lawnmower comes in handy, too!

Cons lived by a moralistic code, and screws remained screws. There were never any nonces (sex beasts) on the wings and grasses were severely served up big time.

The cons did their bird in the way cons should – like men. We worked out hard in the gym. We cooked our own grub. We had lots of sunbathing. We had good visits and we didn't give a fuck.

Parkhurst Prison had a proper riot in 1969 and, believe me, they didn't fancy a second one. That riot was the most violent prison riot of all time. Men like Frank Fraser, Timmy Noonan, Marty Frape, Stan Thompson – proper hardcore cons. The old breed, hearts of lions.

The cons all got smashed up, but so did a lot of screws; one even had his throat cut. That is what you call a riot. Floors drenched with blood. Broken bodies.

Parkhurst held the worst of the worst, but the best of the best, if you follow my meaning. It all depends what side of the wall you are on.

That jail had the 'cream' – the top bank robbers, the mobsters, the fraudsters. It even had its own unit for psychopaths.

I met them all at Parkhurst – the Krays, the Richardsons. Never mind Alcatraz and Capone. This was the place, our very own Devil's Island. And we were doing our bird like men should, our way.

There was respect and a sort of atmosphere like no other jail. Call it menace ... fear ... tension. But it was right in your face – 'Don't fuck with us.'

The place was buzzing, and behind every door there was a story. A dream turned into a nightmare. One day it would be calm, the next there would be a hostage siege.

One week would pass by peacefully. The next there would be four cuttings and two stabbings or a suicide.

But even the suicides were mysterious. I have worked out with guys on a Tuesday, and by the Friday they are dead. Drug overdoses, hangings, slashed wrists.

I once watched a con rip another con's eye out. The guy walked away laughing whilst the other con screamed. One con got a broom handle rammed so far up his arse he ended up with a colostomy bag. Another lost his nose.

Even screws got smashed up there. Cut up ... stabbed up. It was that sort of place.

I remember when Billy Skingle and Cyril Berkett had it away from the SSU. Cyril got caught almost immediately. But Billy got right away and hid in the woods. Sadly, they found him buried under a pile of earth and so had him locked back up.

Billy was serving natural life for shooting a copper seven times in the canister. Billy was a funny fucker, he used to say, 'It was a faulty trigger.' It was years later he died up in Full Sutton Prison. But the truth is, Billy died the day the judge at the Bailey sentenced him.

Parkhurst Prison holds some strange mixed emotions for me. It was while I was there I fell on bad times; I was wrapped up in violence and attempted murder, I also suffered multiple stab wounds and almost

"MAX-Secure".

"
CAGED JUST LIKE A BEAR
BIG BROTHER IS ALWAYS THERE
THIRTY YEARS OF MADNESS
DO YOU REALLY CARE ?
"

PARKHURST.

died. And, to top it all, it was Parkhurst that actually certified me criminally insane.

So, it is a jail that I can never forget. Parkhurst plays a big part in my character make-up today. And some of the cons I met there and fought with and against have become life-long friends and enemies. So how can a man forget? How does a war prisoner forget? You ask those who suffered in those Japanese PoW camps. The actor Peter Wyngarde who played the TV character Jason King in *Department 'S'* was a child prisoner of the Japanese. When the Japs invaded Shanghai, Peter was being looked after while his father was away in India. He spent several years in Lung-hai concentration camp and had both of his feet broken and he was put into solitary confinement.

Well, it is the same as prison. They leave a scar.

To me, Parkhurst has to get good marks, simply is it was my most exciting time in any jail. It was character building. A challenge. And I loved it. Even the bad times were good.

Because, with every act of violence, you fought back with sheer madness. I spent a lot of my time in the dungeon there, battling with the screws. I cut one and I shit plenty up, and I had some good fights that they will never let me forget, but I have no real bitterness or hatred over it.

I was a young man put to the test. Crazy but true and I would love to do it all again, but I can't.

I will give HM Prison Parkhurst 10/10. And I got on their roof. Nice view up there.

HM PRISON PENTONVILLE

This image is an extract from The Millennium Map™ © getmapping.com plc

LOCATION:	Caledonian Road, London.
CAPACITY:	1,100 beds.
CATEGORY AT PRESENT:	Local and Category 'B' – Male.
OPENED:	1842 at a cost of £84,186 12s 2d. Notice from the aerial photo that it was designed in accordance with Jeremy Bentham's panopticon design consisting of a central hall, with five radiating wings (one being the small centre wing), all of which are visible to staff positioned at the centre. This is still apparent in today's layout; very little has changed.
HISTORY:	Again, look at the aerial photo of Pentonville Prison.

The same four cellblocks you can see are the same ones built there over 160 years ago. Fuck all has changed, and you wonder where your taxes go when reformists say prisons have been improved!

Believe it or not, this was the first modern prison and opened in London in 1816 – the new Millbank Prison. There were separate cells for 860 prisoners, which could deal with the rapid increase in prison numbers. This increase was due to the way certain crimes had been dropped from the capital punishment listings and the slowing down of transportation as a punishment.

Pentonville Prison was allowed to be built after two Acts of Parliament were passed allowing for the detention of convicts sentenced to imprisonment or awaiting transportation.

On 10 April 1840, construction started and, by 1842, the prison was ready to open. Originally, Pentonville was designed so that prisoners could have their own cell. This was mainly a punishment consideration. 520 prisoners had their own cells, which measured 13ft by 7ft and were 9ft high.

Pentonville was to become the basic model for prisons in Britain and this prompted the building of a further fifty-four of similar design over a six-year period. Compared to Newgate Prison, conditions were vastly better and healthier.

Life as a prisoner meant that you had to do some sort of work, such as picking coir (tarred rope) and weaving.

I have heard that it costs about £150,000 per year to keep me securely locked up. Compare that to the cost of keeping a prisoner at Pentonville in 1842 – 15s (75p) per week.

Until Newgate Prison closed in 1902, condemned prisoners were not housed at Pentonville Prison. The closure of Newgate meant that Pentonville had to take over the responsibility of executions. This meant that extra cells for the condemned had to be built and the gallows from Newgate were moved to Pentonville. As like the other 'modern' prisons of the day, the execution facilities were housed in a purpose-built shed with a typical brick-lined pit some 12ft deep.

The most uncomfortable of walks for the condemned prisoner was when they had to walk from the prison to the hanging shed. This, again, was typical of most hanging prisons, as public hangings were abolished. Some prisons acted rather sooner than Pentonville in providing hanging cells. Pentonville eventually moved the hanging facilities to within the prison in the 1920s. This saved the condemned prisoner the walk to the hanging shed.

The hanging cells were, as I've already said, on one of the upper floors. This was to allow the body of the condemned to drop the seven or so feet and then to account for the height of the body. So if the person being hanged was, say, 6ft tall and then the drop of the rope was 7ft, then that would be a fair old distance from the neck height of where the condemned was standing. This meant that two or three cells from the ground floor upwards were part of the hanging chamber, comprising a stack of three rooms in the middle of one of the wings. The topmost cell would house the beam from which the rope was suspended from a chain. This rope then hung down through floor hatches.

One of the cells below this cell housed the lever that opened the trap doors and the ground-floor room acted as the pit into which the prisoner was launched. All apart from HM Prison Durham used this type of hanging system.

Would you believe that people actually applied for the job as hangman? The course to be a hangman lasted for one week. Can you see your local college advertising such courses – 'Hangman, a two-day taster course' or 'DIY Hangman for Beginners'?

At Pentonville Prison you could become a qualified hangman. They were taught how to calculate and set the drop, pinion the prisoner and carry out an execution with speed and efficiency using a dummy in place of the prisoner. As mentioned already, one of the most prolific hangmen to ever live was Albert Pierrepoint.

The dummy used by these trainee hangmen was called 'Old Bill'. The trainees practised hooding and noosing Old Bill, getting the eyelet of the noose in the right place and learning the system of what was supposedly humane hanging.

The only humane part of the hanging was when the white cap was drawn over the head of the condemned. What else is humane about hanging someone? After attending the course, the trainees were given a test and that was it – a degree in hanging.

There were 120 hangings carried out in Pentonville Prison from 1902 to 1961. The first to be hanged on the 30 September 1902 was John Macdonald, who was convicted of murder. The infamous Dr Crippen was hanged at Pentonville on 23 November 1911.

During World War II, six spies were hanged at Pentonville under the provisions of Section 1 of the Treachery Act 1940. They were Carl Meier, Jose Waldeburg, Charles Albert Van Der Kieboom, Oswald John Job, Pierre Richard Charles Neukermans and Joseph Jan Van Hove. Hangman Albert Pierrepoint dispatched Waldeburg and Meier on 10 December 1940 and Kieboom a week later on the 17 December by Stanley Cross, having had his appeal dismissed.

The address of 10 Rillington Place sounds familiar, and so it should be. This was the start of multiple murders, which led, first, to Timothy John Evans (9 March 1950) and then, some years later, John Reginald Halliday Christie (15 July 1953) being hanged in Pentonville Prison by Albert Pierrpoint.

The last man to be hanged at Pentonville Prison was Edwin Albert Arthur Bush, aged 21, on 6 July 1961, when he was executed for the murder of shop assistant Elsie Batten.

It was 1976 when I popped in there, well after the last hanging had taken place. I was on my way to Wandsworth from Parkhurst and the van got a call to direct me there. I never knew why; probably a security thing to do with Wandsworth.

Pentonville only kept me three days and moved me on to Wandsworth. So my three days there is a bit short to assess the place, the food and the routine, but the previous hanging history is awesome! Bring back the birch; let's have a whip round.

The seg block was like all the other old blocks in any jail, dark and gloomy with an eerie smell of decay and death. This place is now 162 years old. It looks it, too. The food was pig swill, even the water tasted old.

The screws were typical old school – peaked caps, shiny boots, starched collars, the military swagger. Half the prats never got past the rank of private in the forces. The odd one or two sweated it up to the rank of corporal. But that was only for grassing on their pals. The very few élite may have made it into the SAS. These were the best type of screws. Proper men. They never fucked about with silly psychological games.

The mattress was one of the old straw-filled ones, lumpy, and even the pillow was filled with straw.

Do you know, all these years later, I still can't get used to sleeping on prison mattresses. The very thought of hundreds, even thousands of men being on it before me, wanking, coughing and farting. I still can't face up to that.

I will give HM Prison Pentonville 4/10. Fuck knows why, but I have got to give it something.

PS – I never did go back! Thank fuck.

RAMPTON ASYLUM

This image is an extract from The Millennium Map™ © getmapping.com plc

LOCATION:	Retford, Nottingham.
CAPACITY:	437 beds.
CATEGORY AT PRESENT:	Special Secure Hospital – Male and Female.
OPENED:	1910.
HISTORY:	Opened as England's first State institution for mentally defective people considered dangerous.

Do you know that the now deceased former Prime Minister of England, Winston Churchill, when he was Home Secretary, held views that were no different to those of Germany's World War II Chancellor, Adolf Hitler?

Churchill, like Hitler, was a strong supporter of sterilisation. The extreme views of Churchill were that 100,000 moral degenerates should be given forcible sterilisation! These views were considered so sensitive that they were kept secret until 1992.

Here is what Churchill said:

'The unnatural and increasingly rapid growth of the feeble-minded classes, coupled with a steady restriction among all the thrifty, energetic and superior stocks, constitute a race danger which it is impossible to exaggerate. I feel that the sources from which the stream of madness is fed should be cut off and sealed up before another year has passed.'

(Winston Churchill to Prime Minister Asquith, 1910, quoted by Clive Ponting in the *Guardian Outlook* 20/6/1992)

Rampton Hospital is a high-secure unit with a developing occupational therapy service which aims to provide individual treatment and group work for learning disabilities, mental health, women's services and personality disorder service users. Clients are seen as in-patients on the wards and in day centres.

The occupational therapists facilitate group work in clinical day-service settings. This is proven to be the most appropriate method of meeting a wide range of patients' clinical needs given the finite occupational therapy resource. Staff devise and implement specifically selected and appropriately structured groups in response to the identified needs of the patients.

It was December 1978 when I landed in this funny farm and, believe me, I did not know that any such places existed.

I had just been certified criminally insane over two violent attacks at Parkhurst. One on a con and the other on a screw and it was at Newport Crown Court, on the Isle of Wight, where I was given an indefinite life section, or 'sectioned off'. Such is life.

So there I was at Rampton secure asylum in a world of madness. What an understatement! Total fucking insanity beyond anything I have ever known. Rampton at this time was a brutal establishment.

OK, you are going to say, 'How come? Why is it?' Well, I will tell you. Because it was a place where serious liberties could take place. After all, we were classified as being insane. Who would believe a madman compared to the high rollers from the establishment?

I cannot count on my fingers or toes how many times I was beaten up, but it wasn't the beatings that were the biggest fear, it was something far more sinister than you could imagine ... it was the psychotropic drugs they forced me to take. If I refused to take them orally, I would be attacked and be given these drugs by injection.

The screws in Rampton are, in fact, psychiatric nurses. Now you tell me what sort of nurse wears size 10 boots and a prison officer's uniform? Those nurses are not the sort of nurses you would want looking after you when you're feeling poorly.

But they all got kicked back in the face, as a massive police inquiry took place over the brutality there and many were sacked over it. Had the lunatics dreamed that as well?

Rampton, at this time, was no different from a strict detention centre, or a Borstal. It was run on fear – 'Do as we tell you, or you will be sorry!'

I spent eleven months on Drake Ward, which was the intensive care unit for the disruptive element and, believe me, we got it every day – cold baths, wet towel treatment, kickings, psychological torture, our whole day was made a misery.

We had to scrub floors, wash walls. We were like a load of slaves. There were only twelve of us on the ward. The screws outnumbered us.

At 8.00pm, it was bedtime. We had just a bed and piss pot. We were not even allowed a book to read. Bed was for sleep. At 6.00am, we would be up, slopping our piss pots out, marching about like lunatics.

But do 'patients' do this? So nurses make you do this? To me, Rampton was a hellhole. No wonder the police were brought in. After the police inquiry, and court cases, and sackings, the place cooled down.

Like the Scrubs inquiry, it all cooled down. But in time, they all slip back into hell. Rampton holds a lot of nightmares in the way it treated its inmates. Remember, this is a place that has been around for a good ninety-four years.

It is a gloomy-looking, red-brick institution, where madmen were probably sent to die. I met some old boys there who had been there for forty years and more. They had dead eyes, faces of stone.

Obviously, nowadays, it has all changed. They can't get away with such atrocities.

Did you know that epilepsy was once regarded as a mental illness? And people were locked up for it. Did you know young girls having babies were also locked up in asylums? Our asylums are a disgrace. What they did to people from the 1920s to the 1980s was shameful. Lobotomies, leucotomies, electric shock treatment (without anaesthetic). Please believe it, they are a bloody disgrace. An insult to humanity.

This country should hang its head in shame for the human misery we have caused. But for me, it was the drug abuse. The liquid cosh. What right has anybody got to inject drugs into another human being? Animal rights activists fight for animals. Well, what about the lunatics? Do we not matter?

I have very few, if any, good memories of Rampton. Ask anyone who spent time in Auschwitz if they had any good times. They will spit in your face.

That is how I feel about Rampton. More so, as it was a hospital. So it should not have been like that.

Nowadays, I read, it is a nice place. With sickos there like Beverly Allitt. Discos! Bingo! Gym! TV! Films! Well, I never had any of that, I can assure you.

I will give Special Secure Hospital Rampton 0/10. Sorry, but I would be a madman to give it any more.

HM PRISON RISLEY (REMAND CENTRE)

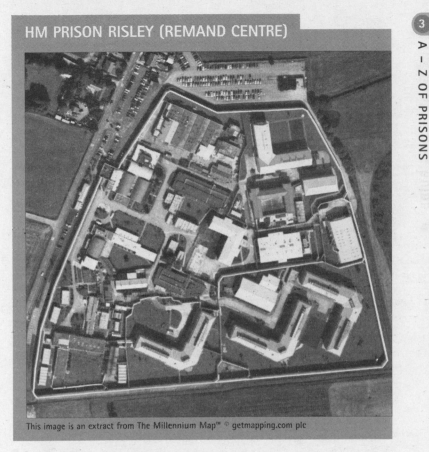

This image is an extract from The Millennium Map™ © getmapping.com plc

LOCATION:	Warrington, Cheshire.
CAPACITY:	1,000 beds.
CATEGORY AT PRESENT:	'C' – Male.
OPENED:	1965.
HISTORY:	Originally opened as a Remand Centre. Always suffering setbacks due to those nasty prisoners committing suicide and always overcrowded. Suffered riots and uprisings as well as poor reports by prison inspectors, this resulted in the prison becoming a training prison. Had a female wing, but this closed in 1999 and became a detox centre for female prisoners

... it soon closed down after a few months.
Operates a sex offender treatment programme. I didn't
know they had gas chambers there? How come sex
offenders are considered more worthy than female
prisoners?

I first landed in Grisly Risley, a shit-hole, in 1969 and I returned there six times afterwards; I must have liked it or something. I could write a book on this place alone. It really was a hellhole. It stunk of death. Suicides. It was a brutal place for youngsters. Some just cracked and topped themselves.

I actually witnessed my first suicide at Risley. And, believe me, it is not a nice sight. I was only a boy myself, seventeen years old, when I saw the lad hanging in his cell. It really had a bad affect on me. Nightmares. It really is not a nice experience. But what is really sick in jail is that once the body is taken out, the next day just goes on as if fuck all has happened.

Screws shouted their fat mouths off. With their big fat arses and beer bellies. I used to watch them and wonder, do they go home and start on and brutalise their own kids like that? Or bash their wives up ... as many are divorced and like a drink?

I changed my whole character just by being in Risley. It all became a game to me. If I could get one over on the pigs ... I would. And I met lads who became life-long 'brothers'.

It's in those places that real criminals are created. We come in naughty boys ... we go out dangerous bastards. It's a fact. That first bit of porridge sticks to you like glue. Does shit stick to a blanket? Does prison stick to a kid?

It sets like rock inside your guts. And you turn to concrete. You become as relentless and ruthless as the screws.

I could not count on my fingers and toes how many times I was beaten up by those pigs. But the reason for that was because I would not stay down, I came back worse. In the end, I think that they gave up and gave me a bit of space.

The cells were tiny. No air. Stuffy. The visits were in closed cubicles behind glass. On one visit, I butted out the glass in frustration. The food was shit. Risley had its fair share of riots. But considering it was a newish jail, built in the mid-1960s, it was a fucking disgrace.

There were rats there as big as cats! One night, I was looking out of my cell window when a guard dog caught one and tore it to shreds. The shriek of that rat went into my soul. It was then that I knew I was in hell.

Another time, I lost the plot and stabbed a guy straight through his eye. That just wasn't me. I could never dream of doing such a nasty thing. But that's what a place like that turns you into.

I burnt nonces with lighters and fags. I cut them. I stabbed them. I jumped on their legs 'til I heard a crack, laughing as I did it. If you live in a hate factory then you become it.

Fortunately, all the scum I ever attacked were either sex cases or grasses, and all the screws I attacked were bullyboys. So I have no regrets. I did to them what ten would do to me, but I did it on my own! And did I do it from behind? No! I came at them face to face. How I enjoy it!

It was in the gym; I felt I had lost my way. I'd got 150lb on the bar for a bench press. I saw this fat nonce come in the gym; he had been in all the papers for raping an old lady. So I thought, 'Yeah, he can have some.'

I called him over and told him to have a go at the bar. As he lay on the bench, I dropped it towards his neck. Somehow, he moved in that split second. He would have died instantly and I would have died with him on a life sentence. I had to get a grip of myself before Risley buried me away with all the dead souls it created.

For a young lad, I was a tortured wreck on a mission to hell. It was years later in 1985 when I almost died in Risley.

But to me, this place was the start of my madness, it scars the brain, warps the mind. I have not really any nice things to say about the place. Only for the smashing pals I met there – Tommy Tedstone, Snowy, Andy Vassal, Sonny Carroll, Johnny Owen, Dominick Gallagher, Chrissy Hendrix, Barry Davis and his brother Ernie. Men I have grown up with. For that I am grateful to have been a part of it all.

A lot of people are not friends. They will leave you in the shit. Even watch you die. A true friend stands with you in times of trouble. My true pals have stood and fought with me against terrible odds. And I love them all for it!

The ones who ran – or stood and watched – I have no bad feelings towards, but they're cowards. It's for them to face themselves. Risley, sadly, broke many. But it couldn't break me.

One of the more bizarre times at Risley Prison was when Keith Hull was sentenced to twelve months' imprisonment for offences relating to her/his shop that was selling items of a sexual nature. Oh, and she got a £6,000 fine on top of the sentence!

Keith had become Stephanie and had truly changed into a female, but she was the only woman on the female wing who hadn't been born a woman. Although she only spent three nights in Risley, it was three nights of hell, sleeping on a mattress on the floor and with nothing but a pot to piss in. After three nights, she was transferred to an open prison.

After three months, she won her appeal due to the sentence being too harsh. Good job she wasn't put on the male wing!

I see Risley is another prison that now mixes sex offenders with normal cons. Many prisons keep sex offenders in separate wings but Risley, which is Britain's largest Cat 'C' prison, integrates them. This has led to the sex cases avoiding other cons by segregating themselves. This is the mentality of prison governors for you, but all the more nonces to get beaten up ... lovely!

I will give HM Prison Risley 3/10 for trying to break me.

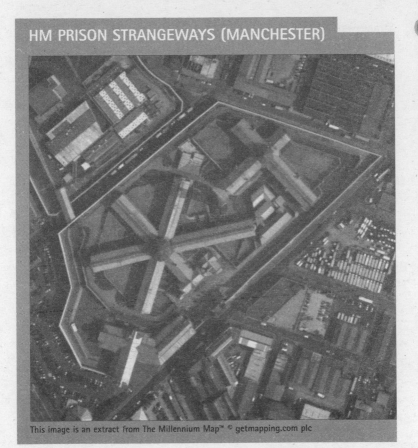

This image is an extract from The Millennium Map™ © getmapping.com plc

LOCATION:	Southall Street, Manchester.
CAPACITY:	1,200 beds.
CATEGORY AT PRESENT:	Core – Male (includes Category 'A' prisoners).
OPENED:	1868.
HISTORY:	April Fool's Day 1990 saw the start of the Strangeways Riot, which ended on 25 April 1990. An event in Strangeway's history that is forever marked by the way it revealed systematic abuse of prisoners and their rights. This riot holds the record as being the longest in British penal history.

Strangeways Prison in Southall Street, Manchester, was built to replace New Bailey Prison in Salford that closed in 1868. Originally opened as 'Salford Prison' in 1868, it housed both males and females in separate units. In 1963, the females were moved out to HM Prison Styal and the unit that housed the women became a Borstal allocation and remand facility.

In 1965, the Remand Centre closed and the remand prisoners were moved to Risley Remand Centre. But by 1980, the prison system was full to the gunwales and prisoners were jam-packed like sardines (four to a cell) and the prison, again, took in remand prisoners.

The prison riot of 1990 caused a sharp improvement to the outdated facilities and much of the prison was substantially rebuilt. The old design was another one of the prisons using the panopticon (radial) concept that was being employed all over Britain at the time. Designed by Alfred Waterhouse in 1861, Waterhouse was assisted by Joshua Jebb, the Surveyor General of Prisons, who had also been involved with the design of London's Pentonville Prison, as previously mentioned.

When construction was completed in 1869, the cost stood at £170,000. Originally, where the prison now stands was Strangeways Park and Gardens, hence the name 'Strangeways'. You can't miss Strangeways with its imposing watchtower and two large gatehouses.

Another one of the execution prisons, Strangeways became the setting for executions for the area after the closure of the original Salford Prison. Like all of the hanging prisons, this prison had the same basic set-up.

When executions were moved inside the prison, it was to be B Wing that housed the killing area. In total, there were 100 hangings carried out within its walls, a nice round figure to end on ... how many of them were innocent?

The first woman to be executed by hanging at Strangeways was Mary Ann Britland, 38, on 9 August 1886.

Remember when I told you about Charlie Peace being hanged at Armley Prison? Well, our Mr Peace had an admirer in the form of John Jackson. The hanging of Peace set Jackson on a whirlwind life of crime that was to end in him being hanged for murder at Strangeways Prison, an execution that was carried out by James Berry on 7 August 1888.

One of only four females to be hanged at Strangeways was that of a namesake of the hangman Harry Allen. Margaret Allen was a butch dyke lesbian who dressed in men's clothes and insisted on being called by a male name, namely 'Bill'.

The execution (for murdering a woman who had come to borrow a cup of sugar) of Allen, 42, was performed by Albert Pierrepoint on 12 January 1949.

Probably the fastest hanging in history took place here when, on 8 May 1951, when James Inglis, convicted of murdering a prostitute, bolted for the gallows from his condemned cell and his escorts had to run alongside him. Executioner Albert Pierrepoint completed the hanging in just seven seconds! This was the nearest thing to a DIY hanging that you could get; Inglis even assisted Pierrepoint in pinioning his arms in the condemned cell ... some people have a death wish!

The last of four women to be executed at Strangeways was Louisa May Merrifield, 46, who had been convicted of poisoning a seventy-nine-year-old, bed-ridden widow who lived in Blackpool.

On the morning of Friday, 18 September 1953, several hundred people wanting to see the death notices displayed besieged the prison. At this time, there was an unwritten rule in the Home Office that poisoners should always hang.

One of the last two hangings to take place in England and the UK was that of John Robson Walby (also known as Gwynne Owen Evans) and took place in Strangeways Prison on 13 August 1964. The hangman was called Harry Allen.

In a bizarre twist, while this was going on, simultaneously in Walton Prison, the second of the two last hangings in the UK was taking place and the name of the man being hanged was Peter Anthony Allen.

Rebuilding work and a change of name hasn't changed the prison's demeanour ... it still looks a gruesome place. Although they renamed the place 'Her Majesty's Prison Manchester', everyone still calls it by the old name.

I can't believe that it is an amazing decade-and-a-half since the most famous riot took place, and I fucking missed it! I was actually in the seg unit in Parkhurst Prison when it all exploded at Strangeways. That was one riot I truly would have loved to have been involved in, but it wasn't to be. Don't life suck!

I first hit Strangeways in the 1970s, again in the '80s and again in the '90s. It is a tough hard jail. It is Manchester's answer, with a vengeance, to Wandsworth Prison in London ... cold and cruel.

Screws in the 1970s and '80s where a brutal, cold-hearted bunch; they ran Strangeways with a rod of iron.

When you hit their seg block, you bounced off the walls. You left your blues behind. Men have begged and cried in that hellhole. Governors and doctors turned a blind eye to it all.

My good pal Tommy Flanagan's head was used as a football; how he survived is a miracle – he was a right fucking mess.

It is no good. There are mugs who say it didn't go on, or it can't go on. The proof is for all to see. Strangeways was a brutal regime, run by evil scum. Basically, the word is 'cowards'. Ten men punching and kicking one defenceless man can't be anything but cowardly, can it?

There was a white line painted on the floor in their seg unit, and the rule was, 'you walk around it ... not on it, or over it'. If you did, they jumped you.

My first spell there, I said, 'Bollocks to your line,' and I can put my hand on my heart and say I never did walk around it nor ever would. Simply because the bullies don't frighten me. I said, 'You can beat the shit out of me, but the first opportunity I get ... I will have one of you snakes.' That has always been my way of life. So fuck their silly white line. And if everybody said 'Fuck it' then there would never be a white line, would there? You are not sent to prison to be humiliated; you are sent there to be punished. A silly white line is a made up thing to degrade you.

Strangeways pushed and pushed and pushed too far. Cons got sick of it. The screws were a disgrace to the prison service, and when it went off, what did the screws do? They shit it and legged it! They evacuated like the cowards they are. That just about sums it up.

The riot opened a big can of maggots; a lot of truths came out, but it cost the ringleaders years of their lives, especially Alan Lord. Alan had already served ten years of a life sentence. Now it is over twenty-four years on and he is still a Category 'A' man and still no chance of getting out. Others copped ten years and eight years and so on. But what did the cowardly screws get for all their violence? Fuck all!

Years and years of torturing cons. The food there was filth; the whole jail was a hate factory. A warehouse full of hatred, all boxed up in little stinking cells, it pumped in hate and spurted out bitterness.

I went back there in the mid-nineties, only for a month, just passing through on a tour of the jails. I must say, the seg unit was clean and the food was brilliant, and the screws were decent to me. It was a completely different place to what it had been.

The cons up there have a lot to thank the rioters for, because they lost everything to make it a better place. But it is sad to have to say it. A good majority of cons today are only shitheads, anyway. Filthy smackheads. They're mugging old grannies to get their next fix. To me, they should be in a dungeon with fuck all. Because they are scum. They give Christians a bad name. What is the code of honour, the morals, the self-respect? The scum would have crawled around that white line and licked the screw's arse for a gram of smack. And Alan Lord lost his freedom for you maggots! It really does sicken me, but that is how it is.

Strangeways to me will always be what it was. It is only a matter of time 'til it falls back into the hole of evil. And with today's cons, it is all it deserves.

As the van rolled out of the gate I thought, 'Why, God? Why did I miss that riot? Am I destined to be unlucky?'

I will give HM Prison Strangeways 3/10, just because it robbed me of the riot!

HM PRISON WAKEFIELD

This image is an extract from The Millennium Map™ © getmapping.com plc

LOCATION:	Wakefield, West Yorkshire.
CAPACITY:	700 beds.
CATEGORY AT PRESENT:	High-Security – Male.
OPENED:	1849.
HISTORY:	Housed local heroes until 1945 when it became a training prison. All that changed when, in 1975, it became a high-security dispersal prison. The majority of prisoners are lifers, some of who have committed the gravest of sexual crimes. Look at the aerial photo and you'll see that there are four wings, one of which houses an assessment centre for the 'Sex Offender

Treatment Programme'. I mean, they honestly think that they can cure a sex offender! And Bronson can fly! A cured sex offender is a dead sex offender.

I first hit here, 'Monster Mansion', back in 1974. Since then, I have been back a dozen times, if not more, and every time to their F Block. I last visited there in 2003 and, as I write the finishing touches to this book, I am still here. No doubt, though, I'll be off on my tours once again, so don't go writing to me here until you've checked my address out on my official website, mentioned at the end of this book.

Let me first describe their cage. It is a cell with two doors, first one door and then behind that a second door, a caged door. The outside door is solid steel. The inner door is an iron gate with a steel mesh on it and a feeding hatch in the bottom. We are fed like beasts in a zoo. Shoes are kept outside the door. We wear a green-and-yellow boiler suit, called a 'Canary Suit' for obvious reasons. Our life is spent, twenty-three hours a day, caged up. You come out for your one hour in the yard, alone. Never less than eight screws wait for the unlocking of the inner door. Some days there are more than eight screws and some days there's a dog, too.

It is the end of the world. You can't go in deeper. This is the belly of the beast! The bowels of hell. This is living in hell. I don't mean that the screws beat you up 'cos this lot in here at the time of writing seem to have left old Bronco alone; can't understand why.

Just because you're not being beaten up doesn't mean that it is a cushy place, you've also got mental cruelty. You look around for things to occupy your mind. You might find a loose button and start to flick it in the air with your thumb, you count how long it stays up for and catch it, but when I've done this in the past, the screws soon cotton on and stamp on it, smashing it to pieces. Anything to stop you using your mind is a bonus to some of them, but you still get the odd gentleman screw, they know who they are.

I spent my time being as mentally creative as possible, anything to keep my mind active. I would train spiders and cockroaches. Now, a spider is a real predator, go to poke them and watch the brave ones rear up to defend themselves. You learn a lot from these things.

You wouldn't think that spiders and insects could learn things; you wouldn't believe that they could be taught, but with time and patience they can be taught many things. I had the time to teach them new things and to keep them occupied, which in turn fed my need to be kept mentally active.

An insect's reflective and inbuilt behaviour can be learned and then used to train them. The secret is this; don't try to teach them to think like a human, you have to think like them. Think like a spider. Think like a cockroach. You have to think 'survival' and think small. In such surroundings, a spider can become a great friend. I had a special one which I called Harry, naturally. Have you ever seen a spider stranded in a bath? He can't climb out 'cos the surface is too slippery. I've heard that people actually buy 'spider ladders' so that the stranded spider can climb out of the bath ... great thinking.

Well, if you use the fact that a spider avoids shiny surfaces, then you can determine where he/she will walk or climb. Now you are starting to think like a spider, see. A spider will not 'web down' on a full stomach, but it will in the evening. So you can start to build on this knowledge.

I had Harry trained to go into his little hideaway when I tapped twice. When I heard the cell door being opened, I would tap on the floor or wall next to him and he'd be off scurrying in to his hole. It took a little while; I'd first set out by tapping and then pushing him in the direction of the hole. The pushing made him fear for his safety so he would be off and, eventually, to avoid being pushed, he would be off as soon as he heard those two taps.

I even trained cockroaches to follow a pre-defined path I'd marked out. The secret is to know how a cockroach thinks. He thinks in terms of safety; he knows that if he's on a light-coloured surface that he's going to be found, so he stays on the dark-coloured surface, whenever he can. So if you mark out a dark-coloured road for him on a shiny surface then he sticks to the dark road. I'd create a dark road by dragging the heal of my boot over the ground, causing a black, dull trail. At mealtimes, I'd put morsels of food down at the end of the black trail and watch them follow the leader to the food. I guess that's enough spider and cockroach training – just because it helped keep me sane, I don't expect you to do it.

Wakefield Prison holds 700 lifers, and it is heaving full to the rafters with sex cases and killers of kids. So, in a sense, it is good I am in a cage and no part of that place. You know when you were a child and, maybe, you believed that monsters existed and lurked about waiting to jump out of the dark and get you, well ... monsters do exist. As they live in Monster Mansion.

The mansion houses the likes of Robert Black, Michael Stone (not the former UFF hitman from Ireland), Howard Hughes (you all remember that bastard with the little girl in Rhyl, he took her out of a tent and killed her), and Duffy the Railway Rapist killer. They are all up there, you can smell the beasts, it reeks of monsters.

Serial sex attackers, old lady rapists and child-killers, they are all there. All under one evil roof. Victor Miller. This piece of shit raped and killed a boy and sexually assaulted twenty-eight others. He has got a colour remote-control TV in his cell. Oh yes, only the best for the worst.

I get a piss pot, and they get spoilt silly. Wakefield is always known as a Monsters' Paradise. Hundreds of them. The prison is also giving out condoms to homosexuals. Can you make this shit up? It is for health and safety, to stop the spread of AIDS. When I took Phil Danielson hostage in Hull Prison, he had previously criticised my art as targeting gays. Well, if that is to be taken in context, then maybe Phil should have a word with Wakefield Prison bosses over this, as they are perpetuating the fact that gays are spreading AIDS. I've got nothing against gays, but when they try and force me to be part of their world then they had better watch out. Just as if a man forces himself on to a woman then he, too, should watch out.

So all these sex killers are humping each other and having a bloody party, while Bronson rots in a cage and is fed under the door as though I am the mad dog with rabies. Somebody tell me I am dreaming it.

Wakefield has had its fair share of murders – Bob Maudsley killed two cons in one day; Tony McUlloch killed a con; John Patton killed a second con. All in all, I would say there have been a good ten murders in the last 30 years there.

I remember when Colin Robinson steamed into a paedophile with a blade, that was in the 1970s. Fuck me, he cut him to bits. The guy lost five pints of blood before they got him sewn up. His face was like King's Cross Station. Awesome! A screw saved him by holding his neck together.

Only recently, the monster who killed little Sarah Payne got stabbed up. That was nice. Let us hope he gets some more of that. Next it will be someone doing his eyes like the ripper had his done.

That was funny when fat Joe Purkuss took a monster hostage. He demanded a six-pack of beer and a box of crisps or he would cut his throat. True to his word, he cut the throat! Ha.

Another time, big Steve Lannigan, a Manchester lad serving life, took a work screw hostage. For that, he got sent to Broadmoor. That was twenty-five years ago. Steve is still inside.

There used to be some sensible screws in Wakefield. Nowadays, they are mostly hobbits. Over-paid and under-worked. But who knows, the odd good one might be lurking about waiting to give Bronco an easy time.

I personally feel the place is now a joke, and giving condoms to sex monsters is like giving me a shotgun. I am a robber; I use a shotgun as a weapon of my trade. They are sex cases. Work it out; what do they use to help them commit a crime?

It is fucking sick and a disgrace. And, you, the taxpayers are buying them condoms, and their TV sets and their nice gyms and nice cosy cells with carpets and curtains.

Who is fucking mad now? And you let me rot in a cage with sod all. But the bigger joke is, they are never to be freed, but I am. So shouldn't I be getting the soft touch, a taste of the rehabilitation? Look, face facts, what good are they? Why not just exterminate the filth?

One sure fact is ... I am no danger to your kids or your old grandmother. And I am not going to climb in your house and nick your TV set or mug your old mam. But it is me who they call a danger to society. I had reports that people were slagging me off on a website guest book, saying they wouldn't want me as a neighbour. Well, I just hope they don't have kids and end up with a sex monster living next-door to them 'cos they'll wish they had me on the other side of them, but maybe when it's too late!

Wakefield is a joke, with double standards. Stuff your condoms up your arses. I mean, this story may help you understand my anger. A screw from Wakefield Prison was jailed in April 2003 for twenty-eight days after he sent sexually explicit material to the husband of his former lover.

The screw, Terry Armstrong, from Monk Bertton near Barnsley, admitted breaching a court order restraining him from contacting the woman or her family. Armstrong scrawled graffiti on walls and a motorway bridge at Higham, near Barnsley after the five-year affair ended, but just over a month after that court appearance, Armstrong sent a sex-aid catalogue to the woman's husband. Wonder if it had any blow-up dolls in it?

I will give HM Prison Wakefield 0/10.

PS. It wasn't like that when Principal Officer O'Hagan was up there. He would have told the Governor what to do with his condoms. Nowadays, screws will lick arse to get up the ladder of success.

HM PRISON WALTON (LIVERPOOL)

This image is an extract from The Millennium Map™ © getmapping.com plc

LOCATION:	Walton, Liverpool.
CAPACITY:	1,600 beds.
CATEGORY AT PRESENT:	Local and Remand – Male.
OPENED:	1855.
HISTORY:	Replaced an even older prison in Liverpool. During World War II, Hitler saw fit to bomb the prison; pity he didn't destroy it all. The aerial shot shows the extensive buildings within the grounds.

It was back in 1974 I first landed here. Well, I tell a lie. I actually first went there in 1970, but that was to visit a friend. This is another prison that has had its name bastardised by the cons. Officially the place is called 'HM Prison Liverpool', but us cons have worked for many years at giving it its real name of 'Walton'.

When I hit there in 1974, the Christmas Number One single was Mudd's 'Lonely This Christmas' ... and by God was it!

This is another big old Victorian prison; in fact, it shares the last execution with Strangeways. They hanged two on the same day simultaneously at Strangeways and at Walton, and after that, hanging was abolished. The Moors Monsters, Brady and Hindley, just missed out! Although I think Hindley went the best way possible, nice and slow and done to a crisp ... anyone for toast?

The prison was infested with rats and cockroaches. It's also one of the old jails that has got five landings, so it is quite tall. I should know better than most how tall it is, as in the summer of 1985, I spent a glorious week up on their roof.

It's a tough old place with old-time rules and a strict regime. But the Scousers are a good-humoured bunch so they just laugh if off. They're just old characters in Walton.

Some of the old screws are a funny lot, witty and jokers. I recall one old screw used to keep a bag of hard-boiled sweets under his hat. He often used to give the cons one.

Another one, they used to call 'Mr G' – I don't know why – but he had been there forty years and in all that time he had never once kicked any con. He used to tell all the old stories of days gone by. I used to tell him, 'Write a fucking book, it would be a number-one bestseller.'

But, sadly, in all jails there are the Gestapo rats with the sliced peak hats and studded boots and Walton was no exception. And that is why I tore their lovely roof off.

The bashing they gave me! My tearaway exploits cost prison HQ a quarter of a million pounds. It cost me more time but it was worth it just to look back on such a victory.

The food in Walton is shit; total and utter shit. Even the drinking water tastes like river filth. The cells are spacious, the good old type of cells. Long and roomy. I believe now they have got toilets and sinks in, but not in my time they didn't. It was all piss pots and slopping out. And jugs and bowls of water. One bath a week.

I remember one morning, I slung a pot of shit all over two screws. Why? Well why not? I just felt like it. They were two dogs anyway.

Always making trouble for us cons. So I shut them up. All the cons cheered. I got a bloody good doing over for that. Yeah, good old days.

Liverpool Prison still speaks of when the cat went missing. It was a big chubby brown cat that all the cons loved to watch through their cell bars when it pounced on rats. The cat was the best rat-catcher in any prison. Cons idolised that cat and some would even give it their rations of milk. Then, mysteriously, the cat disappeared and nobody saw it for ages.

Word went around that a big fat rat had killed it. Rumours had it that a screw's dog killed it or even old age had crept upon it. But nobody knew the real truth until the boxer Paul Sykes walked out of his cell with a Davey Crocket hat on! I don't know if he'd killed and skinned it, but he had it on his head. This story is still being told now.

There was an old picture house in one of the old workshops where they used to show films. It even had an upstairs balcony. We got a film once a week in those days. There was no TV then. It was a movie projector on a big screen. I saw the film *The Magnificent Seven* there, it was brilliant.

During weekdays, we would wear overalls and T-shirts. At weekends we wore what were called 'Greys' – jacket, grey itchy trousers and a cotton striped shirt. You had to wear them, otherwise you were nicked!

There was no gym either. I hear Walton has all changed now. Not before time. But to me, it will always be a shit life. But I will say this much, I really have no bitterness. I actually had some laughs in that place. And let's be truthful, I did have the last laugh when I ripped the place apart.

I will give HM Prison Walton 5/10. Not bad, eh?

HM PRISON WANDSWORTH

This image is an extract from The Millennium Map™ © getmapping.com plc

LOCATION:	Wandsworth, London.
CAPACITY:	1,400 beds.
CATEGORY AT PRESENT:	Local – Male.
OPENED:	1851.
HISTORY:	Originally the County Jail, look at the aerial shot and study the typical radial design; see the wings looking like the arms of a giant windmill. You can also see some separate buildings that were once used to house females; they now house what are called VPs – Vulnerable Prisoners – who are at risk of violence from other prisoners.

When Wandsworth Prison opened in 1851, it was called 'The Surrey House of Correction'. It was another one built on the panopticon design, which allowed for 700 prisoners to have a cell of their own and a toilet of their own, yet all that vanished and it reverted to slopping out piss pots.

The slopping out started in 1870 when the toilets were removed from the cells to make room for extra prisoners. Slopping out came in and stayed until 1996. All for the sake of cramming in more prisoners!

The execution duties were transferred to Wandsworth Prison when Horsemonger Lane Gaol closed in 1878. And again, like all hanging prisons, an execution shed was built in one of the yards and it housed the hanging tackle. From 1878 to 1961, 135 prisoners were to be put to death by hanging. 134 men and one woman.

The hanging shed was dubbed 'The Cold Meat Shed', which remained until 1916, when, like all hanging prisons, the facilities were moved indoors into the cell area where a new facility was constructed within the prison.

Would you believe that this evil lot of bastards kept the gallows there until 1992 just because the death penalty was still a theoretical possibility for the crimes of treason, piracy with violence, mutiny in the armed forces and arson in a naval shipyard. They even tested the gallows every six months, probably with 'Old Bill' right up until 1992. Finally, the gallows were dismantled and transferred to the Prison Service Museum at Rugby. They just can't lay off it, can they? And the old execution chamber ... it's used by cons as a TV room!

William Marwood carried out the first execution at Wandsworth on 8 October 1878 when he hanged Thomas Smithers, 31, for the murder of his wife.

The first woman, and only woman, to be hanged at Wandsworth Prison was Kate Webster in 1879 for the brutal murder of her mistress.

The introduction of the Treachery Act of 1945 stated that: 'If, with intent to help the enemy, any person does, or attempts or conspires with any other person to do any act which is designed or likely to give assistance to the naval, military or air operations of the enemy, to impede such operations of His Majesty's forces, or to endanger life, shall be guilty of felony and shall on conviction suffer death.'

This Act was responsible for the hangings of nine men at Wandsworth. But one of the more bizarre Acts brought into play was the

Treason Act of 1351, which was responsible for John Amery facing treason charges. He was hanged on Wednesday, 19 December 1945.

One of the more infamous characters of the Second World War was the man dubbed 'Lord Haw Haw'. The owner of the voice that became so familiar was William Joyce (1906–1946), a Native American, brought up in Galway, Eire, who had taken up German citizenship during the Second World War before leaving England with a fraudulently obtained passport.

Joyce was born of an Irish father and an English mother in the United States in 1906. He went to Ireland with his parents in 1909, was educated at Catholic schools, and was brought up in a household that was fervently loyal to the British Crown.

For his pro-British stance, his father suffered having much of his property burned in the Irish rebellion of 1916. Maybe this is what gave William the impetus to go against these ideologies.

As the situation in Ireland worsened, young William sought revenge by becoming a youthful informer for the paramilitary auxiliaries, the hated 'Black and Tans'.

By 1921, Michael Joyce took his family to England. William, although not yet 16, joined the regular Army; he gave his age as 18, explaining that he had never been issued with a birth certificate. His army career, however, was short-lived; his real age was discovered when he was admitted to hospital with rheumatic fever and he was discharged after serving only four months. Joyce, being a fighter, made his way back and, in 1923, he entered London University, where he joined the Officer Training Corps.

A year later, he became involved in the embryonic British Fascist movement. In October 1924, during a scuffle with what he later called 'Jewish Communists' at the Lambeth Baths Hall in south-east London, someone tried to cut his throat with a razor. The woollen scarf around Joyce's neck saved his life, but he was slashed across the right cheek from the corner of his mouth to behind his ear, leaving a scar that marred his once handsome features and gave him a rather sinister appearance that enhanced his tough reputation on the political platform.

By the early 1930s, Joyce was heavily involved with the British Union of Fascists, led by Sir Oswald Mosley. But the Fascist cause made little headway in Great Britain and, in 1939, as the clouds of war gathered, Joyce and his second wife, Margaret, emigrated to Germany.

Out of admiration for Hitler, Joyce founded the British National Socialist Party. He fled to Germany before the start of the war in August 1939 and was eventually employed by the Nazi regime in their propaganda war on Britain. The Joyces arrived in Berlin, with British passports, on 27 August 1939. Four days later, Germany invaded Poland. It was then that Joyce received a shock. A friend told him that if war broke out between Great Britain and Germany, he and his wife would be separated and interned!

Joyce tried to leave Germany but a bizarre set of circumstances meant he couldn't use German currency to buy tickets for travelling outside Germany – the Joyces stayed in Germany and eventually William and Margaret Joyce worked for the German Radio Corporation.

Lord Haw-Haw was the name given to Joyce by the *Daily Express* newspaper when referring to a journalist that had written: 'A gent I'd like to meet is moaning periodically from Zeesen [one of the main German transmitters]. He speaks English of the haw-haw, dammit-get-out-of-my-way variety, and his strong suit is gentlemanly indignation.'

And so Lord Haw-Haw he became to the millions of Britons who, anxious for news of the war, tuned in to German radio broadcasts. The voice of Haw-Haw became the most hated voice to come out of Germany, but his was also one of the most fascinating. The legacy of a broken nose, as the result of a childhood fight in Eire, gave him a unique twang. He would pronounce the word Germany with a peculiar intonation so that it sounded more like 'Jairmany' – this became the identifying trademark of his upper-class drawl.

The British authorities became worried about Joyce's contribution to the German propaganda effort. He was clever; often enquiring about the welfare of British personalities. Lord Haw-Haw made his last broadcast to Britain on 30 April 1945, the day Hitler is alleged to have committed suicide. 'Britain's victories are barren. They leave her poor and they leave her people hungry. They leave her bereft of the markets and the wealth that she possessed six years ago. But, above all, they leave her with an immensely greater problem than she had then. We are nearing the end of one phase in Europe's history, but the next will be no happier. It will be grimmer, harder and perhaps bloodier. And now I ask you earnestly, can Britain survive? I am profoundly convinced that without German help she cannot.'

Tentative plans had been laid to smuggle the Joyces out of Germany by Josef Goebbels, the German Propaganda Minister, but Goebbels died in Berlin and the plans came to nothing. They tried to escape to Sweden via Denmark, but Allied forces had landed ahead of them and they were forced to turn back. The end of the war found them in the village of Kupfermuhle, near the Danish border. Their apartment was visited several times by British soldiers, who took them for an ordinary German couple and showed no interest in them.

Joyce was out walking one morning, soon after Germany's capitulation, in the woods. He stumbled upon two British officers who were gathering wood for a fire. He spoke to them in French and walked on. Their suspicions aroused, the officers followed him. One of them, Lieutenant Perry, an interpreter, called out, 'You wouldn't happen to be William Joyce, would you?' Reaching into an inside pocket for his German passport, Joyce looked to be reaching for a weapon. Perry fired his revolver. The bullet passed through both of Joyce's thighs and he fell to the ground.

He was taken to Luneburg, where he spent time in hospital recovering from his wounds, and then to Brussels, where he was detained while the British Parliament hurriedly passed the The Treason Act 1945, which made treachery a capital offence. This was obviously done in readiness for Joyce's trial.

On 16 June, he was flown to London and taken to Brixton Prison. His trial began at the Old Bailey on 17 September 1945. It was a complex business; much hinged on Joyce's possession of a British passport, which as you will recall was obtained by fraudulent means, and his allegiance to the Crown.

His defence argued that, as an American citizen, he owed no allegiance to the Crown and therefore was not guilty of treason. The prosecution's argument was that, as a British passport-holder, he did owe this allegiance. The outcome was never seriously in doubt, and no one showed much surprise when the jury, after only twenty-three minutes, found him guilty of high treason.

His appeal was dismissed on 1 November 1945 and Albert Pierrepoint hanged him at Wandsworth Prison on Thursday, 3 January 1946. The following day, the last execution for treason in the UK took place at Pentonville Prison, that of Theodore Schurch.

To the end, Joyce remained unrepentant. After the execution, Margaret Joyce was interned in Germany while her status was debated.

She died in London in 1972, having regained her British nationality.

Even though there was solid evidence against Margaret (Lady Haw-Haw) to convict her of High Treason by virtue of the fact that she had acted as assistant treasurer to her husband's National Socialist League, in reality, she, too, was a German citizen. Although born in Manchester, England, she relinquished her British citizenship when moving to Germany.

Joyce's daughter, Mrs Heather Iandolo, a schoolteacher from Gillingham, England, fought successfully to have her father's body exhumed from the cemetery at Wandsworth Prison and buried in Eire.

The conclusion to this story could be that argued that because Joyce was not a legitimate British subject, he could therefore not have been tried for treason. If the trial were to have taken place today, maybe the outcome would have been 'not guilty'.

There have been many killers dubbed 'The Acid Bath Murderer', but the original was John George Haigh, 39. Haigh shot three men and three women to death between 1944 and 1949, all for financial gain, disposing of the bodies by dissolving them in sulphuric acid which quite quickly reduced them to a liquid sludge that he could pour down the drain.

Another famous name was hanged at Wandsworth Prison by Albert Pierrepoint – Derek Bentley, who was hanged on Wednesday, 28 January 1953 for his part in the well documented armed robbery which resulted in the shooting dead of PC Sidney Miles.

Eventually, Derek Bentley was finally granted a well-deserved posthumous pardon in 1998.

The only other teenager to be hanged at Wandsworth was Francis 'Flossy' Forsyth who was dispatched through the gallows trapdoor by Harry Allen on 10 November 1960. You hear about gangs of youths running around assaulting people today; well, it happened just as often back in the 1960s. This is how Forsyth came to be hanged, having been part of a gang that attacked and kicked a twenty-three-year-old man to death in a motiveless and vicious attack. One of the other gang members, Norman James Harris, was also convicted of capital murder and, while hangman Robert Stewart hanged Harris at Pentonville, simultaneously, Forsyth was being executed at Wandsworth.

The last man to be hanged at Wandsworth on 8 September 1961 was Hendrick Neimasz, 49, who had been convicted at Lewes Assizes of a double murder.

This is only one of only a few prisons in the English penal system that uses a PO Box address, and are you aware that cons are not supposed to write to PO Box addresses ... not allowed. Yet if you write to a fellow con, which you are allowed, and you write to Wandsworth, then you are breaching prison rules! What a backward system.

I first hit Wandsworth back in 1975. And make no bones about it, it was the toughest jail in Britain. Hard and ruthless, just like the screws. All these hanging prisons seemed to have the same case-hardened screws working in them. The day after I arrived there, I attacked three screws, so my start there was a bad one. A week later, I dived on the Governor and tried to rip his throat out. I just never liked him.

The prison was the last one to remove its gallows, and it was fortunate for one of the prison officers that it was removed and the death penalty for murder abolished. It would have been handy for a prison officer from Crystal Palace who was found guilty of killing a homosexual man by kicking his head in and then, just to make sure he was dead, he put a plastic bag over the victim's head.

The screw, Francis Kavanagh, had been out for the night with other warders from Wandsworth Prison on the night of the killing, four days before Christmas of 2001. Kavanagh was found guilty of murder when the court heard how he flew into a rage after heavily-built homosexual Michael Smith tried to 'touch him up' in a bar near Wandsworth Prison.

But, sometimes, I wonder if he didn't bring it on himself ... Kavanagh had planned to go to a 'school disco' themed night in the West End dressed as a schoolboy! But he violently kicked his fifty-eight-year-old victim with heavy work boots after having an encounter with him.

Kavanagh left the County Arms pub to go to a nearby friend's house to change into shorts for the disco. This is when the victim was seen leaving the pub at 8.30pm to go to his nearby home, and this is when two of Kavanagh's work pals then saw the defendant run towards the block of flats, shortly after that the touchy-feely encounter took place between Kavanagh and Keith Smith. Half-an-hour later, Kavanagh turned up at the pub and continued drinking like a fish.

Wandsworth hanged more murderers than any other jail in Britain. Some should never have swung. The likes of Derek Bentley – that was a disgrace. A public shame. They murdered that boy for nothing. And Craig, the lad who shot the copper dead, he served just ten years and was freed. It shows what a fucking bunch of slags the whole system is. It is so corrupt, it is insane.

The big house, this cesspit of a place, once housed up to 2,000 cons under one roof – awesome ... amazing ... fucking electrifying.

It was 1990, I almost tore that roof off but I got stuck in the wire. What a disaster! What started it off was my Uncle Jack Cronin's funeral in Luton. And the pigs stopped me from going to it. So I made a vow to myself, 'You'll pay for that insult.' I made the climb up ... and got trapped. Such is life. Back in the box. Back to darkness.

Wandsworth is the jail Ronnie Biggs escaped from all those years ago. And what an escape it was, they never did forgive him for that, even now in his old age and close to death, they punish him for it, and show him no respect or compassion as he lies in desperate hope. There's a fight on by Ronnie's son, Michael, to get him released early. I mean, you don't need him banged up the way he is. He's s sick man, but the Home Office holds him as a trophy. This is how heartless they are, a wicked bunch of bastards!

In the last three decades, I have been back there about twenty times. Each stay is short, and I am kept in solitary. I have not actually been back since 1994, as for a time it stopped accepting Cat 'A's. But I believe they do now, so no doubt, in time, I will pass through again; I can't wait. Wandsworth is what it is – a prison. All the screws are what they are – screws. And everybody knows where they are. There is no shit, no falseness; it is a man's jail.

But the seg block has always been hard. More punishments have been dished out there than in any block in the county. The worst I had was back in 1977, and believe me, that was some set to between us. My body was black and blue from head to toe.

I lost over two years' remission in that place in the 1970s. That's the equivalent of a five-year sentence with a bit of parole.

That place cost me a lot of years; it also pushed me over the edge. I even attacked a doctor. Take my advice, never do this; it is like attacking a god. You will suffer afterwards, believe me. And in the seventies, it meant injections.

You can't beat tranquillisers, they can knock an elephant out, they can put a tiger on its knees, so we have no chance.

Violence in this place was a regular issue. Plenty of it. I punched my way through that place. I got so bad, I enjoyed it. And I can hit so hard with a table leg, I swear I thought I killed him. It was the way he fell. His eyes. The way his body landed. I must admit, I panicked, as it was bang on top.

I also had a pop at escaping, but I have been so unlucky at that. I am just not meant to go over the wall; if I had, I would have gone a long time ago.

I met some great guys in this place, 'proper' cons, such as Frank Fraser. I first met Frank in 1975; what a legend. A top man in my book. I also met George Wilkinson there. Who? Yeah, you may well ask. George (RIP) was a giant of man, a Geordie from up north. I rate this man as the most dangerous man ever to walk the prison yard. Forget your Frank Mitchell look-a-likes.

The screws feared George so much that they used to panic and steam into him first. There were always ten on him and with sticks. George took the screws hostage; he also used a lot of violence.

It was 1979 when they drove him out of Strangeways on a journey to Walton. He was, mysteriously, dead on arrival. One of prison's mystery deaths. Read a book called *Frightened for My Life* by Geoff Cugan, it will explain about George's death.

I admired George, as he was fearless, a big man, over 6ft and 19st, a natural strong man. I once met his mother, a small, brave lady. George idolised her and she loved him, too. A bloody sad end.

It was in this jail I cut John Fielding right down his ugly boat. Dirty fucking rat! It was this piece of shit who grassed my escape up to the screws. You won't miss him if you face him. He's got a Mars Bar (scar) from his right eye all the way to his neck. I am just sorry I never ripped his eyes out. I could have gone over the wall if it hadn't been for him. Slag!

Wandsworth is an institution. It's the flagship of all prisons. It will never change its image, too much has gone on there over the last 100 years for it to ever be forgotten. Executions of innocent men, escapes, murders, violence, corruption, brutality, hunger-strikes.

I remember back in 1977, three cons raped one con, a gang-bang in a cell. The poor chap had to have stitches in his arse; he later had a breakdown and tried to end it all. That is Wandsworth in a nutshell – brutal.

It was there I dived on a guard dog just for the fun of it ... that dog bottled it. So did the dog-handler.

It was also there I nicked a big urn of porridge and barricaded up with it ... so the cons couldn't have any. Great days. Funny. Crazy memories. Legendary!

But through all the hell, there were also decent screws like Mr Wells, a PO down on E Wing seg unit. He was a gentleman, a very fair man, a rare breed in that place. I would say to anybody, when you meet a decent screw, 'Respect', because it is in your favour. One day, he may stop you falling into the bottomless hole of emptiness, or from being pushed in.

I will give HM Prison Wandsworth 5/10, just for the sake of Mr Wells. Not bad for such a hell-hole.

Wandsworth 1945 – had not changed right up to when I first visited in 1975

HMYOI AND JUVENILE CENTRE WERRINGTON

This image is an extract from The Millennium Map™ © getmapping.com plc

LOCATION:	Stoke-on-Trent, Staffordshire.
CAPACITY:	110 beds.
CATEGORY AT PRESENT:	Closed YOI (Young Offenders Institution) – Male.
OPENED:	1895.
HISTORY:	Werrington House originally started out as an Industrial School and then, in 1955, it became part of the big system when the Prison Commissioners took it over. In 1957, it became a DT (Detention Centre) and then, in 1985, it became a Youth Custody Centre and changed to a YOI in 1988.

I landed at Werrington back in 1970 with my best pal John Bristow. It's a detention centre that I was in thirty-four years ago ... it sort of makes me look an old git. All our yesterdays ...

Anyway, John and I were sent there for three months. This gaff was run like a military jail. Hard ... spit and polish ... but it was fair.

We all knew where we stood. Step out of line and it was a war zone. The routine was a strict regime with plenty of discipline, plenty of gym, plenty of hard work and plenty of hard whacks. And the food was brilliant. And lots of it. We were all in bed by 8.00pm! And up at 6.00am to the shout of, 'Hands off cocks, on with socks.'

Those were the places you went in as boys and come out as men. You walked in and marched out.

I have got some good memories of Werrington House. But as hard as it was, it did nothing to deter me from a life of crime. It just made me a stronger man. More determined. It was called a 'short, sharp shock', but it just didn't work. The only thing it shocked was your senses; it exploded any grasp of what good order and discipline was all about. It showed that you got what you wanted by violent means.

There was a screw in Werrington House called Mr King; he was a right bastard. A big man, a hard man. I believe he was ex-Forces. For three months, he really put me through it.

But on my day of freedom, he stuck his hand out and said, 'Good luck.' He meant it, too! I shook his hand and said, 'You old bastard.'

I now look back on those three months, and screws like Mr King, and feel a bit proud of that time. But believe me now, it can never work. How can it work? But I had some lovely memories. Hell, I had one of my best ever fights there. It was in the boot room, a proper fist fight – toe to toe! This fight went on for half-an-hour. It was with a Taffy. Could he hit! If that Malcolm Price from Wales was bit younger, then I'd swear it was him, but he didn't go to prison until he was in his twenties, so it must have been someone else.

We were young, and full of it. At that age, we were invincible, or so we thought. It is only with time that those sorts of fights take their toll. Ask Ali how he felt over his classic three fights with Joe Frazier.

Werrington House for me played a big part in my strict self-discipline that has pushed me through such bad times in my life. I really do believe that.

I will give HMYOI and Juvenile Detention Centre Werrington House 8/10. That isn't bad, is it, for a short, sharp shock that was supposed to cure me? It fucking turned me into a raving lunatic!

HM PRISON WHITEMOOR

This image is an extract from The Millennium Map™ © getmapping.com plc

LOCATION:	March, Cambridgeshire.
CAPACITY:	600 beds.
CATEGORY AT PRESENT:	High–Security – Male.
OPENED:	1991.
HISTORY:	This prison occupies a massive site of 90 acres and is state-of-the-art max-secure. All the top geezers have been here, the majority being mandatory lifers with tariffs of over twenty-five years and even up to thirty years. In 1994, a mass breakout resulted in a prison officer being shot.

This is another of the maximum-secure jails and, believe me, one of the maddest places ever. It is so mad, it is unreal.

I first went in there in the 1990s. But it was the first of many times I had landed, each time only to be dragged into the madness.

Whitemoor takes a lot of the Cat 'A' and the high-risk prisoners. I suppose it became infamous over its IRA breakout when five members of the IRA and one Londoner had it over the wall, only to be caught in the area.

Strangely enough, one of the IRA men, Liam McOtter, I smashed over the head some years earlier in Brixton Prison, but it turned out he was a diamond.

Whitemoor must have had more riots than Alcatraz. After the Parkhurst escape in the early 1990s when three cons had it away, but couldn't get off the island, Parkhurst closed down on taking any more Category 'A' and it became a Category 'B' jail.

So all of us Category 'A' cons were shipped to Whitemoor and, believe me, it was Bedlam.

Whitemoor had to handle a lot of frustrated men, as they were happy being at Parkhurst. Now they had to start afresh there ... so it often blew up. Jails often have new ideas. Silly rules. And men are not machines.

We all have a routine, and when routines are smashed – trouble starts. Riots were on the cards. I would say the assaults on screws had to be the highest total of any jail.

Big Ferdi Lieveld was sent to trial over throwing a bucket of cooking oil all down a screw. The screw lost his ears and his face peeled off. Ferdi got a 'not guilty'. The screw was ex-Parkhurst.

Another time, Parnell stabbed three screws; he, too, got a 'not guilty'. Then Charlie McGee stabbed a couple of screws; it was like a war zone. Screws were getting cut up regularly. There were that many shit-ups that the place looked like a sewer. Ronnie Easterbrook was on a dirty protest for two solid years! Phew, where's the air freshener? Then Frank Quinn almost escaped again like he'd done up in Frankland.

I went on a hunger-strike over my art materials being taken away from me. I lasted for forty days, and almost lost 4st. That was long before this David Blaine guy went on TV to do his forty-four-day stint in a box over the Thames. Fuck me, that would have been a pleasure for me, just to see the sights, it would be worth going on hunger-strike again. And while I was doing it, I was in a set to with screws. Throw that into the pot, Blaine, and let a real man show you how to do it. I bet Blaine couldn't do a Bobby Sands.

All I lived on was water, tea and sugar for forty days. The same as Jesus did out in the wilderness. But I bet he had the odd rabbit. I had sweet FA while on the hunger protest; I was rushed twice by the MUFTI (riot squad) and smashed up.

On one of these incidents, when I was thirty days into the hunger-strike, I could barely stand up, I was so weak, and the cowardly scum had a go at me!

That sums those dogs up. It was stated later that I had attacked them! In the weak state I was in, I couldn't attack a bag of crisps properly.

While I was attacked, they left me in the box. My pal, Tony Crabb, climbed up a wall to protest about my treatment, and he, too, was punished for that!

It was a sad day when Dessy Cunningham hanged himself. That upset a lot of people. It was a great day when (Catweasel) Bailey got killed in his cell by two cons. He was a member of the paedophile gang who raped and killed Jason Swift, a young boy from London, along with his cronies, Sidney Cook and Smith.

The two cons who killed Catweasel strangled the fucker. They both, sadly, got life for it. They should have got a medal.

The food at HMP Shitemoor – er, sorry, HMP Whitemoor – is not bad. But it's filth in the seg block; they serve it up cold and it is a fact the screws take the best for themselves; they steal all the cakes and biscuits. You don't have to go on a hunger-strike here, you are starved anyway with the portions they give you.

Yeah, it has all happened in this place, I could write a book on it all. Female screws having sex with the cons! Screws bringing in drugs. Screws using steroids. You don't believe it? Check it out! Go to your library, dig out the stats! Why else are they sacked?

In March 2002, a screw, Andrew Hubbard, 39, from HM Prison Lewes in East Sussex, was jailed for seven years for operating a mini drugs supermarket behind bars. Doesn't that tell you enough? Complaints at Lewes Prison in 2001 led to eight warders being suspended, although they were brought back when assault allegations collapsed.

There are also screws bringing in porn. Some of these screws are sicker than the cons. They have a licence to do it. They hide behind the walls of shame. In all walks of life, there are those who weaken. And screws are no different. If you wipe a bundle of notes in their face ... two out of ten will snap it up.

Why do you think they are any different? Next, you would be saying there are no bent cops, or psychotic soldiers, or alcoholic royalty, or no perverts in religion. Prison is no different to any other way of life. It has got all the pressures and problems of any other walk of life, and there are more bullies than in any other form of life I know of. The Army has its fair share of bullies. Well, remember, a lot of screws are ex-Army, and many have been chucked out of the Army. I rest my case. That is why we know Whitemoor as 'Shitemoor.'

My forty-day hunger strike nearly killed me, so I will give HM Prison Whitemoor 0/10. Sorry, but it is a fair judgement.

HM PRISON WINCHESTER

This image is an extract from The Millennium Map™ © getmapping.com plc

LOCATION:	Romsey Road, Winchester.
CAPACITY:	425 beds.
CATEGORY AT PRESENT:	Local – Male and Female Annexe.
OPENED:	1846.
HISTORY:	Originally the County Jail. In 1964, a YO Remand Centre was built and, in 1992, it was changed for use by Category 'C' prisoners. In 1994, the Remand Centre became a unit for sentenced female prisoners.

I have landed at this prison a good eight to ten times from the 1970s to the 1980s. Only ever been here for short spells, a month at the most, and always in their seg block below A Wing.

To be fair, I only ever got one kicking here, but I have no complaint over that, as I gave as good as I got.

Basically, it is a good old jail; I had very few problems there. Once, I attempted to do a roof protest, but it was quickly stopped.

Another time, I attempted to grab a screw hostage and he broke free. So I barricaded up in the office, where I read my file. You should see the bloody damn lies they've written about me. After I read it, I even thought I was a nasty bastard. I actually thought, 'Is this really me? Or have they got me mixed up with Hannibal Lecter from *Silence of the Lambs*.' On paper, I was a monster; in reality, I am just a cuddly bear.

Another time, they rushed me and injected me; I never did find out why. They must have just thought I was about to explode.

In those days, in the 1970s, it was legal to inject us violent cons. I was injected that many times that my arse was starting to resemble a pin cushion.

But I have some lovely memories of Winchester and I met some decent old screws in that place. I also loved their cells. They always put me in the same cell, Number 3. It was just opposite the steps that lead up to the wing. My cell was a big one, with a high window, which only opened half-an-inch; it used to have dozens of pigeons roosting on my sill. Rats with wings, I call them.

That cell was my gym! My bed frame was my weights. My mattress was my punch bag. My table was for my dips. I'd get library books for my press-ups. Fuck me, did I train in that Number 3 cell. Sweat – buckets of it. Afterwards, I would just bang on my door 'til they let me out for a shower.

Every time I landed there, they gave me a brand-new piss pot, mug and jug. Most nights, about 10.00pm, I would sit on my potty in the back and have a lovely private crap. Just like a little boy on his pot. In the morning, I would march to the recess and shout out, 'Turds away,' and slop out down the sluice. Crazy days, but I enjoyed it all.

I would have a strip wash two or three times a day, plus a shower. I would brush my teeth ten times a day. Clean my boots. Anything to kill the boredom. Read, write, exercise. My life was for ever on the move to just another seg block. I saw nobody. Few ever saw me. But I enjoyed it.

Winchester, in a way, was a part of my making. It made me what I am today with its old regime and harsh ways but, truly, it beat all the soppy jails of today. Winchester was a proper man's jail. It smelt of man. It smelt of brotherhood. The noise was prison. Everything about it was jail. Not like the namby-pamby new jails of today.

Give me a piss pot and a jug of water any day, with my overalls, T-shirt and boots. Fuck all this Mothercare shit of today. Yeah, Winchester brings back some sweet memories, three decades of them. Oh yeah, the good old days. Hard, but sweet.

I will give HM Prison Winchester 8/10, just for old time's sake.

HM PRISON WINSON GREEN (BIRMINGHAM)

This image is an extract from The Millennium Map™ © getmapping.com plc

LOCATION:	Winson Green Road, Birmingham.
CAPACITY:	1,200 beds.
CATEGORY AT PRESENT:	Local and Training – Male.
OPENED:	1848.
HISTORY:	As with most of these Victorian prisons, it is located not too far away from the city centre (3 miles). During the course of this prison's operation, it has maintained a steady role in serving the locality and receiving prisoners from two Crown Courts and, occasionally, from other prisons.

Here's another jail that us cons have bastardised the name of. Officially, it is called 'HM Prison Birmingham', but we call it the 'Green', thus Winson Green. One of the all-time hard jails. A tough city centre jail, full up with all sorts of felons from shoplifting to mass killers.

Talking of mass killers, I was two cells away from one of the murdering duo of Fred and Rose West. As many of you all know, Fred topped himself before he could be tried for the Cromwell Street murders.

It was really fate that he topped himself, because in time someone would have done it for him. Fucking beast. I don't want to rattle on too much about it as I've already covered him in other books, but suffice to say I never gave him a minute of peace.

I never actually hit the Green until the mid-1980s; since then, I have passed through the prison half-a-dozen times. Each time, I have had some fun. One time, I grabbed a doctor hostage; now that was funny. Well, not for him.

I was then assaulted by some sixty screws who were all caught on prison CCTV; this footage was included in my video documentary *Sincerely Yours*, but the then Home Secretary, Jack Straw, threw a wobbler and had it pulled by order of the High Court. Thus any evidence of these nice prison officers assaulting me with two-handed punches and kicks to my body are well hidden away from the Human Rights lobbyists. Just keep on fighting for the likes of Sutcliffe and Brady ... what do I care?

But my best time there was when I nicked the murderer and hostage-taker Michael Sam's leg. Now *that* was funny.

The Green is a place of evil, make no mistake about it. And like all big jails, there are bad screws mixed with the decent screws. And I met them all there.

The best screw I ever met there was SO (Senior Officer) Woodhouse, an old chap in his late fifties, a big old bruiser. He had hands like shovels. He was just what he was. No shit with him. You got what you were entitled to and he made sure you got it. If you had an hour's visit due, you would get it. If you were due to get a boiled egg, you got it. If a tray of spuds were not cooked, he would send it back to the kitchen. By now he must be seventy years old and retired, but I respect screws like him – hard but fair.

When I first arrived there, they wanted me to wear some nonsense clothes. I ripped the lot up. So we did a deal; if I boxed it clever and got my head down, then they would not antagonise me. So we all made it work.

Sure, I had my ups and downs – who doesn't? – but if you were prepared to work on it, there was a solution. The Green, though, has been a bastard to many cons –Johnny Bowden got bashed to a pulp there; Barry Prosser was killed there. Loads got a good kicking there; it was part and parcel of the Green.

Look what they did to the Birmingham Six. Those six Irishmen were battered senseless by screws; even the cons were told to bash them up. But it turned out they were six innocent men! So how do you feel now, bashing them up? Fuck me, that was thirty years ago. Seems like last year to me. I knew them all. Two of the Birmingham Six, Paddy Hill and Johnny Walker, were good pals of mine. Proper nice chaps. It was insane even to think they could plant bombs and kill twenty-one people and injure scores more. It was fucking madness out of control. But the Green tortured them lads, beat them senseless.

There had been acts of evil behind those walls, and you don't know it 'til you have smelt it. But I have this strange belief you have to fight evil with evil to overcome it. You can bend it. Turn it around. I do ... and I enjoy it.

The Green, to me, was a process, a part of the journey. Fuck me, it is not nice to hear it, or see it. Like cons jumping off the top landing and dying, and they do that in the Green. There were a lot of sad endings there.

My pal's brother died there. My pal, Pat McCarthy, loved his brother, but he died in that Green. So did many decent lads. Some through depression and some mysteriously, to say the least.

But that's Winson Green – a hard prison. We are not sent there for a holiday. At least, not back then. Now it is a holiday. TV in your cell is supposed to be a punishment! I think they force you to watch three episodes of *EastEnders*! Personally, I would sooner be flogged than watch three episodes of that dross.

I suppose, if I add my stays up there, I must have spent a good eight to ten months of my life under that roof. And I did get to peep through Fred West's spy hole – or 'Judas hole', if we are to use the proper name. West looked like Benny out of the old *Crossroads* TV series.

And I did get to kick Sam's leg. And I did grab the doctor, if only for a few seconds. OK, and I did use a paedophile as a punch bag in the recess. I caught the fucker by accident as I was slopping out. He should never have even seen all my laundry, let alone been in the recess.

He was in such shock, his mouth dropped open but nothing came out. I suppose a bit like the three kids that he attacked; what goes around comes around, I guess. But it's a fucking liberty bruising your fists on scum like that. We should at least be supplied with prison-issue baseball bats. What are the European Human Rights for anyway?

I will give HM Prison Green 7/10. I just felt happy remembering that paedophile, I suppose.

HM PRISON WOODHILL

This image is an extract from The Millennium Map™ © getmapping.com plc

LOCATION:	Milton Keynes, Bedfordshire.
CAPACITY:	600 beds.
CATEGORY AT PRESENT:	Local, Remand and Category 'A' (SSU Unit) – Male.
OPENED:	1992.
HISTORY:	Constantly in the news relating to the poor regime. The Close Supervision Centre was opened in 1998 at a cost of £3m along with special units at HM Prisons Hull, Wakefield and Durham to hold about fifty of Britain's most potentially disruptive inmates, accused or convicted. With the upgrading of Wakefield's cages at a cost of many millions, this has resulted in some prisons' Secure Units closing down or becoming under-used.

What can I say about this place in the land of the concrete cows – Milton Keynes? This place has been both lucky and unlucky for me. I can go on and on about the bad times. The unit I was on is the most infamous of all the special units.

I spent three years there sleeping on a concrete slab, with no window to open and no fresh air. Even Lord Longford (bless his soul) raised a question in the House of Lords over my cell not having a window. What he meant to say was that my window didn't open. His questions got nowhere and my 'window' remained firmly closed ... summer and winter.

Woodhill Prison has been described as the British answer to Alcatraz Prison in the USA because of its austere conditions and strict code of discipline. Just like Alcatraz, it has a high-security jail within a jail, the SSU, and continues to house many violent and infamous prisoners, many of whom I've met or heard screaming.

The inmates kept in solitary confinement have their cells furnished with cardboard furniture and concrete beds, but if you're clever, like the prisoner Michael Sams who was jailed in 1993 for murder and kidnap, you can make money from the way prison loses your belongings. Sams was going to sue the prison for losing his paintings, which he said were worth £4,000, and for being placed in segregation. He was offered £3,500 to settle both claims.

Incidentally, I think my hostage-taking rubbed off on old Sams, as the one-legged prisoner had a further eight years added to his four life sentences for taking a probation officer hostage at Woodhill.

When you think about how little a screw earns, then it's no surprise to find most of them going on the sick; at times we were left neglected because of staff shortages due to them being off sick. If the screws don't want to work there, then think of us cons ... what is our life like then?

Some of the cells have CCTV cameras, and Ian Huntley, guilty of the Soham murders, had such a cell. The exercise yard is caged and topped with razor wire. When Category 'A' cons are housed in a prison, then you can guarantee that the court facilities in nearby towns and cities are upgraded to accommodate us in case we ever appear there. The courts in Milton Keynes now have bullet-proof glass installed ... I wonder why?

There are three units at Woodhill, all barren areas devoid of any sensory stimulation. Things like plants, pictures, murals or music are conspicuous by their absence. The normal exercise yard is a tarmac-covered bare cage. If you want to sit down, then you have to use the ground. Even the birds avoid this sterile place.

The experimental unit in D Wing closed down when the overly restrictive regime failed. Anyone kicking off with 'dirty protests' were slung into the 'pink room', which had under-floor drainage. The place was like any Nazi concentration camp – evil.

Even the Chief Inspector of Prisons condemned the prolonged isolation of inmates as posing a risk to their mental health. These cells were only unlocked in the presence of six screws in full riot gear, called a 'riot unlock'.

My time at Alcatraz – er, sorry ... Woodhill – was spent there in what is called 'basic' level. A Wing has cells furnished with a sink and toilet, a concrete plinth for a mattress, a cardboard table and chair, and a fixed mirror made of plastic – that's your lot. Mind you, they did allow you up to twelve photographs, and up to six library books a week. And, my, oh my, a dustpan and brush is issued on request.

For the normal cons, life begins in B Wing, which has sixteen cells on two landings, with a shower room and toilets on each level. The regime is supposed to allow about seventeen hours of what is called 'constructive activity', which for those lucky enough to mix with other cons includes time in an association room with a television, a table tennis table and cardboard and plastic tables and chairs.

Now if you are a real arse-licker then you can progress to the third unit, C Wing! This wing provides what is called an 'intervention programme' for a minimum of twenty hours a week. After that, if you survived being nice to the screws, you are supposed to be transferred to Monster Mansion (HMP Wakefield). Now can you see why I don't comply? And then if you lick some more arses, you are considered tame enough to be returned to the ordinary prison system.

A High Court ruling was responsible for D Wing closing down. After the then Home Secretary Michael Howard was responsible for the Special Therapeutic wing in Parkhurst Prison closing down, it was then that the special unit in HMP Woodhill opened. They hoped to be able to use a pioneering therapeutic approach to dealing with the most potentially disruptive prisoners. How the fuck they could think this, I just don't know.

The Special Therapeutic wing in Parkhurst was run by Dr Bob Johnson and, in the time he ran the place, violence had dropped by 90 per cent and the use of tranquillisers had dropped by the same. Then they go and close it and kick Dr Bob in the teeth!

So it was no surprise to find that in the first year of this unit at Woodhill opening, that there was a desperate need for the 'pink room' due to so many cons going on a dirty protest and refusing to co-operate. Since then, the regime at Woodhill has been the subject of repeated human rights challenges.

It was then decided that 'control and containment' should be the first priority of the Woodhill units, and it was even considered necessary to discuss whether guard dogs should be introduced.

Once, I managed to rush out of my cell and I smashed the unit up. The MUFTI squad, sixty riot screws, were called in to restrain me. Yes, sixty. I have had the riot screws come and get me off the yard after I was involved in a five-hour standoff in July 2000. I can go on and on about it all. But I am choosing to do the good thing because, you see, Woodhill helped me find my angels. Two beautiful angels came into my life from nowhere. It just came to me in January 2001, a brand-new year.

A mystery letter arrived from Saira Rehman. She wrote to me. Who was she? What was she? Who was little Sami? Then my brother John died, and it ripped me up. I was so low and depressed. Days later, Saira completed all the formalities and paperwork and eventually visited me. Then she brought her ten-year-old daughter, Sami, on a visit. Then, on 1 June 2001, on Saira's birthday, we married. It all happened in a few months. Now Sami is our girl. She is special to me, and calls me 'Dad' too! It is a love and joy that I long forgot about, it is a truly beautiful feeling to possess.

Then my wife Saira ... she just takes away all my pain and fills me with so much love. I am now full of love and faith. My wife has hair like black silk; her eyes are so deep I can swim inside them; her skin glows with love. Her smile lights up the sky and from her toes to her head is the body of an angel. Her movement is graceful. Her aroma is that of a flower. She is so gentle and loving. Her life, her journey has not been an easy ride. It has been full of pain and despair. But what we have is a true love that I have never experienced in my fifty-one years of being alive.

My whole life has changed for the better, I feel good inside, I even like myself better, my heart feels fresh, my dreams are alive. I have responsibilities, they both need me. Now I think more, I am more in control; I am a proper man, like any dad and husband out there.

So, some good does come out of prison, after all. It really is a miracle how it happened. One day I am in a hole grieving my brother John's death, and then I am on top of the mountains grabbing a rainbow.

Sure, it is fate telling me to be thoughtful and to slow down. It is now nearly three years since we have been married and my violence is coming to a stop. I no longer get urges to hurt people, neither do I dream of robbing banks.

Woodhill unit is no Butlin's holiday camp. It can be as cruel and lonely as the rest of the jails. But it sure saved my ass. Because I was on a journey to hell. Now I am first-class all the way to paradise. Singing all the way.

Only love can change a man's direction, nothing else. I mean, look at how Jimmy Boyle turned his life around, all because of a woman! Only love can cure a broken heart and fill you with hope. It is a miracle. But until the prison HQ can accept it and believe it, I remain in solitary confinement. I remain the label, the Bronson myth, the double danger man, your very own Hannibal the Cannibal. But it is all behind me. 'Pass the cucumber sandwich ... two sugars in my china cup, please.'

I will give HM Prison Woodhill 10/10, just for sending me my two angels.

HM PRISON WORMWOOD SCRUBS

This image is an extract from The Millennium Map™ © getmapping.com plc

LOCATION:	Du Cane Road, London.
CAPACITY:	1,400 beds.
CATEGORY AT PRESENT:	Local and Lifer Centre – Male.
OPENED:	1890.
HISTORY:	Inmate labour was used to construct this memorial to prisoners' suffering. Note the design from the aerial photo; it broke away from the radial arm design. Looks like a battery hen farm and was often as overcrowded as a tin of sardines. In 1998, allegations of prison officer brutality against inmates resulted in over twenty prison officers being brought before the courts; some were given prison sentences.

This place to me is just evil. Always has been. Always will be. I call it the bullyboy outfit.

When I first hit time in the 1970s, it was a hole then. My last spell here was in 1994, and it was no different to the way it was in the 1970s. I have never been up on the main prison wings. They just kept me hidden away in the seg block.

There, they are big old cells, 14ft long and 10ft wide. There are cages on the windows. It was all slopping out back then. You became potty-trained in these old jails. But those cells are the best for a workout, plenty of room. Why can't they make the modern jails like those old ones? Have they got no sense at all? You would think that they had to pay a land tax per square foot the way they make prisons these days!

The Scrubs, as we called it, has been around for years. It is capable of holding a good 1,500 cons. So it is a big place that is run by fear. They try to intimidate the cons. But it has the opposite affect on me. It doesn't work. It never will. Like I say, all they can do to me is kill me, and they haven't done it in thirty years. So why now?

They don't scare me with their show of force, opening my cell door fifteen-handed, all glaring at me, some with shields, some with sticks. I'm not in the urban theatre; I'm in the urban jungle! It becomes a fucking joke; it is basically a waste of time. Because one decent screw could open my door and I will be polite and respectful. But if fifteen open my door, I will just abuse the cowards, because there is no sense in it. And I don't play games like that. That is all it is, one big game.

It was 1985; I almost lost my arm in the Scrubs. I smashed up a recess and started throwing sinks and toilets about. Then I punched through an 'unbreakable' glass window. My fist went right through it … then it happened. Blood was squirting out like a fountain. I panicked, and started to chase the screws. But the blood was coming out so fast that I just collapsed.

Someone must have taken pity on me, because I actually awoke in hospital. But that was only the start of it. My injury went bad and, eventually, a big lump of puss grew in my wrist. Anyway, I had to be operated on; it was touch and go whether I would lose my arm. I was very lucky, but I broke the glass. It took me years to build the power up in that fist. But I overcame it.

It was also in the 1980s that I tried to kill the Governor by strangling him. Fortunately, the screws were on me and I spent all my time in restraint over that. Wherever I went, I had to be put in a body belt. It was at this period of my life I was at my most dangerous and unpredictable.

I would dive at a screw for just looking at me and they would dive at me if they thought I was getting bad. They, in fact, had a licence to attack me on any day they felt like it. Many times, that is just what they did ... if they felt like a fight, then it was that day I would get served up.

My life, my world, was now a war zone. If I got through a day without an incident, I would pray to God and say 'Thank you'. But in the morning, it would be a new struggle. The struggle was now my sanity.

It was in 1974 when the Scrubs really took a liberty with me, at a time when I was on my knees. My dad had just died. I was devastated. I was in a daze, lost, empty. Tearful. My whole life was in shock. And I just felt hopeless.

All I really needed was a friendly talk, some sort of compassion. A cup of tea and a nice chat. And all I got was a bashing. They brutalised me. It was an act of evil. I have always been able to shake it off, and get on with it, but this beating was totally unjust and unnecessary. There was just no sense in it. I was smashed with sticks; stomped on, and even had my 'tash ripped out of my lip. I was stripped naked and secured in a body belt. And left.

Days later, I was picked up and put in a van. I could barely walk as my toes were all bruised and bent, even the nails had been ripped off. I left the Scrubs like my dad ... dead. They had killed my heart. It did not matter to me where I went. I just felt I was buried.

A few years later, a lot of Scrubs screws were sacked. Some were sent to jail over the brutality there. So don't tell me it doesn't happen. It does. But with Bronson, there is a licence kill. It is all part of my journey.

Obviously, you get over a beating, it is just physical – it is like a bad head or a storm, it clears up and the sun shines. But mentally, it stays. You have nightmares, you lose trust. You lose faith in humanity and it rips up your soul. I think it does make you a stronger person. A more determined person. But you are never the same, as you become 'cold'.

I will give HM Prison Wormwood Scrubs 0/10. Fuck 'em! It is all you deserve.

No hard feelings to any of the decent screws there, as I am sure that there are lots. And it may well be a better jail now that the scum have been sacked. But the stigma never dies, too much shit has gone on there. It needs pulling down and rebuilding. A new plan, a new regime, a new bunch of staff. To me, it is the same as it always was.

HOSTAGE HELL

If you asked any of my hostage victims what the experience was like, I'd bet most of them would say, 'Hell'. I don't want to cover old territory, as that's already been covered and well documented in my other books. So what I intend to do is to let some of my hostages speak out for themselves.

It isn't easy being Bronson. People expect so much of you and yet, at times, I can't give what they want. Expectations of my behaviour means that certain things are expected of me when situations like taking a hostage materialise. This is what prison can do to you; it can make you mad or make you break down. You have to have an inner resolve to get you through it.

For the ordinary prisoner, they can go and speak with a number of support staff, but what can I do when the pressure gets too much? I've cracked and taken a hostage or two! God knows, I've resisted temptation so many times.

Although my hostages may have feared for their lives when initially taken hostage, by the end of the siege they knew I wouldn't have carried out any of what I said. That's why I've included these statements from three of my hostages; these have never before been seen in print.

All of the statements have one thing in common – the hostages say that they were threatened with some sort of violence, but read each statement and you will see that nothing but the minimum of force was applied to them ... they all lived to walk away from the siege. I was the one to pay for each siege with extra prison sentences being continually added on.

Although I've taken many more hostages than these three, I feel that these key individuals represent the effect of my thoughts and actions at the time. But all walked away in one piece; this is what duress can do to a man. That is why they were taken hostage ... duress of circumstance. I was not in control of my actions and I was not in control of what was said to them, but I did my best to fight the urges and I often harmed myself rather than harm the hostages. I believe I was harming the hostages by proxy. If I was to slash my head with a broken bottle, then that saved me from doing that to a hostage; that is how much I fought not to harm them.

When you get settled into a prison and then face the threat of being moved to another prison, it can set all sorts of alarm bells ringing. You know that when you get to wherever it is that a reception committee will be waiting for you, so you do your best not to go to such a place. I do not receive the usual helping hand from the prison administration, they've given up on me. I am under the control of Prison Service HQ; the prison I am in has to do the bidding of the grand masters in HQ, they are just tools. I am then forced to react because of the way these orders are carried out without any compassion; you're body belted and marched off to a van ... and you don't know where you're going.

That is what most prisoners go through, the fear of where they are going, the fear of leaving the safe haven of the establishment that they're in and the fear of having to make new acquaintances when they arrive at their destination. For me, when I feel another prison move is coming on, then it does cause me concern. I am being led by the blind, they do not see what I can see, they have not experienced the degradation and violence that my body has felt. This can set off a chain reaction that I have no control over, as happens with many other prisoners in the system.

The main difference between my moves and that of a 'normal' low-security being moved is that they are told in advance of the place they may be moved to. They may get a slip under their door at night telling them that they're going to such and such a place tomorrow; that doesn't happen with me. I am simply ghosted away. No warning, no nothing.

It doesn't mean that all prisoners do not feel some sort of concern about the move. Some prisoners look forward to being moved to 'open' conditions and, therefore, do not mind the move ... they crave the move. But some prisoners do not like certain establishments and do genuinely feel fear about the impending move and think of all sorts of devious plans to remain at the prison they are in. What devious plan can I come up with other than to resist with my physical self?

I leave you with the hostages to have the last word in this chapter, as they deserve it and here they tell you what happened.

ANDY LOVE

Crown Court, Luton
The Queen v Charles Bronson

Charles Bronson is charged as follows:

> Count 1
> *Statement of Offence*: False Imprisonment
> *Particulars of Offence*: Charles Bronson on the 26th day of May 1993 assaulted and unlawfully and injuriously imprisoned Andrew George Love and detained him against his will.
>
> Count 2
> *Statement of Offence*: Blackmail, contra to Section 21(1) of the Theft Act 1968.
> *Particulars of Offence*: Charles Bronson on the 26th day of May 1993 made an unwarranted demand of an inflatable doll, a cup of tea, weapons and a helicopter from Sarah Irvine with menaces with a view to gain for himself or another or with intent to cause loss to another.

Handwritten letter from Andy to someone he calls 'Sweetheart':

Sweetheart,

Thanks for your message – it really helped. And thanks to Mary [can't make out name ... Marje?] for being with you.

I'm OK except that they're not feeding us or telling us what's going on. This may go on for some time but I don't think I'm in any immediate danger – I know lots of people are working for me, somewhere. Keep the kettle ready. I'll leave it up to you to decide whether or not to tell my mother or anyone else. There's news on Horizon every hour.

I'm thinking of you and XXXX and love you both, keep strong and stubborn.

Love you,

Andy

Statement made on 28 May 1993 by Andrew George Love:

I am employed by Buckinghamshire County Council in the position of Librarian at Woodhill Prison, Milton Keynes, and have been so since July 1992 when the prison opened. Most of the inmates are able to go to the Prison Library and select their own books. There are about ten units that are not able to attend the Library for various reasons; one such unit is the segregation unit which is really a punishment wing. I then select some 300 books, place them on a trolley and take them to these units for the prisoners to select.

On the morning of Wednesday, 26 May 1993, I went to the segregation block with my trolley of books, arriving at about 9.30am. I parked the trolley by the Good Order and Discipline part of the prison. Officers would bring one prisoner at a time to the trolley where they would exchange books.

At about 9.50am, Charles Bronson came through the gate leading to the exercise yard and the officer was just locking the gate when the prisoner Bronson approached me quickly from behind and placed me in a strangle-hold with his right arm. It was on very securely and constricted my throat; it was locked against his left forearm which was behind my head; I was having trouble breathing.

He said something to the effect of, 'Don't do anything silly and you will be OK ... if you try anything silly I will snap your spinal cord.'

This was spoken in a quiet, rational way. I knew what a strong, powerful man he was and was aware of his reputation. I had no doubt that he meant his threat and I was in fear of my life. I was terrified.

He began moving me towards his cell which was situated on the ground floor. I recall Bronson saying, 'This is a hostage situation.' I can't recall a lot in those split seconds until he got me in the cell and banged the door. I was in a state of shock. He slammed the cell door shut with his boot. I was still in a head lock. He took me over to the back of the cell. He said, 'I am going to sit you down on the chair. I want you to be quiet and stay there.' This I did.

He stood behind me, still having me in the strangle lock. He shouted out that he wanted to see the Governor. I am a bit confused as to the order of things. I recall him saying he would snap my spinal cord if his demands were not met. He asked for someone to write down his demands. He made numerous threats on my life. I remember Prison Officer Sarah Irvine turning up as negotiator and speaking to Bronson.

After five or ten minutes, Bronson released me from his grip. He did not grab hold of me again throughout tie siege. His demands started off at a blow-up doll, and a cup of tea for both of us.

He made continued threats to the prison officers outside that he would snap my neck and kill me, but this seemed to be for their benefit mainly and was directed to them.

As time went on – I do not know what time, I do not wear a watch – he said that he would not harm me, but this was after several hours of me being in the cell.

He went into a number of rages when he thought negotiations were not going his way; at these times my anxieties increased. He made unreasonable demands at these times for a helicopter, gun and bullets. He seemed to have a number of grievances about the time he had spent in solitary confinement and the denying of visits.

But he really just seemed lonely and wanted company, and was concerned as to the possible outcome of his forthcoming trial. He encouraged me to write a couple of letters later on. This I did. I wrote one letter to my wife exhibit AGL/1 and one to Sue Shilling, a prison Governor, whom we had heard speaking on the Horizon radio as Bronson had a radio playing in his cell.

I was very intent on not showing Bronson that I was frightened and tried to build up a relationship with him. This was fairly easy, as he knew me from my library job. Towards the end of the siege, I feel that I understood his position and I believe he had built up some respect for me as I had not cracked. I believe he expected his demands to be met.

At the end of the siege, it was arranged that I would go to the cell door, he would stay at the back, I would be released and he would be given a rub-down search and then moved to another cell.

Just before the cell door opened, he shook my hand, apologised to me and told me I was in the wrong place at the wrong time. The cell door opened and I was released. I was taken to the adjudication room and seen by some medics. I was later seen by a psychologist and debriefed.

I was held for some fourteen hours. In the early hours, I was terrified and frightened for my life. I really believed that if Bronson's demands were not met, he would kill me. As the hours went by, I realised that this was less likely to happen. I did not consent to being taken into the cell or being kept or being kept there against my will.

ADRIAN THOMAS WALLACE

I am the above named and I am employed by the Home Office as Deputy Governor, Her Majesty's Prison, Hedon Road, Hull. I have been engaged in this capacity at Hull for two years, three months and have worked within the Prison Service, working my way through the ranks, for about twenty-three years. My duties have taken me all around the country and, prior to my current post, I was based at the Northallerton Prison. My current position at Hull is as the Head of Operations and part of my time is spent supervising the Special Unit on A Wing.

This unit houses only four inmates. They are categorised as special prisoners and are placed on this unit because they cannot interact with the mainstream prisoners. The unit is specially contained and they are given more independence in an attempt to replace them into routine prison life.

The four prisoners on the unit are Anthony McUllagh (DoB 21/4/67), Paul Flint (DoB 21/4/64), Edward Slater (DoB 28/4/64) and Charles Bronson (DoB 6/12/52). This latter prisoner changed his name to Bronson from Michael Gordon Peterson. He has been at Hull since November 1993, previously being at Frankland Prison. Bronson is an extremely large man. He is about 5ft 11in tall but has a huge physique, like Geoff Capes. He has a shaven head and a large handlebar moustache. He is an extremely fit man, spending a lot of time working out. He is currently serving an eight-year sentence for conspiracy to rob and has spent the vast majority of his adult life inside institutions. He is presently awaiting trial for a previous incident in which he took a librarian as hostage. [The siege involving Andy Love.]

The other three prisoners are all serving life sentences but even they are frightened of Bronson. It is fair to say that I am and have been aware of his potential for being dangerous since he came to Hull.

Part of my duties, as stated previously, involve the regular visits to both staff and prisoners on this block. During the last few weeks I have been aware that Bronson has been more and more agitated as his trial approaches. I have been informed that he had spoken recently about taking a hostage, this information being passed on to me by other prison staff.

Shortly after 9.00am on Monday, 4 April 1994, I commenced my duties on A Wing. I walked into the block and everything appeared perfectly normal, just like any other Monday morning.

As I walked into the block I became aware of the prisoners filing out of the kitchen, to my left. I said, 'Good morning,' to them. I noticed that Bronson was at the rear of the group but as soon as he saw me he pushed the other prisoners aside and rushed at me. He grabbed me around the neck and pushed me towards the wall. Bronson was behind me with his forearm around my neck, pushing my chin up. He had come at me so quickly that I did not have time to avoid him and similarly the other prison staff did not have time to react.

Bronson held me tightly around the neck applying pressure to my throat. He shouted at the staff, 'Don't come near or I'll break his neck.' He then dragged me backwards, walking with his back to the wall, along the corridor and dragged me to the TV room (TV room 2). He threw me down in the TV room and then sat me down, telling me to put my hands behind my neck. Bronson was extremely agitated and was not in any sort of state to be questioned or upset. Bronson then began barricading the door with the tables and chairs in the TV room.

I remained sat on the chair in the middle of the room. The chair was a tubular metal chair with a thinly padded vinyl seat. Initially, I was sat facing the door of the TV room and I recall Bronson speaking through the windows with one of the prison officers, Roy Kirk. Bronson was saying that I was a bastard and that nobody liked me. He said to me, 'If you move, I'll kill you.' There is no doubt that I took this threat seriously, bearing in mind the man's history and mental instability. I was frightened, and was in a situation that was completely out of my control. Bronson was able to do anything to me.

I was dressed in a blue pin-stripe suit, brown-and-white striped shirt, tie and a pair of black shoes. Bronson was wearing dark tracksuit bottoms and a sleeveless vest and yellow-painted prison boots. He took my tie off and tied my hands together behind my back but not fastened to the chair. Bronson was still very agitated at this time and I realised that my best option was to act quiet.

Bronson punched me a few times across my right cheek and also to the back of my neck, knocking me to the ground. He dragged me back up by the scruff of the neck and put me back on the chair. Bronson was telling me I was a 'bag of shit' and said nobody liked me and that he was going to kill me. He was pacing around the room. He told me that he knew there would be police sharp-shooters brought in and that I would be killed as well.

Bronson rifled my pockets. He took my prison radio from me and asked me how it worked. He put all the items from my pockets on to the table in front of me and then threw the items around the room and on to the floor. He took my prison keys out of my pocket and, as he took my wallet, he ripped my trousers down the right side.

He picked up my wallet from the table and began throwing the credit cards around the room and started ripping up the notes. He picked up an iron that was in the room and held it close to my face. He said, 'I'm going to batter you with this, cunt, and stave your head in.' It is difficult to put into words my thoughts and feelings while this was going on but I honestly felt in fear for my life.

All this that I have described took place in the first few minutes of the incident. Bronson then turned me around on the chair so that I was facing away from the door. The windows of the room were therefore behind me.

The room in which I was is about 10ft square. The chair was placed along the wall to the left about 4 or 5ft from the door. Most of the time I was sat facing the sidewall or the back wall. Bronson told me not to speak and kept pacing up and down behind me. He was kicking the furniture around and snorting. Bronson asked me how the prison radio worked and I explained to him.

About thirty minutes into the incident, Bronson told me to get on the radio. He told me what to say and I passed a message saying that he wanted us both to leave the prison together, that if there were any SAS or Royal Marines in the prison that they had better shoot us both. I told the communications room that Charlie had done jungle warfare and was not 'fucking' about. Bronson held the radio while I spoke into it.

I continued to sit quietly on the chair facing the TV. I was aware that Roy Kirk, the prison officer, was watching through the glass windows. I could not see Bronson but could hear him pacing up and down behind me. He told me to sit still and not to speak. Bronson turned the sound up on the TV. The station was tuned into pop music and when he turned it up it became very noisy.

Shortly after, Bronson asked for a cup of tea and he asked me if I wanted one. I told him that I did because I didn't want to upset him any further. He shouted his request to the officers in the *corridor and a few minutes later Bronson partly moved the barricade and the cups of tea were pushed through. I told Bronson that I wouldn't be able to drink my tea with my hands tied and so he undid them. He told me, however, to keep one hand in my pocket, which I did. I expected that later he would re-tie my hands but he never did.*

I had a watch on but was unable to look at it in case Bronson saw me. However, I heard Bronson talking with Roy Kirk about an 11 o'clock deadline and said that he wouldn't hurt me until that time had elapsed, as he was a man of his word.

During the incident, although I had full sense of my faculties, I was not in control at any time. Many things went through my mind about the things Bronson could and would do. I recall at one point, which I believe was after the 11 o'clock deadline, that Bronson stood behind me, I could not tell how close he was, but I heard him unzip his trousers. My first thought was that he was going to inflict some form of sexual abuse on me but instead he urinated in a bucket. As soon as he had finished, I thought the bucket would be poured over my head and prepared myself for it, but it never came.

A few minutes later, Charlie got back on the radio. The radio had been switched on all the time and we could hear the day-to-day running of the prison continuing on it. Charlie called up saying that he wanted the prison closing down and that he didn't want any further talk over the radio. He made some reference to having some mushrooms stolen last week, but I couldn't make much sense of that.

Shortly after that, Charlie told me to get on the radio. He told me to ask for his blow-up doll and that he wanted it dressing up in a black skirt, black tights. I asked the communications officer to acknowledge that my message had been received, which he did. Charlie had told me to do it right and threatened me with violence if I didn't comply.

Charlie picked up my prison security keys and asked me about them. He wanted to know which doors they fitted and said that he was going to try them on the doors. By this time, Charlie had calmed down a bit but, because he is so volatile, I thought it best not to try and engage him in any sort of conversation.

I was aware, however, that the officers outside were trying to negotiate with him and I kept my mind active by running through the procedural matters that the negotiators would be going through in order to resolve and contain the situation. I myself have been in incidents of this type before but obviously the situation is completely different when you are the hostage. I do recall thinking that I shall have the windows in the TV room replaced with glass that can be broken should the need arise. The windows are presently fitted with unbreakable glass.

A while later, again I cannot say what time, but assume it was about lunchtime, Bronson told me to call up on the radio and ask for two steak and chips, one for himself, one for me. Bronson said he wanted it in five minutes. Again, I passed this message to the communications room.

I then became aware that Bronson was becoming more and more agitated. He began pacing up and down and seemed to be working himself up. For the first time for quite a while, I became frightened again. Bronson smashed one of the chairs in the room, an armchair, and took the padded seat of the chair, he placed it across my chest, strapping it in place with a sheet which he tied behind my back.

Bronson had told me that he knew police tactics and knew that they would soon start drilling holes into the walls to listen to him and see what was going on in the room. He told me that he was going to move me. He picked me up again, grabbing me around the neck. He moved the barricade out of the way and opened the door to the room. He walked me out into the corridor, again warning the other prison officers to keep away. Bronson had me tightly around the neck and was stood behind me. I assume he had placed the chair seat on to my chest to act as some form of protection in case someone tried to shoot him.

Bronson walked me along the corridor and then dragged me into the adjoining TV room only a few yards away from the first room. Again, he barricaded the door to prevent the prison staff getting in, using two chairs and a table; however, the barricade was not as heavy as the first one.

Again, Bronson sat me down and shouted for another cup of tea, which was brought a few minutes later. I felt I had to drink it just to keep him happy. Once I'd finished it, I said to him, 'Can I put it down?' but Bronson snorted back, 'No, I'm in charge!'

He started to puff and puff and snort and somebody came to the window and he shouted, 'Fuck off. I don't want to talk to you.' He was becoming more and more excitable and grabbed the radio. He said he was going to come back on the radio in five minutes, that he wanted the communications room to get a tape recorder and record his message that he was going to give. He said he was going to sing a song and said he wanted it playing at his funeral. He said he wanted a copy sending to his solicitor in London.

I could sense Bronson was building himself up and expected something serious to happen. It crossed my mind that I would be killed. Minutes later, Bronson again spoke on the radio. This time he said that he knew he was going to die today and that he was prepared for it. He said he expected to be shot by a police bullet. He said he was going to sing a song, which he wanted playing at his funeral. Bronson then sang a song called 'I Believe', which he sang at the top of his voice.

This must have lasted for a few minutes and when he finished I thought he was going to hurt me. Bronson then started singing some Christmas carols and hymns; he picked up the TV, smashing it on the floor alongside me.

He dragged me to my feet again and walked me to the door of the room, pushing aside the barricade. He again began dragging me back along the corridor and it seemed as if he was taking me back to the first TV room we had been in.

Bronson was again behind me, walking with his back to the wall, feeling his way along as we approached the first TV room (TV 2). He shouted to the prison officers, who were stood only a short distance away, asking them about his steak and chips. One of them shouted that they were unaware that he had asked for any food.

I realised that once we got back into the first room it would be more secure than the last one, so I was reluctant to go back in it. As Bronson reached out trying to find the door handle, I felt his grip loosen around my neck, ever so slightly. As it did so, I saw my chance and pushed with my foot against the door frame knocking Bronson slightly off balance. I pushed as hard as I could and Bronson fell backwards with myself falling over with him. As we fell, he released his grip on me. We landed and I jumped straight to my feet, kicking Bronson on the body and face a couple of times. Within a second, a number of other prison officers jumped on top of Bronson and one of them took hold of me and led me away. I was taken to the command post in the Governor's office.

I was extremely highly charged at this time and was grateful that I had been dragged away because I feel I would have done some harm to Bronson if not moved.

I went to the Governor's office and was sat down. Everyone was very nice to me but I felt as if I was being pampered and didn't want all the hassle. I felt I just wanted to be left alone to try and sort the many different feelings out that were going through my mind. I sat and talked the situation through and slowly started to come down from the incident.

PHIL DANIELSON

The prison officer was sat where Tim had been sat, but I was unable to identify the officer because the officer was reading a tabloid newspaper which was covering the officer's face. I was not happy with this because I felt the officer was ignoring me and not paying any attention to my safety and I felt very vulnerable and that I was being put at risk. I could not see any other officers from the classroom and therefore believed other officers could see me.

I then heard the sound of footsteps on the stairs which lead up to the 2s [2nd floor level] near to Room 23. Fred Lowe said, 'That's only Charlie doing part of his exercises.'

I looked over my shoulder but didn't see Charlie. I thought to myself, 'I don't like this, I'm off.'

Still, I could not see any prison officers paying any attention to me. I then thought about getting out and over to the stairs which lead to the exit door on 2s. I turned back to Fred for an instant when suddenly there was crash and the door to the classroom flew open and then I felt an enormous thump to the right side of my upper face. Initially, I didn't know what had happened because it all happened so quickly.

I fell to my left side on to the carpeted floor. As I fell, I hit the floor with my chin or lower part of my face causing my lower teeth to become slightly dislodged. I may have lost consciousness for a few seconds as it took me some time to focus and to realise what had happened.

I was laid on the floor behind my desk at this point completely out of view of the prison officer due to the solid area at the bottom of the wall.

My glasses had been knocked from my face but I am only slightly short-sighted and once I managed to focus I could see clearly.

I remained very still on the floor as I realised that I had been hit by Charlie. I saw Charlie stood astride me looking down at me. He was holding a knife in his right hand. I could not see the handle but saw the blade which was about 6–8in long pointing down towards me.

I then heard Charlie say, 'Now I've got you, take your last breath because this knife is going in you.'

I remained very still. I was absolutely terrified. I thought Charlie was going to kill me. I didn't dare move. I tried to appear dazed and knocked out.

Charlie then went down on one knee level with my waist and jabbed the knife into my ribs. I felt the point through my shirt but I don't believe it went through.

Charlie then held the knife at my ribs and said, 'You are the bastard that slagged my cartoon off.'

I made no reply to this and remained very still. I knew what Charlie was referring to. Charlie had designed a poster with various cartoons exampling 'healthy living'. One of the cartoons was titled 'Safe Sex'. Charlie's example explained how gay men should use condoms to prevent the spread of diseases.

When I had seen Charlie's poster in the education department I commented on the poster to a member of the education staff when Charlie was not present. I had felt that the poster inferred that gay men alone were responsible for spreading sexually transmitted diseases, and I did not feel that this was acceptable on a poster.

This comment had somehow reached Charlie and he had obviously taken offence at my comment.

Charlie then got up off the floor and left me but I still remained very still. Charlie then started to knock the computer equipment on to the floor, the keyboard, the terminal and the other equipment with it. Ray and Fred left the classroom very quickly. From the position I was laid in, I could see Charlie throwing the equipment around and yanking cables from the computers. At one point, a printer hit me on my legs but did not cause me any injury.

Charlie then came back over to me, stood astride me and then pulled both of my arms behind my back. He then tied my wrists together incredibly tight with the computer cable. This hurt my upper arms as well as my wrist due to the tightness.

Charlie then moved down my legs and tied my ankles together with another piece of cable. This was also tied very tightly. Charlie moved very quickly and I offered no resistance to him because Charlie was holding the knife in his teeth while tying me up and I still thought he was going to kill me.

I then saw Charlie look out of the classroom window and then bend down and pick me up. He placed me around his shoulders with my legs on one of his shoulders, my body around the back of his head and my head over his other shoulder. Charlie then carried me out into the middle of the ls.

I looked around for someone to help but I couldn't see a single soul ...

... I wasn't too concerned because I didn't have cell keys but on the other hand I didn't know where the other inmates were. This I feel was an indirect threat from Charlie because Fred is well known for being a dangerous inmate.

Charlie seemed to have calmed down a little by then. He then said to me, 'Tell you what, if we don't get what I want, I'm gonna kill you and then I'm going to kill myself, they can carry both of us out in body bags.'

I had the feeling of absolute terror. I believed Charlie meant what he said. Charlie then said, 'You wait here.'

Charlie then left me on my back on the table. Over the next twenty minutes, Charlie proceeded to trash the entire floor of the wing. He systematically went from room to room and smashed and turned everything over. I managed to move my head around so that I could get a good view of him.

I saw Charlie go into the kitchen, room number 1, and return with a deep freezer over his head. He then chucked it up the staircase which leads to point 29. The freezer landed halfway up the stairs and slid down to the bottom. He did the same with a cooker and other similar items and then did the same on the staircase near to the snooker table which leads to point 24. The noise was incredible.

Charlie was also making loud noises, shouting, swearing, cursing and making monkey-like noises. He was acting and sounding like a crazed madman.

It was quite clear to me that Charlie was barricading us on the 1s. Charlie used anything he could find large enough to block the stairs.

At one point he began to throw the dumbbells from the gym at the glass panels of the classroom. Charlie was unable to break these as the dumbbells just bounced off and broke from the impact.

It was then that I passed out, I think from fear and adrenalin. I don't know how long I was unconscious for. I kept drifting in and out of consciousness. I don't believe Charlie had knocked me out, I just mentally and physically gave up.

During Charlie's moments of destruction, Charlie climbed on to a metal cupboard he had dragged out earlier, stood on it and reached up to the security camera above the snooker table and placed a block of butter over the lens.

I watched Charlie and tried to work out what he was doing. I was beginning to lose track of time. I had been on the table for a long time so I decided to speak to Charlie. I said, 'Charlie, where are you?' because I couldn't see him at that time.

Charlie replied, 'Shut your fucking mouth, speak when you're fucking spoken to.'

To me, that was a hint he was not going to kill me yet, but at a later time.

I said to Charlie, 'I promise I won't speak again but hear me out on this one, will you, please, go and see if you can find my glasses 'cos I can't see a bloody thing without them.'

I could see clearly, but I wanted Charlie to show some sympathy towards me.

Charlie replied, 'It won't make much difference in a bit.'

... From room 28, Charlie marched across the ls over to the kitchen. I managed to inch my chair around to watch him. Charlie then went into the utility room which is attached to the kitchen. There is no door on the utility room so I had a good view of him.

I saw Charlie pick the washing machine off the floor and begin to yank it away from the wall. I then head a loud gush of water and saw a small stream of water run from the kitchen over to where I was sitting. I became concerned because the washing machine is hard-wired into the wall and there was a danger of electrocution if Charlie kept pulling at the machine.

As I saw the water getting closer to me, I lifted my feet up from the floor. Then, suddenly, I saw an enormous flash and I heard a loud bang come from the utility room and Charlie let out a scream and a groan.

I thought to myself, 'Brilliant, he's electrocuted himself.'

Then there was silence and I thought Charlie was either dead or he was knocked out. I remained perfectly still in case someone was going to come into the wing to get me.

I remember looking at my watch at this time and I think it was about 6.00pm, to time him to see how long he remained quiet for. I wondered if there was enough power in the power point to kill him.

I then heard a groan from Charlie so I inched my way back

around to face room 30. I had the confidence to move because I knew Charlie was very short-sighted.

I called to Charlie, 'Charlie, are you all right, what was that loud bang?'

Charlie replied, 'I got hell of a shock from that thing then.'

Charlie then emerged from the kitchen looking very white and ill. He then came over, pulled up another chair and sat beside me.

I told Charlie that my legs were beginning to hurt. Charlie asked *if I wanted another chair to put my feet up for a while. I told him I would, so Charlie placed another chair in front of me so that I could place my feet on it, but my ankles remained tied ...*

'Charlie', I said, 'we must have been down here for three hours now and no bastard has even been to see if we are OK.'

This felt like a first step with Charlie, as though he and I were in this together. I was trying to build some sort of rapport/relationship with him to take the focus of him killing me away.

I then shouted up the stairs for someone to get me some cigarettes. I saw prison officer Tim come to the 2.1 gates. I shouted at him for some cigarettes and the Governor. I was getting very angry at this point, mainly through fear.

Alfie Stockman, another prison officer, then came to 2.1. I shouted the same to him and I was told he would relay my message.

During the first few hours of this incident, Charlie made two demands of me. I cannot remember which came first or at what time Charlie made the demands.

The first was to write two notes; one was a note to his girlfriend, Joyce Connor, and one was to my partner, Richard. Charlie dictated the notes to me while I wrote them. I cannot remember the contents of the notes; I only remember them being bizarre. I also cannot remember if or how they were passed out.

The second demand was for me to cut off Charlie's ear. He was pissed off that he couldn't go to his grandma's funeral so he wanted me to cut it off and take it out with me and bury it with his grandma. I was horrified but so scared that I would have done it if he had made me. Luckily, Charlie forgot about this and it was never mentioned again.

After I had finished shouting upstairs, Charlie said, 'These fucking lights are doing my head in,' indicating the fluorescent lights. Charlie then untied my body from the chair and lifted me from the chair and replaced me back on the snooker table. Charlie then, with a snooker cue or a brush handle, I'm not sure which, proceeded to smash every light. There was glass flying everywhere but I was slightly protected by the snooker table's overhead light. This went on for about ten minutes. I had my hands and arms covering my head and face from the glass ...

THE GOOD PRISON GUIDE

... I told him I couldn't go to the toilet because I was still tied to the chair.

Charlie came over and lifted my chair up so that I could stand with the chair still tied to me and then he moved me a couple of feet toward room 28 and then Charlie told me to pee on the floor.

Even though I was tied I managed to pee because my hands were slack enough which gave me sufficient movement. I was then returned back to point A. This procedure was the same each time I told Charlie I needed to pee.

This was a humiliating act by Charlie, especially because I was still tied and because he didn't allow me to use a proper toilet.

There was an occasion while I was at point A when Charlie got a saucepan, poo'd in it and then threw the pan and its contents up the stairs, which I found disgusting.

I felt that I had to keep a rapport going with Charlie to try and save myself. I told Charlie that I had been deserted and then I started shouting to the prison officers upstairs. This was for the benefit of Charlie because he relished in my anger when I shouted at the prison officers because it was as though I was shouting out against the establishment, the prison and that we were in this together. This was the first glimmer of hope that I could actually do something with this situation.

Charlie then disappeared for some time. When he returned, he had a clear glass bottle in his hand similar to a Newcastle Brown bottle. He came over and stood a few feet in front of me. He held the neck of the bottle and smashed the base of it on something. I don't know what it was.

Charlie then leant over to me and unbuttoned my shirt to my waist and then pushed my shirt and jacket apart so that my chest was exposed.

I feared that Charlie was going to cause me some serious harm with the bottle. Charlie then held the broken bottle to my chin and then to my chest. The bottle was only a few inches away from me.

Charlie made no sound, he was just staring. I was absolutely petrified. I was as scared then as I had been at the beginning when I had the knife held at my ribs.

The bottle was held at me for a few seconds and then Charlie stepped back from me. I began to then button up my shirt but was having difficulty because my hands were shaking so much through sheer fear. Charlie was stood in a very macho position with his legs astride, shoulders back with his arms by his side.

Charlie was still holding the bottle. He then, without making any sound, put the bottle to his head and scraped the jagged edge of the bottle down his bald head. Blood gushed from the cut down his face and on to his shoulders, chest and then on to the floor. I just sat there, too terrified and shocked to do or say anything.

Charlie then left without saying anything and began to wander around the floor. I tried to watch him as much as possible. I was also concerned that the cooker ring was still on and that he might harm himself or even me with it.

There was complete silence for about ten minutes and Charlie walked around.

I saw Charlie pick up a cloth from somewhere and mop his head. The cut did not appear serious. I now believe that the incident was for a dramatic effect to try and put the fear back ...

... Charlie then began to sing so I joined in. He complimented me on my voice and asked me to sing a song for him. I sang, 'You'll never walk alone,' and Charlie adored it. He kept asking me to sing it over and over again. The singing went on for about half-an-hour. I believe I may have fallen asleep at this point as I do not recall any significant events.

I do remember feeling as though I had been deserted, as I had heard nothing from the prison officers for some time.

Charlie then decided that we would go for a walk. I was now feeling drained, exhausted and cold and stiff from being in the same position for so long. I also told Charlie that I needed a shit but there was no way that I was going to do it on the floor.

Charlie then undid my arms and legs but kept the rope around my neck. Charlie walked ahead and led me over to the stairs near to the snooker table, point 24. I was then made to climb up the side railings of the stairs due to Charlie's blockade preventing us from walking normally up the stairs.

Charlie went first, still carrying the spear and somehow holding on to the rope around my neck.

... *Throughout the episode Charlie told me that thirty-five was his cell but I never went in.*

Charlie tied me to the railings outside his cell and then he disappeared somewhere and returned a couple of minutes later with a clean mattress and a pile of about six green blankets. Charlie then threw the mattress on to the suicide net.

Charlie said to me 'On there,' and indicated to me to go over the railings and on to the net.

He then said, 'Over there and sleep.'

Charlie then untied the rope from the railings and I climbed over the railings and jumped on to the net and climbed on to the mattress.

I believe Charlie's idea was to disorientate me and torture me because I felt like I was hanging over the edge of a cliff. Charlie then tied the other end of the rope on to the netting to restrict my movement and to prevent me from getting up.

I laid on my back and looked up at the ceiling and saw that it was becoming light so I guessed it was about 7.30am. Charlie was stood leaning against the railings talking to the inmates in their cells. He spoke to them for about an hour mainly about their moves to different prisons.

I drifted in and out of sleep but I couldn't sleep properly because I was still terrified.

I remember Alfie shouting to Charlie saying he wanted to talk. Charlie shouted back that he wanted food for the other prisoners. He never asked about any food for me, and didn't seem concerned about me.

I faced the security camera and mouthed, 'I'm not all right, get me out.'

After some time, Charlie jumped on to the net which jarred my neck due to being tied still. I felt like I was being treated like a dog on a lead.

Charlie untied the rope from the net and held on to it. He then told me to stick the mattress and blankets down through the edge

The only reassurance I felt was that the prison officers were at gate 2.1 and that I could be seen by a security camera which was situated at the end of the wing on the 3s.

... *Julie (trained negotiator) shouted again, 'Are you all right?'*

Charlie was laid on the sofa and said, 'You go and talk to them.'

I asked him if he meant I should go to the gate and speak to them. Charlie then had a tremendous outburst, 'Of course I don't fucking mean that.'

Charlie told me to go to the door while he held on to the rope around my neck and I talked through the gap of the door. I realised that I was still dealing with a lunatic.

Julie asked us how we were both doing. I told her we were fine but tired. Shortly afterwards, we heard some noise coming from outside. Charlie jumped up, led me from room 33 and into room 5.1, the wing office. He opened the window which looked out on to D Wing where the YPs (Young Prisoners) under-21 inmates were chanting, 'Charlie, Charlie.'

I asked Charlie to stop them. I could hear them shouting, 'Have you done him ... is he dead?' plus other similar things.

Charlie then shouted back a most unusual reply, 'Look, you lot, do you realise what a good man this is, because I've just had a heart-attack and Phil has just brought me round and given me the kiss of life.'

Some shouted back, 'Oooh.'

Charlie then collapsed on the floor in fits of laughter.

The YPs shouted to see me so I stuck my head out of the window. I heard shouts of, 'Are you all right, Phil?' and 'Phil, you're gonna get it, you'll get your throat slit.'

Charlie then told the YPs to 'Shut up' and they did. I became even more fearful because I thought they might provoke Charlie into killing me.

We then went back to the gate and sat chatting for a couple of hours.

I think it was about 5.00am by now. We went back to room 33 for some time. I remember thinking about my family and home and how I was missing them and I looked at my watch and thought, 'Five hours to go.'

We both just laid on the easy chairs looking out of the window and watching TV.

After a total of forty-four hours, I gave myself up and Phil Danielson was released to safety unharmed. He was awarded £65,000 in compensation and I was awarded a life sentence.

STARS BEHAVING
BADLY

The public expects the typical prisoner to look like the old Victorian murderer Charlie Peace – gnarled face, walking with a limp and shabbily dressed. That is the typical image conjured up, that is how criminals are perceived to be. This is, sadly, very far removed from the truth.

I've compiled a listing of well-known characters who have had run-ins with the long arm of the law; some you will know about and some you may not. Many of them were the victims of false accusations, some were never charged, many were acquitted, and some of them did a bit of porridge

I have collected the details of these characters over time and only now have I the opportunity to reveal them to you. Some of the characters only gained notoriety after being imprisoned, but that still makes them a celebrated person. Some of those listed have merely been in the wrong place at the wrong time – a bit like my hostages!

ALI, MUHAMMAD (boxer) – Refused to fight for his country in the Vietnam War, served five years behind bars and was fined $1,000.

ANT, ADAM (real name Stuart Goddard, New Romantic singer) –

Received a 12-month community rehabilitation order and was also ordered to pay £500 compensation to an injured pub musician when he appeared at the Old Bailey on charges of affray following an incident when he brandished a starting pistol and threatened drinkers in a North London pub after they mocked his clothes. The court accepted that Goddard had suffered a temporary spell of mental illness. This is what I was getting at when I mentioned duress of circumstance, but what was he doing carrying a starting pistol; who was he going to race?

AITKEN, JONATHAN (Member of Parliament) – Was imprisoned after being convicted of perjury following an unsuccessful libel case. While in prison, Aitken found God ... wonder where he was hiding?

ARCHER, JEFFREY (Author) – A well-known geezer, jailed because of his perjury, received a four-year prison sentence. He could be stripped of his Lordship if a new Act is passed and backdated outlawing the likes of him.

BARRYMORE, MICHAEL (TV personality) – Mad or sad? The partially naked body of Stuart Lubbock, 31, was found floating face-down in the swimming pool of Barrymore's luxury home. Before Lubbock drowned, it was alleged that he was party to some rough gay sex, which had, it was claimed, caused some internal damage to his anus. There was reference to the date rape drug Rohypnol. Police suspect Mr Lubbock of having purchased some.

A late-night party developed after Barrymore and his gay lover, John Kenney, claimed that after Mr Lubbock was discovered in the pool he ran off with two other men into the nearby village. Kenney called his lover, Barrymore, a coward for running off. Although no charges were brought against Michael, the mud still sticks.

BENN, NIGEL (former Super-Middleweight Champion) – He was arrested for assault charges in a nightclub. His alleged victim needed a lot of stitches to his face and nose. Benn, it was claimed, had supposedly punched and kicked Ray Sullivan, a ticket agency owner, while he was on the ground.

After a week-long trial, the jury of six men and six women took six hours to clear Benn of wounding with intent to cause grievous bodily harm. The lesser alternative charge of unlawful wounding was decided on some twenty minutes later, with the jury finding him 'not guilty' on all counts.

BERRY, CHUCK (singer) – He hired an under-age hat-check girl who had also set up as a prostitute at a nearby hotel. Charged with transporting a minor over State lines, Berry went through two trials and was sentenced to two years in a federal prison.

BEST, GEORGE (ex-international footballer) – Jailed for drink-driving and has never looked back since ... he dare not!

BOYCOTT, GEOFF (former Test cricketer and commentator) – Geoff Boycott was dropped as a commentator by newspapers and broadcasters following the outcome of a court case in France. He was found guilty of punching Margaret Moore twenty times after an argument in a hotel, in Antibes, in the South of France in October 1996.

BRAMBELL, WILFRED (actor – deceased) – The co-star of the BBC's 1970s television series *Steptoe and Son* was once caught by the police for 'cottaging' in public toilets (ironically, near to the BBC studios, in Shepherd's Bush, London).

BROWN, JAMES (soul singer) – The Godfather of Soul, the master of ... etc! Drug use, gun charges and driving offences, but a great singer in spite of this. South Carolina officials pardoned him for his past crimes in that State. Brown served a two-and-a-half-year prison term after a 1988 arrest on drug and assault charges, and was convicted of a drug-related offence in 1998.

Now this man is a man after my own heart! He entered an insurance seminar near his office and asked seminar participants if they were using his private restroom ... he had a shotgun with him at the time! The police chased Brown for half-an-hour from Augusta, Georgia into South Carolina and back to Georgia. Brown was high on PCP. The only way the police could end the chase was by shooting out his tyres. And this for a man of sixty-four years old means I'm still in with a shout. Wonder if they'll grant me a pardon?

BUTT, NICKY (Premiership footballer) – The Manchester United midfield footballer was arrested for alleged assault. A mum of two was punched in the face during a nightclub flare-up, which led police to question Butt who spent two hours at a Cheshire police station. No charges were brought.

CAPRIATI, JENNIFER (professional tennis player) – With all of her money she had to go and do some shoplifting. What is it with these rich chicks? Then she goes and gets involved in drug-taking ... these women are flawed!

CHARLES, CRAIG (actor and TV presenter) – The star of UK television's *Red Dwarf* science-fiction series, presenter of *Jailbreak* and *Robot Wars* spent some time on remand in prison while awaiting trial over allegations of rape and sexual assault. And all over a bacon sandwich! Charles and friend, John Peploe, decided on the spur of the moment to pay a visit to a former Soho stripper who was also Charles's former girlfriend.

This visit resulted in Charles facing heavy charges when the former Soho stripper accused him of leading a drug-induced gang rape on her for a 'bacon butty' breakfast.

When the case got to court, the comic actor said he visited the flat of the woman, a one-time girlfriend, in the early morning, on the 'spur of the moment' hoping that she would rustle up food for him and the co-accused, John Peploe.

On hearing that Charles planned to marry his then ex-stripper girlfriend, the woman, aged thirty-eight, gave them cocaine and became sexually aggressive, Charles told Southwark Crown Court.

The woman claimed that Charles arrived at her flat in Clapham, London, with Peploe and a third man called Roger, who has never been traced. She said they then raped and sexually assaulted her.

As Charles stood in the witness box, his voice frequently came close to breaking as he denied the charge and explained how the woman had ripped off her own shorts and knickers, and then inserted various items inside her body – namely a biro, an olive oil bottle and an orange!

Charles went on to tell the court, 'No sex took place with this woman. I have got nothing to hide and he (Peploe) has got nothing to hide.' He also insisted that there was no third man. 'Would I have wrecked my life and gone to prison for four months if I had something to hide?'

The woman making the accusations lived with Charles for about two weeks and after that they saw each other occasionally for about three months, but by then the sexual relationship had then finished and he then dated another woman for about four years.

The Liverpool-born comic described his alleged victim as 'weird' and she appeared to 'have a thing' about him.

The prosecutor, Jeremy Carter-Manning QC, questioned Charles repeatedly about why he had decided to visit this woman for a bacon butty, saying, 'I suggest there are many places you can get a bacon butty from.'

In answer to this, Charles responded, 'There are also many places you can get sex from. You don't have to rape a woman for it. You can try and make me look as guilty as you want, but I am innocent.'

Surprise, surprise ... before the complainant had even signed a police statement, details were released to the press. Charles and his co-accused, after a lengthy trial, were acquitted of all charges.

CROSBY, DAVID (rocker) – Rocker Crosby is a man who has lived the hard rock life – drugs, guns and served time in prison. A real rocker, not that I'm advocating drug use ... a drug mug is always a drug mug.

DENNING, CHRIS (former Radio One DJ) – Discovered the 1970s pop group the Bay City Rollers, was a good friend of convicted paedophile and pop impresario Jonathan King. Denning served three-and-a-half years in a Czech Republic prison for sexual offences against young boys; he left Prague rather sharpish after a failed attempt to extradite him to Britain.

Now living in exile, he is wanted for a series of alleged child sex offences in Britain. The name of Jonathan King was mentioned by one of the boys involved in the Czech trial; this prompted the investigation of King by British police.

DODD, KEN (Diddyman and funny man) – Faced tax evasion charges and was looking at the same sentence as Lester Piggot, but won his case and was acquitted.

DOWNEY JR, ROBERT (actor) – Another drug mug! Caught red-handed carrying a gun and in possession of drugs (heroin and cocaine) in 1987.

He deserved to be locked away because he failed to keep attending rehab.

ELVIS (singer/actor now deceased) – The Legend. It's amazing what turns up all these years later! He was arrested for supposedly fighting with two petrol pump attendants in Memphis, Tennessee, in 1956, although he was cleared of all the charges. Rumoured to have been on the payroll of the FBI; not surprising that he got off with the charges.

GLITTER, GARY (real name Paul Gadd, glam rocker) – Engaged in downloading child pornography, received a short, sharp, four-month prison sentence and went on tour of countries, including those frequented by paedophiles, in his boat. He was acquitted of having underage sex with a teenage fan. Hope the bastard drowns.

HOPPER, DENNIS (actor) – Arrested for driving offences and, later on, in Canada, for possession of marijuana; the drug charges were later dropped.

KING, DON (boxing promoter and manager) – Has a rap sheet longer than my arm, a true Teflon Don.

CAPONE, AL (known as Scarface, gangster, deceased) – Now here was a man with Teflon coating. In the end they couldn't get him on racketeering charges so they got him on tax evasion! Capone was born on 17 January 1899, in Brooklyn, New York, USA. Before he was fourteen years old, he was a member of two gangs. He received his infamous facial scars and the resulting nickname 'Scarface' when was attacked by the brother of a woman he insulted where he was working.

Capone personified what a gangster was all about and he filled the country with fear. The most notorious killing he was involved in was the St Valentine's Day Massacre of 1929. Yet, when he finally served his first prison time in May 1929, it was simply for carrying a gun. Soon, he became what was known as 'Public Enemy Number One.'

In 1931, the Internal Revenue Service indicted Capone for income tax evasion for the years 1925–29. He was also charged with the misdemeanour of failing to file tax returns for the years 1928–1929. Capone was said to owe $215,080.48 in taxes from his gambling profits. But even after all of this, the jury only managed to find Capone guilty on five charges out of the original twenty-three counts. For this, he was sentenced to a total of ten years in federal prison and one year in the county jail.

During his imprisonment, Capone was still able to run his crime organisation from his prison cell, but his timing was off. Prison wardens everywhere were being asked to recommend their most troublesome inmates for transfer to the not yet notorious Alcatraz. Capone was ghosted out.

Alcatraz, the Rock, proved to be an impenetrable place for Capone and he lost touch with the outside world. The only way out for Capone was if he earned time off for good behaviour, so he decided to be a model prisoner, even refusing to become involved in prisoner rebellions or strikes.

Although Capone was working towards legal escape, he could not escape the ravages of syphilitic dementia; the rest of Capone's sentence was spent in the prison hospital.

Having completed the ten-year tax evasion sentence, Capone was transferred, on 6 January 1939, to Terminal Island, a Federal Correctional Institution in California, to serve his one-year misdemeanour sentence.

After his release, his mind and body continued to deteriorate and, on 21 January 1947, he had an apoplectic stroke and died from cardiac arrest.

COLEMAN, GARY (actor turned security guard) – Played Arnold in the US soap *Diff'rent Strokes*. Sentenced to ninety days in a California jail after pleading no contest in a case where he was accused of assaulting a female autograph-hunter. This hard-as-nails (not) geezer who is 4ft 7in tall hung his head and wept as his lawyer plea-bargained with the judge. He was also ordered to attend anger management classes.

DICKINSON, DAVID (raconteur, antiques dealer and presenter of BBC's *Bargain Hunt*) – In the early 1960s, the 'cheap as chips' TV presenter set up a fraudulent company, Deansgate Mail Order, with his business associates. The scam involved buying goods on credit, selling them at a slight loss and recycling the money back into the business to gain a better credit rating. This resulted in David serving four years in good old Strangeways Prison, in Manchester.

DIDDY, P (formally known as Puff Daddy, real name Sean Combs, rapper) – The allegation was that after a rival 'dissed' him by throwing money in his face, the millionaire rapper pulled a gun out in a crowded nightclub and opened fire. Puff, who was with his then girlfriend, Jennifer Lopez, was said to have blindly fired a single shot into the ceiling of a New York rap venue. After a lengthy trial, the rapper was found 'not guilty' on charges.

DIOUF, EL-HADJI (Premiership footballer) – Liverpool footballer El-Hadji Diouf was fined £5,000 for assaulting a Celtic fan by spitting on him during a UEFA Cup match. Diouf pleaded guilty at Glasgow Sheriff Court to assault under provocation. Diouf said that it was like fighting at the Battle of Britain; he can spray that again.

ELECTRA, CARMEN (real name Tara Leigh Patrick, *Baywatch* star) – Was arrested in 1999 on assault charges after she had a fight with her former-husband. Neither wanted to press charges, and both were released on $2,500 bail; the judge ordered that the two should stay at least 500ft from one another.

EMINEM (Real name Marshall Mathers III, rapper) – The Grammy-winning rapper was given two years' probation for carrying a concealed weapon. Further weapons charges resulted in the rapper being sentenced to a further year of probation to run concurrently with the first probation order imposed.

FONDA, JANE (actress) – You have probably seen the tabloid photos of Britney Spears spilling the contents of her bag across the floor of a UK airport; slimming tablets are supposed to have been part of the contents. Nothing wrong with this, but a similar incident occurred in which the contents of a handbag nearly ended up with Ms Fonda being charged with drug smuggling! In 1970, Ms Fonda was discovered to have some dodgy-looking pills in her bag at Cleveland Airport, USA, but the charges were dropped when the pills turned out to be nothing more sinister than vitamins.

GRAMMER, KELSEY (US TV sar) – The star of *Frasier* was jailed in 1990 for cocaine possession but escaped a second prison term for drink-driving after agreeing to go into a rehabilitation clinic

GRANT, HUGH (actor) – Tuesday, 27 June 1995, at 1.45am, Hugh

Grant, 34, arrested in Hollywood and booked 'on suspicion of lewd conduct in a public place' after being caught having his knob end polished by a prostitute, Stella Marie Thompson (AKA Divine Brown), 25, in a rented white BMW convertible. Tuesday, 11 July, Grant pleads 'no contest' to a charge of having sex with a Hollywood prostitute and is fined $1,180 (£800), given two years' probation, and ordered to submit to an AIDS test.

GRANTHAM, LESLIE (actor) – Jailed in the 1970s for killing a German taxi driver in a bungled robbery attempt, consequently served twelve years.

HALLIWELL, GERI (ex-Spice girl) – At 17, she was convicted of theft, shoplifting and handling stolen goods.

HUCKNALL, MICK (singer) – Simply Red singer Mick Hucknall was cleared of rape allegations within 24 hours of being detained and interviewed by the police.

JONES, DAVID (football manager) – The former manager of Southampton football club, David Jones, was cleared of care-home child abuse when his trial collapsed amongst other unsatisfactory evidence. An alleged victim refused to give evidence. The judge made clear that David Jones left court without a stain on his character.

KEACH, STACEY (actor) – Arrested and jailed in England for cocaine smuggling.

KELLY, R (R&B singer) – Arrested in 2002 on twenty-one counts of child pornography. The arrest was based on a videotape. He is denying all charges.

KING, JONATHAN (pop impresario) – Given a seven-year prison sentence for four indecent assaults on teenage boys throughout the 1980s.

KING, LARRY (US talk-show host) – Arrested for larceny on 20 December 1971, but the charges were dropped.

LEE, TOMMY (heavy-metal drummer) – All minor charges, not a true rocker. Given a six-month prison sentence for assaulting his then wife, Pamela Anderson. Was also given a thirty-day prison sentence to run concurrently for assaulting a bouncer at a rock concert.

LEWIS, JERRY LEE (rock singer) – Once showed up at Elvis's house drunk and started waving gun around and was arrested several times throughout his musical career.

LESLIE, JOHN (TV presenter) – The former *Blue Peter* and ITV presenter who was cleared of allegations of sexual assault is still suffering at the hands of the media moguls as he waits in the wings for a TV comeback. Some say that there is more chance of Michael Barrymore making a comeback than Leslie.

The prosecution at Southwark Crown Court, London, said no further action would be taken against him and offered no evidence, adding that it had 'come into possession of further material that has led to the charges against the defendant being reviewed.'

Why shouldn't Leslie be given another chance? He's been cleared of all charges and therefore his slate should be wiped clean.

LONGMUIR, DEREK (band member) – Admitted possessing child pornography, but unlike Gary Glitter, he was spared from going to jail. Why? A founding member of 1970s Scottish teeny band The Bay City Rollers, Longmuir, the former drummer, was sentenced to 300 hours community service for possessing indecent films, videos and photographs at his house. In defence, Longmuir told the court that although the material was in his possession, it belonged to an American friend.

LOPEZ, JENNIFER (singer) – Was arrested along with her then boyfriend Sean 'Puffy' Combs, for criminal possession of an unlicensed and stolen gun. The charges against Lopez were dismissed.

LUALUA, LOMANA (Premiership footballer) – The £2.25m striker admitted the devastating charge of not having a TV licence and was fined £175.

MARSH, TERRY (World Champion boxer) – Arrested, tried and acquitted of the 1989 shooting of boxing promoter Frank Warren.

MICHAEL, GEORGE (singer) – Arrested for 'lewd' behaviour in a public lavatory, in Will Rogers Memorial Park, in Beverly Hills, USA. Temporarily restarted the crooner's career.

MOORE, DUDLEY (actor – deceased) – Arrested on domestic violence charges against his girlfriend who later retracted her claim and went on to marry the actor.

MORRISON, JIM (rock 'n' roller – deceased) – Arrested after a concert in Miami, Florida, for exposing himself to the audience and using profanity. He was sentenced to eight months in prison.

MORRISON, MARK (R&B singer) – Earned two jail terms in just a few months – sentenced to a year in prison after using a body 'double' to dodge a community service order for his part in a street brawl which left a student dead. Just three months into that sentence and he was sentenced to a further eighteen months for his involvement in a nightclub fracas. Arrested on further charges in 2002.

NEVILLE, RITCHIE (real name Richard Dobson, band member) – Ordered to give £3,000 to charity after he admitted breaching the peace to a Dublin court after pleading guilty to being drunk and disorderly at a public bar. This means that the pop star gets no conviction, unless further crimes are committed.

NOLTE, NICK (actor) – Arrested after his luxury car was spotted veering towards oncoming traffic and failed a field sobriety test administered by the State police.

O, STEVE (*Jackass* stuntman) – Arrested in Scandinavia for a *Jackass* drug-smuggling stunt when the madcap extrovert swallowed a condom of marijuana and was found to be in possession of Ecstasy when police in Sweden found Ecstasy and five grams of cannabis in his hotel room. The no-holds-barred stuntman was locked up for one week after Steve O claimed in interview that he swallowed a condom full of marijuana before entering the country.

PACINO, AL (actor) – In 1961, Pacino was arrested for carrying a concealed weapon. Charges were later dropped after Pacino claimed he was en route to an acting gig and was to use the gun for the scene.

PAYNE, CYNTHIA – At her trial, Ms Payne was given sympathy from the public and was sentenced to eighteen months' imprisonment, in Holloway Prison. The charge of 'keeping a disorderly house' found distinguished supporters falling over themselves leaping to her defence.

PENN, SEAN (actor) – Jailed in 1987 for assault after attacking a film extra.

PERCY, HENRY (9th Earl of Northumberland) – Now this geezer really was a man after my own heart. Shared his imprisonment with Sir Walter Raleigh. He was lodged in the Martin Tower on suspicion of plotting against the Crown (Gunpowder Plot). While in prison, he renovated the place, even making the windows larger and having a bowling alley built in the garden. He also made hooch from his own still. Now that's what I call prison!

PHILLIPS, JASON (So Solid Crew member) – Jailed for four years after being found guilty of possessing a loaded handgun; Phillips is the second member of the notorious group to receive a custodial sentence for possessing a gun. The band faced repeated claims that they glamorised gun culture.

PIGGOT, LESTER (Royal jockey) – Jailed in 1985 for a year for failing accurately to declare tax on his earnings. Was also stripped of his OBE ... but what about Ken Dodd?

REEVES, KEANU (actor) – Arrested for driving under the influence, he decided to straighten his life out after seeing his police mug shot.

ROSE, AXL (heavy-metal singer) – Arrested for assault, property damage and in a separate incident he threatened an airport security guard who was searching his bags.

ROSS, DIANA (diva) – Arrested on board the ill-fated Concorde after an altercation with an airport guard. In a 'tit for tat' fracas, Ross grabbed the security woman when she was humiliated after the guard gave her a thorough frisk when her belt set off a metal detector.

RYDER, WINONA (actress) – Found guilty of shoplifting £3,500 worth of goods from an exclusive department store in Beverly Hills. In her defence, Ms Ryder had allegedly gone to the Saks Fifth Avenue store prepared for a shoplifting spree – armed with scissors, a big bag and tissue paper to wrap the stolen goods in after a film director told her to do it as preparation for a movie role.

When security guards confronted her, she said, 'She came, she stole, she left. End of story.' The court sentenced Ms Ryder to three years of supervised probation for two felony convictions and also ordered Ms Ryder to complete 480 hours of community service, complete drug and psychiatric counselling and pay up some $10,000 in fines and restitution.

SHARIF, OMAR (actor and gambler) – At seventy-two years of age, this guy is a real handful. After he had been gambling at the Enghien-les-Bains casino in the suburbs of Paris, over the course of the evening he had lost 30,000 Euros. He then got into an argument with the croupier and a policeman was called. Sharif then insulted and headbutted the policeman. Sharif was given a one-month suspended prison sentence and fined 1,500 Euros.

SIMPSON, OJ (actor) – Simpson was charged with first-degree murder in 1994 for allegedly killing his ex-wife Nicole Brown Simpson and her friend outside her LA home. OJ was acquitted of the charges, but he was held liable for the killings by a civil jury and was ordered to pay $33.5m to the victim's survivors.

SINATRA, FRANK (crooner/actor – deceased) – Arrested for 'Breach of Promise'! He was locked up for sixteen hours in the Bergen County Jail back in 1938. Broke off an engagement, but hell hath no fury like a woman scorned! She had Sinatra arrested, but the charges didn't stick to the Teflon Don Juan!

SLATER, CHRISTIAN (real name Christian Michael Leonard Gainsborough, actor) – Arrested for assault and battery in a domestic incident. He was reported even to have tried to grab a policeman's gun.

Also arrested for driving under the influence of alcohol, and again in 1994 for attempting to take a gun on a plane.

SMITH, ANNA NICOLE (pole dancer and filthy rich widow) – Arrested for the US charge of DWI (Driving Whilst Influenced).

STROUD, ROBERT (Birdman of Alcatraz) – Probably the most famous inmate ever to reside on Alcatraz. Portrayed in the film *The Birdman of Alcatraz* by Burt Lancaster, Stroud was shown to be a sad and badly done to prisoner. But, in reality, he was a totally different character.

In 1909, he viciously murdered a bartender who had failed to pay a prostitute he was pimping for. Stroud shot and killed the bartender and then he took the man's wallet as compensation for the prostitute.

In 1911, Stroud was convicted of manslaughter, and he was sent to serve out his sentence at a federal penitentiary in Washington State called McNeil Island. While at McNeil, he was a violent prisoner.

A hospital orderly had grassed on Stroud for trying to get drugs by threats and violence. For this, the orderly was viciously assaulted. I don't agree with grassing, but I don't agree with drug use ... so I'll call this a draw between Stroud and the orderly. I wouldn't have been able to beat the orderly up, but I could have certainly pushed him off a cliff. On another occasion, Stroud chivved a fellow con.

Stroud had a six-month sentence added on for the stabbing and he was ghosted out of McNeil to the nice Leavenworth Federal Penitentiary in Kansas, USA.

Now, one of the things that screws shouldn't mess a con over is his or her visit! The screws refused Stroud a visit with his brother, so he stabbed a guard to death in front of 1,100 cons in the prison Mess Hall.

Sentenced to death for first-degree murder by hanging, Stroud was banged up in solitary confinement awaiting his sentence. In 1920, Stroud's dear old mum managed to convince Woodrow Wilson, the President of the United States of America, to commute her son's death sentence to life imprisonment without parole.

Because of Stroud's unpredictability, he was permanently placed in the segregation unit, to live out his sentence in total solitary. After 30 years at Leavenworth and after finding an injured bird in the recreation yard, he developed an enthusiastic interest in canaries. The prison allowed Stroud to breed birds and maintain a lab inside two adjoining segregation cells.

Eventually, having raised nearly 300 birds in his cells, Stroud wrote two books on canaries and their diseases. He even developed and sold medicines for various bird ailments. But didn't old Stroud go and get caught with a still which he used to make prison hooch; he made the still out of some of the equipment he had requested for his canaries.

In 1942, Stroud was transferred to Alcatraz, where he spent the next six years in segregation in D Block and then eleven years in the prison hospital.

In 1959, he was transferred to the Medical Center for Federal Prisoners in Springfield, Missouri.

On 21 November 1963, at the age of seventy-three, Stroud died from natural causes. The original Birdman had never been permitted to see the film in which Burt Lancaster depicted Stroud as a Mr Nice, which was a far cry from how Stroud had actually spent his fifty-four prison years in solitary ... beats my thirty years of time served!

TOWNSHEND, PETE (rocker) – Insisted he entered a child porn site as part of a research project on paedophilia. Received a caution. Townshend had been caught when his credit-card details had appeared among 7,272 names handed to the police by the US Postal Inspection Service.

TYSON, MIKE (World Champion boxer) – Former Heavyweight boxing champion was arrested in 1991 for raping Desirée Washington in his hotel room. Tyson was sentenced to ten years in prison.

VAUGHAN, JOHNNY (TV presenter) – Jailed at the age of twenty-four after being found guilty of possessing cocaine and 'concerned with the supply'.

VICIOUS, SID (real name John Ritchie, punk rocker – deceased) – Arrested in 1978 for the murder of his girlfriend, Nancy Spungen, in a New York hotel. He was gang-raped while awaiting trial and was then released on bail and it is thought that the trauma of this and the loss of his girlfriend caused him to go into a severe depression. Prior to going to trial, he died of a drugs overdose. Rumoured to have had his ashes spread on his Jewish girlfriend's grave in a covert operation carried out by Sid's family.

WEILAND, SCOTT (singer) – Violated his probation conditions on his conviction for heroin possession in 1998 and was jailed in 1999.

WILDE, OSCAR (poet/writer – deceased) – He found himself in a homosexual affair with the Marquis of Queensberry's son, Alfred Douglas, whom he left his wife for in 1895. The Marquis of Queensberry accused Wilde of being a 'ponce and sodomite'. Nowadays, he'd call him a 'butt fuck'.

Wilde lost a libel case against being called this and then found himself prosecuted and imprisoned for homosexuality under the terms of the Criminal Law Amendment Act.

Wilde was first imprisoned in the notorious Newgate Prison and then transferred to Pentonville Prison. Eventually, Wilde was released from Reading Prison in 1897 and moved to France. Prison ruined his health, cutting short his life, and he died in 1900.

The only things Wilde and I have in common are that we've both served time, we both despise the system and we're both well-known poets. OK ... Wilde's a bit better known than me! A piece of work that was inspired by Wilde witnessing an execution is as follows:

Dear Christ! The very prison walls
Suddenly seemed to reel,
And the sky above my head became
Like a casque of scorching steel;
And, though I was a soul in pain,
My pain I could not feel.

I only knew what haunted thought
Quickened his step, and why
He looked upon the garish day
With such a wistful eye;
The man had killed the thing he loved,
And so he had to die.

Yet each man kills the thing he loves,
By each let this be heard,
Some do it with a bitter look,
Some with a flattering word,
The coward does it with a kiss
The brave man with a sword!

WOODGATE, JONATHAN (Premiership footballer) – He was found guilty of affray in connection with the attack on an Asian student, Sarfraz Najeib, in Leeds. During the trial, fellow team-mate Michael Duberry dramatically turned the tables when he changed his story from a previous version given. Woodgate was ordered to do 100 hours' community service.

WYNGARDE, PETER (real name Cyril Louis Goldbert, actor) – Caught committing an act of gross indecency with another man, Richard Jack Whalley, 24, in the public toilets of Gloucester bus station on the evening of 8 September 1975. Caught red-handed in the act by police, the pair were arrested. Appearing at Gloucester Magistrates' Court on Friday, 17 October 1975 under his real name of Cyril Louis Goldbert, he was fined £75 for the gross indecency.

BRONSON VS. THE SYSTEM

The following chapters concern the threat of legal action in the form of a judicial review brought upon the Secretary of State for the Home Department by Charles Bronson's legal team on 14 March 2003 following an alleged assault by prison staff at HMP Full Sutton and subsequent refusal by the governor of HMP Whitemoor to allow external medical staff deal with Charlie's medical needs. Dr Bob Johnson and Isabella Forshall were acting on the instructions of Charlie's legal team. This case was never proved in court and throughout the prison service maintained that they had done nothing wrong and it has never been proved otherwise in court. A police investigation (Humberside Police) into the alleged assault at HMP Full Sutton ended with no prison officer being charged with assaulting Charlie.

What happens when you're all alone in a prison environment and the staff mess around with you?

I was severally assaulted in HM Prison Wormwood Scrubs in 1994. Below is a report from one of my legal teams at that time. I hope this provides details so that you can see there was an agenda within HM Prison Service to do me harm. Why wasn't my case added to the many prisoners' cases who put a multi-party action in against HM Home Office Department? So many people have failed me in my bid for justice.

I want to show you how prison deaths are possible to cover up. If major assaults against a high-profile prisoner such as me can be covered up, then so can prison deaths. I have already requested that my legal team carry out an investigation if I should die behind bars for any reason. Even if I were accidentally to slip in the shower and bang my head and then die ... they are to bring in a private team. None of my organs are to be removed and carted off – I make that clear here and now. All are to be examined by my legal team's nominated party, not the Home Office vets!

RE: CHARLES BRONSON
ADVICE ON MERITS AND QUANTUM

1. I am asked to advise Mr Bronson on merits and quantum in relation to an assault upon him by prison officers at Wormwood Scrubs.

For the last three or so years, Mr Bronson, a serving prisoner, has been the subject of a regime known as continuous assessment. The reality of this regime for him is that he seldom spends more than a month in any prison, always segregated, and in conditions of extreme security.

2. THE FACTS

On 29 October 1994, he was being held on the block at Wormwood Scrubs. He had attended a memorial service for his father (whose funeral was being held the same day) the day before. He was feeling understandably oppressed by the conditions of his confinement and, as often in the past, Mr Bronson wished to spend the day in the strong box. He had requested to do so the day before in a note to the Senior Officer. In the morning, he slopped his cell out, naked, as is his frequent custom, and said to the prison officers with him – not a group he was accustomed to seeing on the block – 'Let's go to the box.' He was then attacked by the officers with sticks, boots and fists. While they were attacking him, the officers taunted him, 'Hit the bastard ...', 'We'll teach you ...', 'Your mum's dead,' 'Smash his hands,' 'You won't work out with Belmarsh screws,' and so on. He was put into a restraining belt, but it was taken off to shouts of, 'Get the small belt ...' There was then a struggle to squeeze Mr Bronson into the small belt, during which he became unconscious.

3. He woke up alone in an unfurnished cell, very tightly belted, with swollen wrists and fingers, vomit on his body and blood on his body and on the floor. He was in pain, felt as though his chest was on fire, his breathing was heavy and neck stiff. He believed he was having a heart-attack. The belt was removed after about nine hours. Mr Bronson spent the next three days in this cell and on Monday, 3 October 1994 was moved to Wandsworth.

4. EVIDENCE OF INJURIES

At Wormwood Scrubs, it seems from medical records that Mr Bronson was visited by a doctor at 9.45am on 29 September 1994 in order to decide in accordance with procedure whether he was fit to continue to be restrained. The doctor's note records: 'Because of this man's violent state, he was unable to be examined. Looked through the cell window. Lying on the floor, restrained.'

Nevertheless, shockingly, the doctor recorded his view in the Register of Non-Medical Restraints that there was 'no clinical contra-indication to continued restraint.'

The next day, Mr Bronson refused to see the same doctor, who described him, memorably as, 'lying comfortably on the floor'. It has been Mr Bronson's way over many years of prison confinement to give a wide berth to the Prison Medical Service. These two visits explain eloquently why.

5. After his arrival at Wandsworth, Mr Bronson was able to get in touch with his solicitor of the time and she arranged for him to be visited by a non-Prison Medical Service doctor that day, the 3 October 1994. Sadly, neither party treated the visit as a forensic medical examination. Mr Bronson agreed to the doctor's request to show him his right index finger which was visibly infected, and accepted topical antibiotic medication for it.

6. On 4 October 1994, Mr Bronson saw his solicitor, Margaret Morrissey. She listed his injuries seen by her, without asking Mr

Bronson to remove his clothes, as follows:

HEAD

1. Bruised red end swollen right cheekbone.
2. Bruised left eyelid, small mark under right side of eye.
3. Bruised right eye 'under the lid' towards the nose.
4. Cut inside lower lip.
5. Bruise in middle of upper lip.
6. Graze to right-hand side of chin.
7. Swollen left temple.
8. Lump and bruising behind right ear.

HANDS

9. Swollen and bruised right middle finger.
10. Nail of right index finger missing; blackish and red in colour, green around the edges.

FEET

11. Swelling, discolouration and bruising on left instep.
12. Right instep swollen and bruised.
13. Big toe nail coming off.
14. Swollen right ankle.

From the Polaroid photographs taken that same day by a sympathetic officer at Wandsworth, we can add the following:

15. Large area about 5in in diameter of bruising to the underside of the right upper arm.
16 Area of bruising about one-and-a-half inches in diameter to upper right quadrant of right buttock.
17. Large area of bruising about 4in across and 2in down to upper left quadrant of left buttock.

7. On 5 October 1998, police surgeon examined Mr Bronson on the instructions of a Police Sergeant Wells investigating the incident at Ms Morrissey's instigation. Photographs were taken of his injuries. These are presently with the police. We know, however, that the photographs were said by DS Wells in a conversation with Ms

Morrissey to be of good quality and to show clearly injuries to Mr Bronson's 'hands, feet, arms, bum, legs, face, eyes, cheek and wrists'. The FME (Forensic Medical Examiner, or police surgeon) apparently took the view that the injuries he saw 'could have been caused by falling, or other causes than direct injury, or by direct injury'.

OTHER INFORMATION
8. We have two current accounts of this incident through official prison service channels. According to the Report of Injury to Inmate form, 'Mr Bronson refused to return to his cell, assaulted a member of staff and had to be restrained.' According to Sir Derek Lewis's letter to Sir Graham Bright, MP, 'When he was unlocked for breakfast, Mr Bronson headed straight for an unfurnished cell and pushed aside a member of staff who barred his way. He was restrained by staff, placed in a body belt and returned to his own cell ...'

9. Ms Morrissey was telephoned in the aftermath of this incident by a prison officer who chose to remain anonymous. The account he gave Ms Morrissey in his calls to her was that Mr Bronson had humiliated a Deputy Governor named Gareth Davis at Wandsworth by calling him a tea boy and demanding to see his boss. This same officer had decided to set up a confrontation with Mr Bronson, had recruited a young and inexperienced control and restraint team, had briefed the team that Mr Bronson was making outrageous and unreasonable demands (when, in fact, he was following custom and practice in his case), and had further briefed them to humiliate Mr Bronson in order to take him down a peg or two in the eyes of other prisoners. Of course, the officer's evidence is not available to us.

10. There are a number of other salient features of this case. Firstly, Mr Bronson was not disciplined for the alleged assault, proceedings being abandoned at a very early stage under the 'no useful purpose' rule, despite the facts recorded by the officers at the time, and echoed by Sir Derek Lewis. Secondly, it has never been alleged that any officer was injured in the course of the incident. Thirdly, no officer chose to say anything about the incident when interviewed under caution.

MERITS OF MR BRONSON'S CLAIM

11. The information provided to Ms Morrissey by her anonymous source means that we have knowledge of a shocking moral background to this incident, which we are quite unable to prove in Court. So what we have to go on to do is to consider the prospects of success of the case on the evidence we know will be available to a Court.

12. The question for a Court to determine is whether we can prove on the balance of probabilities that, on this occasion, the officers concerned unlawfully assaulted Mr Bronson, or whether, on the balance of probabilities, they are able to show that they used no more than necessary force in carrying out their duties as prison officers.

13. Mr Bronson's case, of course, is that the officers concerned failed to give him any indication of what was required of him that morning, let alone to warn him of the consequences to him of failure to comply, and that they treated his words to them as a pretext for a violent attack upon a man who had used no force on them.

14. I take the view that Mr Bronson's injuries go some way to confirming his account. None of them is grave, particularly when one bears in mind that Mr Bronson had no clothes on at the time of this incident. But the bruises to Mr Bronson's buttocks and arms are in common sense far more consistent with being beaten with sticks while on the ground than they are with a fall (which, of course, is not in any event the explanation raised for them). It strikes me also that the injuries to fingers and toes including loss of nails bespeak a fierce, concentrated, blunt impact and are not the sort of marks one would expect ordinary restraint to leave behind.

15. Mr Bronson, however, would, I know, be the first to agree that he is really quite extraordinarily strong and that his behaviour can be very volatile. He would, I think, agree that necessary force in his case might, in some circumstances, be extreme. In addition, with the burden of proving his case to discharge, in a non-jury

action, Mr Bronson's twenty-year history of confinement in prisons, and at times in special hospitals, leaves him with some difficulties in asking a Court to prefer his unsupported evidence to that of a group of prison officers.

16. For the present, I take the view that Mr Bronson's claim should be pursued on his evidence and the confirmatory evidence provided by his injuries; however, once the Governor at Wormwood Scrubs files a defence, I take the view that we would need to seek the assistance of a consultant pathologist on all the evidence, including that currently in the possession of the police, as to whose account of their causation is preferable.

QUANTUM

17. As I have already said, none of Mr Bronson's injuries, taken in isolation, was grave. However, there was a large number of them and the manner and circumstances of their infliction are aggravating features of the utmost gravity. Damages are at large in this case and, though not specially substantial for the injuries themselves, if a Court found that the attack on Mr Bronson amounted to oppressive arbitrary or unconstitutional action by the servants of the government (as it should in my view if Mr Bronson's account is accepted) then the award would fall to be increased by a substantial sum of exemplary damages.

In the circumstances, the course I propose is as follows:

1. That Mr Bronson's solicitor, Lucy Scott-Moncrieff, again request from the Metropolitan Police copies of the photographs of Mr Bronson taken on 5 October 1994 and the FME's report, reminding them that after issue of proceedings we intend to apply under Section 34 of the Supreme Court Act for disclosure of these items to us.

2. Whatever the outcome of that final attempt to assemble the evidence and assess it before issuing proceedings, that we then see Mr Bronson in conference to finalise his instructions.

3. Once we have issued proceedings, seen a defence and, if necessary, obtained disclosure of the police evidence of injury, we

can seek the advice of a pathologist on Mr Bronson's injuries, and on whose account of their causation is preferable.

4. At the close of proceedings, we will need to assess again the prospects of success of Mr Bronson's claim.

Isabella Forshall
14 November 1996

11 Doughty Street
LONDON
WC1N 2P6

BRONSON VS. THE SYSTEM (II)

What follows are two reports by Dr Bob Johnson. The first one was produced to show that I am suffering from PTSD (Post-Traumatic Stress Disorder). This report was based on Dr Johnson visiting me at HM Prison Durham. Read this and see the way he was disrespectfully handled by the dogs who work in the prison.

The report was to show why I took a hostage at HM Prison Hull and my reasoning and state of mind at the time. Dr Johnson backs up everything I have claimed; he is a man of knowledge, a man with letters after his name and a man who knows what dogs these prison officers can be. For the first time, an authoritative academic supports what I have long claimed – that prison brutality does exist ... believe me.

CONSULTANT PSYCHIATRIC REPORT
On Charles Bronson BT1 314 (formerly Peterson, currently Ahmed)
Durham Prison, Old Elvet, Durham DH1 3HU

Born 6 December 1952, age 49

by Dr Bob Johnson
Consultant Psychiatrist
GMC Specialist Register for Psychiatry
Formerly Head of Therapy, Ashworth Maximum-Security Hospital,

Liverpool Consultant Psychiatrist, Special Unit, C Wing, Parkhurst Prison, Isle of Wight.

MRCPsych (Member of Royal College of Psychiatrists)

MRCGP (Member of Royal College of General Practitioners)

Diploma in Psychotherapy Neurology & Psychiatry (Psychiatric Inst New York)

MA (Psychol)

PhD (Med Computing), MBCS, DPM, MRCS

Approved under Section 12(2) of the Mental Health Act 1983

Member of Royal College of General Practitioners

I examined the above on Monday, 13 May 2002, in the prison stated and found as follows:

PSYCHIATRIC OVERVIEW

The psychiatric perspective on Charles Bronson is crystal clear – he is suffering from as clear a case of Post-Traumatic Stress Disorder (PTSD) as you would expect to find. Having been assured by a senior official from the Prison Service with whom he had been well acquainted over many years, that he could expect to stay at Hull Prison for a further 3 or 4 years, he was abruptly informed that this was no longer the case, that he now had to chose which of the Segregation Blocks, or Punishment Cells he would select for immediate transfer. Charles was all too familiar with all available Segregation Units having been moved from one to another every six weeks or so in a desperate and clumsy strategy on the part of the Prison Service to contain his outbursts – it has been estimated that he was subjected to 66 such destabilising moves.

This sudden and unanticipated change in his management strategy was a serious shock to this man. He had been greatly relieved to be off the 'magic roundabout' as it is known – thus, suddenly to find that his living quarters were again to be totally disrupted in an arbitrary fashion was too much for his system. He tells me that he has been severely beaten on a number of occasions during his time in prison – thus this threatened return to his earlier unsettling treatment appeared to him to be 'a threat to the physical integrity of self' as the text describes it. (See below.)

PTSD, as detailed below, represents the effects of a traumatic shock upon a vulnerable individual. In essence there must be (a) a threat, as above, (b) persistent intrusive thoughts of the trauma, (c) avoidance of circumstances of the trauma, and (d) heightened vigilance against the trauma recurring. When these are present for longer than one month, then the diagnosis of PTSD as described in the standard psychiatric text, the DSM-IV (Diagnostic and Statistical Manual of Mental Disorders 4th Edn. 1994) becomes inescapable. I include below a complete description of the disorder, as it appears in that text.

Even now, Charles displays all three. He has (b) flashbacks of the many beatings he suffered, which his abrupt change in management presaged. He avoids circumstances (c) that remind him of the threat, in so far as his restricted routine permits it. And (d) he has an inability to sleep, and cannot put the matter out of his mind. Every time he hears a van door slam, he immediately thinks that he is about to be moved again and trembles for the consequences he fears. When he walks to the exercise yard for his hour out of cell, he holds himself in readiness to be 'jumped upon' – whether the threat of this occurring is real or otherwise.

The legal issue applicable in this case, as I understand it, turns on the question of 'duress of circumstance or necessity', in which 'the words or actions of one person break the will of another'. The necessity is generally seen in the context of applying to 'a person of reasonable firmness'. Thus in one suffering from PTSD, as here, the impact of the duress of circumstance becomes more severe. By virtue of his having PTSD, Charles Bronson is rendered more susceptible than normal.

Three criteria have been suggested to me as being of relevance – (a) the act was done only to avoid what appeared to him to be an inevitable or irreparable evil, (b) that no more was done than was reasonably necessary for that purpose, and (c) that the evil inflicted by it was not disproportionate to the evil avoided.

I have not the least wish to intrude upon the legal process in which my qualifications are meagre – indeed, I only comment on these points strictly from a psychiatric point of view, in the hope that this might assist that process.

DURESS OF CIRCUMSTANCE

The phrase 'break the will of a person' has an unfortunate ring in this context – any reasonable person would seem bound to conclude that moving this man's living accommodation without any notice, 66 times in a short space of time, never allowing him to stay in one spot longer than a few weeks, can only be seen as a deliberate policy of wearing him down. Whether this goes as far as a strategic attempt to 'break his will' I leave to others to judge – it certainly cannot be seen as an attempt to settle him down, to give him due encouragement to mend his impulsive ways, and to see if something more in the way of a carrot might not succeed better than too much stick.

Given this background it is not difficult to see how desperate the abrupt change of prison policy would appear to Charles Bronson. Having been confidently reassured that his 'travelling days' were over, that he would have the opportunity to settle for a number of years in one place, get on with his art work, and put down roots – this is suddenly and arbitrarily whisked away from him, and he is exposed to what he has, over the years, come to fear most – perceived violence from prison staff directed at him personally.

(A) AVOIDING AN INEVITABLE OR IRREPARABLE EVIL

In this context, the act to be avoided, namely the recommencing of the 'magic roundabout' would appear to Charles both an inevitable and an irreparable evil. What else could he do? What other avenues were open to him? After 28 years in prison, he knows only too well that verbal protests on his part would avail him nothing – even assurances from senior prison personnel, such as he had recently received, had been shown to be short-lived. The evil he perceived was again a direct consequence of his long familiarity with prison conditions – and whatever the facts in the case, there can be absolutely no doubt that Charles Bronson was terrified of receiving further violence in the manner he feared. He tells me he feared being killed – and from my knowledge of the man and of the prison service, I find this belief, however regrettable, entirely credible.

(B) NO MORE WAS DONE THAN WAS REASONABLY NECESSARY FOR THAT PURPOSE

While he agrees that he has been impulsive, he assures me that he has never killed anyone, nor intended to do so. It is clear to me from my previous knowledge of him, and from my examination of him this week, that this is entirely correct. He has a pattern of kidnapping, indeed, in my personal knowledge he once kidnapped a solicitor's clerk which did nothing to improve his legal case on that occasion. So it did not surprise me that he had impulsively reacted in this way again. It should be noted that he did not actually physically harm his victim, and that he promptly released him on speaking with his solicitor.

Damage, especially of a psychological kind, could well have been done to his victim. However, had Charles been like so many other violent prisoners in my direct experience, then serious physical harm would have been committed almost as a matter of course, given the widespread level of violence prevalent among the general run of prisoners. Violent injury was not offered, nor, as I see matters, was it intended.

(C) THE EVIL INFLICTED WAS NOT DISPROPORTIONATE TO THE EVIL AVOIDED

Charles Bronson's fear of being killed by a kaleidoscope of changing prison staff is, as I say, entirely credible in my view. He was thus impelled to take remedial action. Though the fear of death to himself was paramount, he had no intention of murder in his mind. It would seem to me from this, that the offence he committed was not disproportionate to the fear he had in his mind.

In concluding this section, it remains to add that sending a prisoner to a Segregation Block or Punishment Unit commonly follows arbitration by the Governor as retribution for an infringement of prison rules. In the present case, there had been no such infringement. It would thus appear entirely unfair to Charles Bronson on this occasion. The prison service was here punishing him for doing what they must surely want him to do, namely settle and mend his impulsivity, which is precisely what it appeared he had been doing in Hull up to the critical moment. In a word, they were dispensing punishment when reward would have been more sensible.

GENERAL PSYCHIATRIC CONDITION

When I first examined Charles Bronson on Friday, 5 July 1991, in my then role as newly appointed Consultant Psychiatrist in Parkhurst Prison, there was not the slightest evidence of PTSD, nor of any other major psychiatric disorder. What I did find on that occasion, however, was a degree of Delayed Emotional Maturation, or Attachment Disorder. In other words, in my opinion then, he was still suffering from excess emotional dependence on his mother. This has caused him considerable distress over the intervening 11 years – especially when a member of his family became ill, or in his grandmother's case, died.

It may be noted that his outbursts of impulsivity became very much worse on these occasions when his family were in trouble. Since that first consultation in 1991, he has repeatedly requested that I provide him with treatment for this condition; indeed, at times, his letters to me were desperate, even suicidal. Despite my repeated approaches to the Home Office, his request for medical treatment of his choice was denied. Had it been acceded to, I have not the least hesitation in stating that his time in prison would have been considerably calmer – indeed, many incidents could well have been averted altogether

At that earlier time (i.e. in 1991), it was perfectly clear to me from my examination of Charles Bronson that he was not in the same category of dangerousness as the majority of other long-term prisoners under my care – he knew what he was doing, he was generally in better control, and the pressure of his internalised aggression was far weaker than the 60 murderers including 6 serial killers I got to know really well at that time. The fact is that he has never committed murder, his offences have generally been against property, and his harm to his victims has fallen a long way short of that all too commonly observed among the 100 or so dangerous violent prisoners I was regularly called upon to treat in Parkhurst Prison. In view of this relatively small destructive element in Charles Bronson, taken in conjunction with the point made about his emotional maturation in the next paragraph, the prognosis from a psychiatric viewpoint is decidedly bright; though I must add that the psychological damage he inflicted was perhaps greater than he was aware of.

I discussed our first session of July 1991 with Charles this week, and he now agrees that at that time his emotional response and indeed his dependence upon his mother was excessive. He tells me that since his recent marriage, he has become very much more stable, and more mature. He describes the death of his father, which still moves him today. It is my professional opinion that he has indeed become emotionally mature, and that therefore his risk of impulsive behaviour is now diminished to negligible proportions. He also suffers from bereavement for his father, for which treatment is clearly indicated.

From a psychiatric point of view, it is ironic that his conditions of imprisonment are now of a level of security, and indeed of social deprivation, which is far in excess of his level of risk – in terms of expense alone, this would merit re-evaluation. In terms of the damage it does to Charles Bronson's mental health, there is perhaps a case to be made for his punishment being excessive – the phrase 'cruel and unusual' comes to mind. For the last eight months he has been confined to a single cell – he has 60 minutes' exercise outside the cell in 24 hours. He is denied all social contact with his fellow prisoners. His visits are 'closed' which means that he remains behind a gate of iron bars, to which a net of one-inch squares has been secured. He is allowed no physical contact with his wife nor his stepdaughter – apart from touching finger ends, poked through these one-inch gaps in the wire netting. As a result of this excessive restriction, he can no longer face the humiliation of visits from his wife and stepdaughter, which therefore no longer take place – a further increment to his retribution.

My own psychiatric examination had to be conducted in a noisy corridor, with contact restricted as above. I regularly video my interviews with the object of showing the court, especially the jury, the inner workings of the mind. Permission to video this interview though applied for, was denied, or at least a decision deferred until after the critical time had passed – could it be that the Prison Service was as anxious as the trial judge to keep from the wider scrutiny the precise details of the conditions under which he is incarcerated.

From a psychiatric viewpoint, his current conditions of imprisonment are highly relevant. They remind me of the sensory deprivation experiments carried out in the mid-twentieth century, when exploring the origins of schizophrenia. Sensory and indeed social deprivation of this order are well recognised as highly destabilising to mental health – man after all is intrinsically a social animal. Clearly, his fears of precisely this type of treatment underlay the terror he experienced when the '3 or 4 years' he was promised at Hull were explicitly dashed.

As an earnest example of the maturation mentioned, and of the reduced level of risk he now poses, he was pleased to give me a copy of a Gist Report to CSC Committee. This, he tells me, is one of a series of monthly reports detailing his conduct during the preceding month. For eight months, he has had clean reports – no infringement of the prison rules has been recorded. Though this confirms my prognosis of his future behaviour, it throws into an odd contrast the notion that the cell he now occupies is generally used as a 'punishment cell' – though the infringement for which he is now suffering is unclear. It could be that he is being denied the maxim of being innocent until proven guilty – here he is being treated as guilty before the event. Should not the principles of natural justice be more obviously applied?

MY OPINION AND RECOMMENDATION

It is my considered psychiatric opinion that Charles Bronson suffers today from Post-Traumatic Stress Disorder (PTSD). The psychiatric evidence in support of this is overwhelming in my view. It is also supported by Dr Kennedy's report dated 24 January 2000, page 16, para 1.3. The detailed reasons for this are given above and below. Nor is there any doubt in my mind that the terror he had of the dangers posed to him by the proposed abrupt departure from Hull was the trigger for this disease.

From a psychiatric viewpoint therefore, it seems entirely reasonable to me that he was acting under duress of circumstances, or of necessity, such that he committed one crime to avoid a worse – namely his own immolation.

In so far as my psychiatric opinion is relevant, it is also abundantly clear to me that the three criteria suggested above apply in full. Namely – (a) the act was done only to avoid what appeared to him to be an inevitable or irreparable evil, (b) that no more was done than was reasonably necessary for that purpose, and (c) that the evil inflicted by it was not disproportionate to the evil avoided. The psychiatric evidence available to me at this time fully supports this contention.

My recommendation is that his current conditions of imprisonment be reviewed as a matter of urgency, not only with regard to the application of natural justice as mentioned, but more significantly with regard to the damaging effect such wanton social isolation is well known to inflict, even on the strongest constitution. It would seem to me that the Prison Service is failing in its duty of rehabilitation by imposing such drastic conditions of social isolation, especially in view of the fact that their own data show that he has not infringed any rules in the last eight months.

I would also need to add that he does require Bereavement Therapy to help him cope with the recent death of his father – it is entirely unreasonable, in my view, to deny him the expert assistance he requests and requires in this regard.

MY BACKGROUND

I have been medically qualified since 1961, and a Member of the Royal College of Psychiatrists since 1973. I am on the GMC speciality register for psychiatry. I have extensive training in psychotherapy, notably having obtained a Diploma in Psychotherapy, Neurology and Psychiatry from the Psychiatric Institute in New York in 1965. I have wide experience of psychotherapy, especially in the forensic area, both in Parkhurst Prison, and latterly in Ashworth Special Hospital, and also for 18 months in the trauma unit at Charing Cross Hospital. I have an MA in Psychology from the University of Cambridge, and a PhD from Manchester University. I have been approved under Section 12(2) of the Mental Health Act 1983, this approval now extends to 2003.

For almost five years, from July 1991 to January 1996, I worked as Consultant Psychiatrist in Parkhurst Prison, initially attached exclusively to the CRC Special Unit, C Wing, which accommodated those long-term prisoners too violent and too ill-disciplined to be easily contained in the system in general, or in Broadmoor. The majority were convicted of murder; of the remainder, there was a liberal sample of rapists, arsonists, child molesters, and other sexually deviant behaviours, all of whom I was able to get to know very closely, and whose underlying pathology I had wide experience of. Latterly, I was asked to see and to treat others in the prison in general and in particular those who persisted in harming themselves for whom I developed a degree of expertise, which was by and large successful.

I worked with Dr Felicity de Zulueta at her express invitation at Charing Cross Hospital Trauma Centre for 18 months when she was Director there.

I was one of 14 national experts invited to submit evidence, twice, and indeed to testify before the Fallon Inquiry into the Personality Disorder Unit at Ashworth Hospital, which reported last year – a transcript of my evidence and testimony is available on the internet.

I was recently Head of Therapy in the Personality Disorder Unit at Ashworth Special Hospital, Maghull, Liverpool. I had been specifically invited to work there; indeed, the post of Head of Therapy was especially created for me, to accommodate my experience and expertise. I have now provided Court Reports for a wide variety of cases, and approach this one with a background of 40 years' clinical experience.

EXPERT DECLARATION

1. I understand that my primary duty in writing reports and in giving evidence is to the Court or other Statutory Bodies, rather than to the party who engaged me.

2. I have endeavoured in my reports and in my opinions to be accurate and to have covered all relevant issues concerning the matters stated which I have been asked to address.

3. I have endeavoured to include in my report those matters which I have knowledge of or of which I have been made aware, that might adversely affect the validity of my opinion.

4. I have indicated the sources of all information I have used.

5. I have not, without forming an independent view, included or

excluded anything which has been suggested to me by others (in particular by my instructing solicitors).

6. I will notify those instructing me immediately and confirm in writing if for any reason my existing report requires any correction or qualification.

7. I understand that:

(a) my report, subject to any corrections before affirming as to its correctness, will form the evidence to be given under affirmation

(b) I may be cross-examined on my report by a cross-examiner assisted by an expert

(c) I am likely to be the subject of public adverse criticism by the judge if the Court concludes that I have not taken reasonable care in trying to meet the standards set out above

8. I confirm that I have not entered into any agreement where the amount or payment of my fees is in any way dependent on the outcome of the case.

QUESTIONS I AM ASKED TO ADDRESS IN THIS REPORT

To establish:

1. Whether he is in fact suffering from Post-Traumatic Stress Disorder (PTSD).

2. Whether his condition would have led him to take the hostage.

DOCUMENTS AVAILABLE TO ME AT THE TIME OF WRITING THIS REPORT

The following are available to me at this time:

Record of PACE interview of Mr Charles Branson dated 27 April 1999. Handwritten verbatim notes of prison officers who witnessed the incident at HMP Hull.

PSYCHIATRIC REPORTS:

Psychiatric report at Broadmoor hospital dated 11 July 1996.

Psychiatric report from Park Lane Hospital dated 12 June 1984.

Psychiatric report from Bethlam Royal Hospital dated 18 January 1984.

Psychiatric report from Dagenam Royal Hospital dated 18 January 1985.

Report from Dr Tenant dated 15 April 1985.

Psychiatric report from Dr H Kennedy dated January 2000.

Psychiatric report from Dr Chandra Ghosh dated 24 September 1999.

Summing up and verdict dated 17 February 2000 at Luton Crown Court before his Honour Judge Moss.

Witness statements – Schedule attached.

Psychological Report by Hilary Laurie, Principal Psychologist, Durham Prison, dated January 2002.

Probation Report by Rosemary Kirkby, Probation Officer, Luton, dated 11 February 2002

BACKGROUND AND PERSONALITY

Asked how he saw his parents as a child, he [Bronson] said simply of his father that 'I loved him'. He was strict, being a Navy man, one whom he looked up to. He says he misses him a lot, following his recent death. He also sometimes thinks he has not died; indeed, he went so far as to admit he does not want him to have died. These jumbled emotions are typical of bereavement, and require expert Bereavement Therapy to correct, since untreated they will inflict unnecessary pain.

Of his mother, whom he describes initially as a 'lovely lady', he now sees that he had been too emotionally dependent upon her. Two events have contributed to his gaining insight into his family configuration – firstly, he sees things much more clearly since his father died, and again he has had renewed confidence and esteem following his marriage.

PRESENT PSYCHIATRIC SITUATION

On examination, Charles is entirely straightforward. Conditions of this examination were less than ideal, as noted above – indeed, I am tempted to describe them as disgraceful. But given these constraints, Charles Bronson related extremely well – there was good eye contact, and no sign of major mental disease such as psychosis or schizophrenia. Indeed, given all the psychological ill treatment he has received, and continues to receive, he has shown astonishing mental stability to cope with it all.

He struggles for the word to describe his earlier offending

behaviour; I suggest 'impulsive' and he grasps it with alacrity. He also displays to me, and agrees when I put it to him, that he is now vastly more emotionally mature than when I examined him in July 1991 – an event he remembers in remarkable detail.

I took it upon myself to address the question of his possible emotional reaction should his mother die – since from my first consultation with him, I was well aware that this was liable to precipitate a major emotional upheaval in him. Indeed, I had endeavoured to warn the prison authorities of this likelihood, though to little apparent avail.

In the event, I was delighted by his response – not only did he agree that this had been a serious potential flash-point in the past – it would have 'smashed me' he said. But he went on to say 'I have grown up. I've matured,' which I could see from his reaction that indeed he had.

He told me that he had known he had had problems – indeed, his abundant letters to me over the last decade show this – and that he needed to sort it out. He says that earlier he wouldn't accept it, but now he is no longer fighting the system – he no longer has a need to.

POST-TRAUMATIC STRESS DISORDER – PTSD

Since the presence of this condition in this individual is the major point of psychiatric interest in the case, I include here the official description of it from the definitive psychiatric text copied directly from the DSM–IV (Diagnostic and Statistical Manual of Mental Disorders 4th Edn. 1994). I have underlined the sections which I consider applicable to this case, and comment in more detail on them below.

DIAGNOSTIC CRITERIA FOR 309.81 POST-TRAUMATIC STRESS DISORDER

A. The person has been exposed to a traumatic event in which both of the following were present:

1 the person experienced, witnessed, or was confronted with an event or events that involved actual or threatened death or serious injury, or a threat to the physical integrity of self or others.

2. the person's response involved intense fear, helplessness, or

horror. Note: In children, this may be expressed instead by disorganized or agitated behaviour.

B. The traumatic event is persistently re-experienced in one (or more) of the following ways:

1. recurrent and intrusive distressing recollections of the event, including images, thoughts or perceptions. Note: In young children, repetitive play may occur in which themes or aspects of the trauma are expressed.

2. recurrent distressing dreams of the event. Note: In children, there may he frightening dreams without recognisable content.

3. acting or feeling as if the traumatic event were recurring (includes a sense of reliving the experience, illusions, hallucinations, and dissociative flashback episodes, including those that occur on awakening or when intoxicated). Note: In young children, trauma-specific re-enactment may occur.

4. intense psychological distress at exposure to internal or external cues that symbolise or resemble an aspect of the traumatic event.

5. physiological reactivity on exposure to internal or external cues that symbolise or resemble an aspect of the traumatic event.

C. Persistent avoidance of stimuli associated with the trauma and numbing of general responsiveness (not present before the trauma), as indicated by three (or more) of the following:

1. efforts to avoid thoughts, feelings, or conversations associated with the trauma

2. efforts to avoid activities, places or people that arouse recollections of the trauma

3. inability to recall an important aspect of the trauma

4. markedly diminished interest or participation in significant activities

5. feeling of detachment or estrangement from others

6. restricted range of affect (e.g., unable to have loving feelings)

7. sense of a foreshortened future (e.g., does not expect to have a career, marriage, children, or a normal life-span)

D. Persistent symptoms of increased arousal (riot present before the trauma), as indicated by two (or more) of the following:
1. difficulty falling or staying asleep
2. irritability or outbursts of anger
3. difficulty concentrating
4. hypervigilance
5. exaggerated startle response

E. Duration of the disturbance (symptoms in Criteria B, C and D) is more than 1 month.

F. The disturbance causes clinically significant distress or impairment in social, occupational, or other important areas of functioning.

Specify if:
   Acute: if duration of symptoms is less than 3 months
   Chronic: if duration of symptoms is 3 months or more
Specify if:
   With delayed onset: if onset of symptoms is at least 6 months after the stressor.

As indicated, Charles complies with the above criteria, as follows:

A. He has been exposed to a traumatic event in which both of the following were present:
1. he experienced an event that involved actual serious injury, or a threat to the physical integrity of himself.
2. his response involved intense fear, helplessness.

The terror from being threatened with arbitrary and instant removal from the relative comfort and sociable atmosphere of Hull Prison to a further sequence of Segregation Units, which he had long known and weathered in the past, put him quite explicitly in fear of his life.

B. The traumatic event was persistently re-experienced in two of the following ways:

1 to 4

Charles shows symptoms in all these categories in B, except perhaps the physiological reactivity.

C. He persistently avoids stimuli associated with the trauma and numbing of general responsiveness (not present before the trauma), as indicated by three of the following:

1. efforts to avoid thoughts, feelings, or conversations associated with the trauma

2. efforts to avoid activities, places or people that arouse recollections of the trauma

3. inability to recall an important aspect of the trauma

4. markedly diminished interest or participation in significant activities

5. feeling of detachment or estrangement from others

7. sense of foreshortened future

Charles is less stressed by these now than immediately after the event – yet his sense of a foreshortened future, as a direct result of having the 'magic roundabout' inflicted upon him once again, especially after having been promised that it would not be – this caused him to doubt he had any future at all. Happily since then, the two events mentioned have assisted him in becoming more emotionally mature, and better able to cope.

D. Persistent symptoms of increased arousal (not present before the trauma), as indicated by two (or more) of the following:

1. difficulty falling or staying asleep

2. difficulty concentrating

3. hypervigilance

4. exaggerated startle response

His sleep difficulties are, at times severe. His hypervigilance, that is to say his excessive alertness, afflicts him every time he is taken for exercise – he fears, even now, being 'jumped upon' and attacked, beaten and even killed. I hasten to add that there is no evidence that his current warders have given any concrete evidence to justify these fears – on the contrary, he has warm words for them, given the restraints under which they operate.

E. Duration of the disturbance (symptoms in Criteria B, C, and D) is more than 1 month.

F. The disturbance causes clinically significant distress or impairment in social, occupational, or other important areas of functioning.

Criteria E and F speak for themselves.

IN CONCLUSION

Given these psychiatric findings, the diagnosis of PTSD becomes inescapable.

COMMENTS ON THE DOCUMENTS AVAILABLE TO ME

1. Record of PACE interview of Mr Charles Branson dated 27 April 1999.

2. Handwritten verbatim notes of prison officers who witnessed the incident at HMP Hull.

These are of interest but not of direct relevance from a strictly psychiatric point of view.

3. Psychiatric reports: (detailed above)

These are extensive, and in view of the length of this current report, I shall curtail my comments upon them. Dr Kennedy as mentioned, suggests the diagnosis of Post-Traumatic Stress Disorder (PTSD) – though it would seem that I place greater reliance upon this than he does. Dr Ghosh, who has known him longer than I have, concludes that he suffers, or did suffer when she examined him, from a Personality Disorder. As will be clear from my comments above, at the time of my examination, he was considerably more mature emotionally than previously, was in good control of his more powerful emotions, and showed excellent insight into where those emotions had come from – accordingly, I would no longer support the diagnosis of Personality Disorder in this case. Far more striking to me was the prevalence of PTSD symptoms, as described. The other psychiatric reports predate this incident, as also my first consultation with Charles Bronson – much has changed since they were written.

4. Summing up and verdict dated 17 February 2000 at Luton Crown Court before his Honour Judge Moss.
This has more direct legal interest than psychiatric.

5. Witness statements – Schedule attached.
This has more direct legal interest than psychiatric.

6. Psychological Report by Hilary Laurie, Principal Psychologist, Durham Prison, dated January 2002.
This is a decidedly unusual report. Frankly, I am surprised that it has been submitted at all. From the signal fact that Ms Laurie asked Charles Bronson not a single direct clinical question, it is hard to see how any of her current recommendations can be given any weight at all.

In her para 1.2 she writes 'when he stated the grounds for declining to see me'. She omits to mention what these grounds were. Charles Bronson tells me that he was acting under legal advice in so declining. The mere fact that a man is a prisoner surely does not remove his right of consent to psychological examination by the examiner of his choice.

In para 2.2 she concedes she is unable to quantify any changes in attitude that 'may have developed over time'. Given this fact, we are then invited to review a history of how he has been in the past – what is of pressing clinical, indeed legal significance, is how he is now, as I have alluded to in the body of my report.

Her recommendations (page 4 of her report) para 6 do not merit significant weight in my view, for the reasons just given. My own conclusions, as noted above, are that considerable amelioration has occurred – and I base this on direct, pointed and robustly put questions, to which the replies given were clear, open and to the point, as described.

7. Probation Report by Rosemary Kirkby, Probation officer, Luton, dated 11 February 2002.
Mrs Kirkby comments, para 7, on the dearth of therapeutic input, though he informed her that he was willing to participate in any such programme. She comments too on the improvement that appears to have taken place in his behaviour since the relationship

with his wife 'has given him the stability and determination to work for his Parole'. If Mrs Kirkby can make this observation, one wonders why Ms Laurie cannot.

MY RESPONSE TO QUESTIONS I AM ASKED TO ADDRESS IN THIS REPORT

1. Does he suffer from Post-Traumatic Stress Disorder (PTSD)?
The evidence that he does indeed suffer from PTSD is overwhelming, as I have described above.

2. Would his condition have led him to take the hostage?
The evidence, in my view, is stark and clearly in the affirmative. In order for him to avoid a desperate situation, namely a return to the insecurities and dangers as he saw it of being repeatedly and arbitrarily moved from Segregation Block to Segregation Block, he undertook the equally desperate measure of kidnap. The two are clearly linked in his mind, and I see no possible medical reason to doubt that this was the sole reason he undertook this offence. He was more susceptible at the time of the offence, since he was already suffering from flashbacks, avoidance and over-reactivity (hypervigilance) which are entirely characteristic of this awesome disease.

MY OPINION AND RECOMMENDATION

These have been given above, at the end of the Psychiatric Overview.
If I can assist in any other way, I should be more than happy to do so.

Dr Bob Johnson
Wednesday, 15 May 2002

BRONSON VS. THE SYSTEM (III)

What follows is a 'medical report' from Dr Johnson; I do not want to say anything other than all of his 'urgent' medical recommendations were ignored. This is HM Prison Service at its finest!

GENERAL MEDICAL REPORT
on Charles Bronson BT1 314 (formerly Peterson, currently Ahmed)
Durham Prison, Old Elvet, Durham DHI 3HU

Born 6 December 1952, age 49

by Dr Bob Johnson
at HMP Full Sutton, York

I examined the above on Thursday, 6 February 2003, in the prison stated and found as follows.

I am sending a copy of this report directly to the above, as is my invariable custom, though at his special request, via his solicitors as noted.

GENERAL MEDICAL OVERVIEW
This is an unusual case in several respects. Firstly, this is the first occasion a High Court Order, or its equivalent, has been required for me to gain medical access to a patient.

Secondly, there is clear medical evidence of damage arising from injury which has not been receiving the appropriate medical attention it so obviously urgently needs.

Thirdly, there is disturbing evidence that these injuries were caused by a deliberate assault of prison staff upon this patient while he was under their care.

And finally, and perhaps most troubling of all, there is the suggestion of an under-culture of physical brutality which may run something as follows – if a prisoner smashes prison property (as here, the shower room) then the prison staff 'are expected to' smash the prisoner. This latter, of course, is a most serious allegation which would require more time and resources to establish than are available to me at this time. However the very possibility of its existence would, in my view, warrant it being investigated by the highest authorities, so that they can determine whether or not such a climate of brutality did operate on this occasion, and just how widespread it might be if it did. The legal team instructing me might consider sending copies of this report to the Governor of the prison, the Director General of the Prison Service, the Home Secretary, the Chief Inspector of Prisons, the Prison's Ombudsman and others whose statutory duty it is to uphold the highest standards of care in our prisons, which represent a rather obvious basis by which our very civilisation can and should be judged.

1. LEGAL CONSIDERATIONS

As I understand it, the fact that I was permitted to examine this patient, after earlier strenuous prohibitions, relies on the fact that the Human Rights Act entitles the individual to a doctor of his choice. The fact that in the absence of such extensive legal endeavours this report would simply not have been possible – the Prison Service almost glibly prohibiting my visit – this reflects poorly on the statutory duty of the Prison Service to care for those for whom it is responsible.

1.1 CONSIDERATIONS OF TRUST

The stand taken by my legal team receives immediate and ample justification from my medical findings. A patient needs first and foremost to trust their doctor – in the absence of trust, medical practice evaporates, as here. Charlie Bronson refused to have his lacerations stitched by the prison medical staff – what clearer indication could there be that a stable, trustworthy doctor–patient relationship is the sine qua non of medical practice. No trust between both parties leads inexorably to no treatment. Both parties are thereafter wasting their time.

In a superficial sense, blame for refusal by a patient of treatment offered, in this case suturing of an obvious wound to the thumb and elsewhere, can readily be laid at the patient's door. However, since all medical practice since the dawn of time has relied upon a robust doctor–patient relationship, then the medical staff of the prison must bear a measure of responsibility for the failure of that bond to materialise, as here.

Again, the prison medical staff do not operate in a cultural vacuum – I have worked for five years in Parkhurst Prison so I am well aware of the pressures on professionals working in prison, endeavouring to maintain the highest standards of their profession. Thus the responsibility for the manifest failure of medical care is shared among all three parties here – the patient, the doctors, and the prison ethos for which the prison Governor, the prison staff and indeed the Prison Service as a whole is clearly responsible. I see little value in allocating percentages of blame in this respect to each of these three parties – suffice it to say that the failure of a therapeutic medical context should be entirely unacceptable in this age, and steps should be actively taken to remedy this medical disaster area.

1.2 THE MEDICAL RECORD AS EVIDENCE OF LACK OF TRUST

Evidence that there is some justification on Charlie's part not to trust the prison medical staff comes from a review of his medical record. Here we see clear entries dated as follows:

4.1.03 'smashed up shower block this a.m. multiple lacerations to both hands. Inmate refused examination and treatment.'

5.1.03 'injuries abrasions / contusions to Left front-temporal area, less to Right, ditto. Hands Right ?? bony injury, needs X-ray. Left 2.5cms and 1.5cms laceration to thumb. Refuses suture.'

The second entry, dated 05.01.03, records extensive injuries to his head. There is no record of where these came from. Obviously, they are unlikely to have arisen from the patient's own actions, unlike the injuries to his right hand which he used to smash the window and the basin.

No full medical history is recorded here, no suggestion that these head wounds were inflicted by others and not by the patient. The medical record is incomplete, and seriously so. The reason why it is incomplete is readily deduced – were the prison doctors to document actions entailing staff violence, then the doctor's working life would become decidedly difficult. Siding with the prisoner against the prison staff is not a comfortable position – there is thus clear evidence in the deficiency of this medical record of a conflict of interest operating inside the medical profession. This in itself is readily registered by the patient, who here withdraws his trust.

Thus Charlie's refusal to trust the medical staff has some justification since they show themselves in these medical records to be less than 100 per cent on the patient's side – perhaps in-house medical staff would find this difficult or impossible to achieve. Where medical personnel cannot, for whatever reason, put their patients' interests first, then medical practice fails, as here. If prisons concentrate heavily on punishment, then treatment, which is its antithesis, takes a back seat, as here.

I have a relationship of trust with this man, built up since I first examined him on 5 July 1991. As evidence of this, I had no trouble in obtaining a urine sample – and entering the result for the first time in his medical record. It occurs to me that this is the first occasion when the entry of a normal urine test result is of such medical significance.

Confirmation of this breakdown in medical care comes from the following. The patient and the patient's wife both assured me that he had been passing blood in his urine following his injuries. If I knew of this most ominous symptom, why is there no record of it in his medical notes? Again, the answer reflects on the parlous quality of the doctor–patient relationship. No doctor can practice medicine in the absence of a clear history from the patient – indeed, medical skill and expertise consists largely in successfully eliciting significant clinical items from troubled individuals.

Here a combination of the three factors mentioned eliminates entirely the medical consideration of this dire symptom. Since the doctors do not know about it, have no access to it, cannot raise enough of a trustworthy relationship to acquire it – they cannot offer treatment, nor, inexorably, can Charlie receive any possible medical assistance with it. Here then is clear evidence of a breakdown in medical care, arising from three sources mentioned, but nevertheless resulting in a complete vacuum of care for this individual at this time.

1.3 CONSIDERATIONS OF CONFLICT OF INTEREST

I would wish to emphasise that I have some measure of sympathy for the doctors in this matter. I know what attempting to provide medical services in a prison can entail. However, there is clearly a conflict of interest here – preserving amicable relations with colleagues among the prison officers, while endeavouring to conduct an ethical medical practice requires support and diplomatic skills which are not generally included in the medical curriculum.

Where these two powerful factors conflict, as here, then one or other must suffer. Thus, where the prison staff appear to be the cause of the medical problem, then only by confronting this thorny issue can the doctor hope to gain the patient's trust, and thereby access to the vital symptoms on which alone medical practice can progress.

Here, as the medical records clearly show, this particular nettle was not grasped, the whole issue of possible staff violence is simply ducked, placing this particular patient in a dire condition, with an untreated kidney injury of major clinical significance. Again, timely intervention of legal procedures may well have circumvented a dire outcome that no one could possibly wish for.

2 INJURY DAMAGE STILL UNTREATED

In examining this patient, it was clear that damage still remained from his injuries. He told me he was deaf in his left ear. This again has not been recorded in the medical record. There is a clear possibility that this deafness arose from injuries received. He needs urgent examination of his eardrum, something that was quite inappropriate for me in a confined cell, with six officers standing at one end. He needs a full ENT evaluation, with inspection of his eardrum. He also needs a full set of hearing tests.

He gives a clear history of continuing pain in his back; this is so severe it has prevented him for exercising since the date of his injury. This is a major setback, since exercise for this man is vital to his mental health. When I examined his abdomen, I clearly observed that his Left kidney was enlarged, it was swollen to a larger size than it should have been. It was also tender – again a serious medical indication of major kidney damage.

Enlargement of the kidney, taking into account the clear history of haematuria, or passing blood in the urine for some five days after the injury, is entirely consistent with a diagnosis of bleeding internally. He requires urgent investigation. He may even require an operation to relieve the possible haematoma, or accumulation of blood within the capsule of the kidney.

Failure to record the least suggestion of traumatic kidney disease is obviously of the gravest medical significance. Happily, the legal processes enabled me to exercise the already fruitful medical relationship I have with this man, to elicit this potentially lethal symptomatology, hopefully in time to limit long-term damage to his kidney. I need scarcely add that were both kidneys to suffer such damage (of which I have no evidence to date) then the outcome could be dire indeed.

3 EVIDENCE THAT THE INJURY DAMAGE WAS CAUSED BY ASSAULT
Charlie clearly used his right hand to smash the window and the basin. He did not use his left hand for this. However, it is his left hand, especially his left thumb, which suffered most severely. Accordingly, this is a medical indication to look for a different origin for the injuries to his left hand. His Left thumb in particular, as his medical record shows, was split from top to bottom. When I examined him, there was a longitudinal scar running the full length of his left thumb. There would appear to be only one possible explanation for this, namely that his thumb was crushed, possibly under a boot. Certainly the scar I examine yesterday is entirely consistent with his thumb being powerfully stamped upon.

This conclusion is further bolstered, not only by the patient's clear history of being assaulted but also of there being clear photographic evidence to confirm this. I was myself prevented from my explicit wish to photograph Charlie's current condition. Nevertheless, several references have been given to me that photographs taken at the time clearly show boot marks on his head. I have not, as yet, seen these photographs myself, the urgency of the medical considerations means I am completing this report before seeing them, however I am assured that this is the case both by his wife who has seen them, and his solicitor also. There is only one way that boot marks can appear on the scalp.

4 IS THERE A SUB-CULTURE OF 'AUTOMATIC PRISON BRUTALITY' ?

I did not put this point directly to Charlie, but I am sure he would take it as read that his smashing up the shower room lead directly to his being injured. For the record, he tells me that on the day in question, he was told by staff that he would be denied his one hour exercise on that day because the locks were frozen. Later, he says, witnesses saw the locks being readily used without difficulty. He tells me that the staff said this in order to watch a TV programme.

He was frustrated by this, and smashed up the shower room. Clearly, this is an immature thing to do, but given his recent history, mentioned further below, then his manifest lack of making progress in the system must be taken into account.

Were Charlie's allegation that his exercise hour had earlier been denied him on that day, then the staff should bear some measure of responsibility for his subsequent outburst – not 100 per cent, of course, but when dealing with violent and potentially dangerous pensioners, arbitrary changes of the rules should be avoided at all reasonable costs, as again I know full well from my five years' work in Parkhurst Prison. And where they are changed, then care should be taken to explain fully the reason for this disadvantage to the prisoners, an explanation that should make at least some sense, otherwise an understandable air of grievance is likely to be raised.

He tells me again of his fear of being jumped upon whenever he is out of his cell. Indeed, this fear is of a size that means he is frightened of being killed. Given the extent to which he has already suffered kidney damage, perhaps this is not so far-fetched after all.

Again, a further happy outcome of the legal intervention in this case, is that his fear in this regard is now reduced by the certain knowledge that he will be able to invoke outside medical assistance of his own choice, backed, if need be, by High Court action. This greatly reassures him. It shows him that there is a wider authority that can be applied even in a Segregation Block than the say-so of the local prison staff.

MY OPINION AND RECOMMENDATION

I have had cause to examine this man on several occasions now, notably on 5 July 1991, and it really is little short of disgraceful how little has been done to rehabilitate him. I reported in May 2002 on a substantial change in his underlying personality problems, as evidenced also by his marriage to a highly supportive wife. Surely he should now be expecting to move on to conditions of more normal prison life, and eventually taking such steps as are necessary for his sensible eventual release.

As this particular episode demonstrates we have managed to build up a level of trust which is not easy given all the circumstances. This fact alone argues in favour of allowing me to continue to treat this man over a period of time. It is highly significant that as I was discussing his general situation, he spontaneously asked me if I would undertake to see him, say, monthly, in order to continue the treatment we had started many years ago, and which he has requested in writing on almost a yearly basis since.

He has clearly indicated his preference for me as his doctor. Does this preference have weight in law? A prison doctor would have a huge mountain to climb to reach the level of trust we now enjoy. We have a history of a developing relationship – a positive history. Sadly, the prison doctors he has met have a similar length of history, though rather less fruitful, as the present episode so clearly shows.

My pattern of counselling or treatment has a measure of uniqueness in itself – every psychotherapist, like every artist, brings his or her own unique flavour to what they do. Charlie Bronson has clearly stated that he likes my 'brand' – perhaps some legal way may be found for me to answer his continued requests.

It is my considered opinion that Charles Bronson suffers from severe injuries, notably damage to his Left kidney, and his left ear.

My recommendation is that these two medical conditions be given urgent and expert medical attention from an ENT specialist, and from a renal expert. If these are not undertaken within seven days, then I would have no hesitation in advising my legal team to return to the High Court for assistance.

On the wider issues, it is clear to me, and has been for some time, that the current policy of moving him on, at random, with no notice from one maximum-security wing to another, for shorter or longer periods, apparently at whim, is entirely counterproductive.

This is not only on medical grounds, or humanitarian grounds, but also on simply pragmatic grounds.

This man states that his recent marriage has helped stabilise him. Has the prison service capitalised on this? Has it encouraged this family relationship to flourish? Have they expedited increased contact between this husband and his wife and stepdaughter?

Surely it is time to combine humanitarian strategies with prison security strategies. It must be obvious that to build a measure of permanence into this man's prison stay together with increased contact with his new family must surely make the prison staffs' job easier.

Is this a case where legal, penal and medical strategies can come together to stabilise this man's condition for the first time in his 26 years in custody?

If I can assist in any other way, I should be more than happy to do so.

Dr Bob Johnson

Dr Johnson continues with his specialist work and has recently written a book, Emotional Health (ISBN: 1904327001), which can be purchased from the James Nayler Foundation at PO Box 235, York, YO1 7YW, UK, for the price of £14.99 (includes P+P) or further details from website of: www.TruthTrustConsent.com.

BRONSON VS. THE SYSTEM (IV)

What follows is further evidence on my behalf in supporting what I claim, a skeleton argument for the High Court constructed by my legal team. When you see what the Home Office are like in respect of my treatment and ignoring many, many requests by my solicitor and legal team, then you will understand where I am coming from. Let what follows speak for itself and for all those prisoners in the future who may need to follow the same path ... let it be of help to them.

IN THE HIGH COURT OF JUSTICE
QUEEN'S BENCH DIVISION

ADMINISTRATIVE COURT

Between The Queen
(on the application of Au Ahmed, formerly Charles Bronson)
Claimant

- and -

The Secretary of State for the Home Department
Defendant

Skeleton Argument of the Claimant

URGENT APPLICATION

1. The Claimant seeks judicial review of the refusal of HMP Governor of Whitemoor to allow the Claimant access to urgently needed medical examination and treatment in accordance with the recommendations contained in the medical report of Dr Bob Johnson dated 7 February 2003 (Appendix 3, doc 1) and the addendum thereto (App 3, doc 7).

2. In spite of oral requests made on 7 March to the Prison General Manager by the Claimant's solicitor, Mr Richard Mallett, and subsequent letter to the Governor dated 11 March sent by fax (App 3, doc 2), the Governor has not responded. Such response is

treated as a refusal for the purposes of this application. The effect of no response is of course tantamount to a refusal in terms of its impact.

3. Solicitors on behalf of the Claimant were only instructed in this matter on Sunday, 2 March 2003. In an attempt to exhaust all remedies before issuing this application they wrote to the Directorate of High-Security Prisons on Wednesday, 12 March requesting a response within 48 hours (App 3, doc 3). At the time of lodging this application, no response has been received. The Directorate has also received a copy of the Letter before Claim.

FACTUAL BACKGOUND
4. The Learned Reader's attention is drawn to the Chronology at Appendix.

5. The Claimant was transferred from HMP Wakefield to HMP Full Sutton in or about January 2003. On 4 January he was assaulted by prison officers and sustained serious injuries. Earlier that day he had been denied his one-hour exercise period and, frustrated by this, he had smashed up the shower room in the Segregation Block. It was following this incident that he was assaulted. On 16 January, Humberside Police were instructed to investigate the assault. The outcome of those investigations are not yet known.

6. On 9 January, the Claimant was visited by his former solicitor, Mr Peter Boddy. A request was immediately made to the Governor for the Claimant to be seen by Dr Johnson. According to Mr Boddy, this was strenuously refused by the Prison (see correspondence at App 3, doc 4). Dr Johnson was eventually given access to his patient on 7 February after threatened High Court proceedings.

7. Having examined the Claimant, Dr Johnson concludes that not all of his injuries were sustained as a result of smashing up the shower block: 'A second entry dated 05.01.03 records extensive injuries to his head. There is no record of where these came from. Obviously they are unlikely to have arisen from the patient's own

actions ... the medical record is incomplete, and seriously so. The reason why it is incomplete is readily deduced – were the prison doctors to document actions entailing staff violence, then the doctor's working life would become decidedly difficult.'

8. The learned Reader's attention is drawn to page 6 of the Report. It lists the injuries suffered by the Claimant as a result of the assault:

1. a swollen left kidney indicating major damage of a life-threatening nature:

'He requires urgent investigation. He may even require an operation to relieve the possible haematoma or accumulation of blood within the capsule of the kidney ... Failure to record the least suggestion of traumatic kidney disease is obviously of the gravest medical significance.'

2. deafness in the left ear necessitating a full ENT evaluation with inspection of the eardrum and a full set of hearing tests

3. a left thumb split from top to bottom 'entirely consistent with his thumb being powerfully stamped on'

The doctor concludes that the Claimant: 'suffers from severe injuries, notably damage to his left kidney and his left ear. My recommendation is that these two medical conditions be given urgent and expert medical attention from an ENT specialist and from a renal expert' (p. 9).

9. Photographs of the Claimant's injuries are exhibited at App 3, doc 5.

10. 15 February; the Claimant was further assaulted by prison officers sustaining injuries to his back and neck. The incident was recorded on CCTV and a copy of the video requested by his former solicitors. A copy was not provided. Mr Boddy was informed that the footage had been sent to the Directorate of High-Security Prisons.

11. In early March 2003, the claimant was transferred to HMP Whitemoor. He has not been seen by Dr Johnson or any other external doctor since his transfer. However, Mr Mallett has been

informed by the Claimant's wife that the Claimant was recently visited by the prison doctor, Dr Nandi. Dr Nandi has confirmed to the Claimant that his injuries need to be seen by an external specialist but that this course of action had not been approved by the Governor.

12. Mr Mallett is unable to provide this court with first-hand information on the well-being of the Claimant as he has been unable to visit him. This is because HMP Whitemoor have stipulated that the Claimant may only be seen on a 'closed visit' basis. The Claimant has refused to see Mr Mallett in those conditions as he regards them as claustrophobic and is confident that he would not be able to hear Mr Mallett through the glass partition due to a combination of his ear damage and the physical impediments provided by the closed hearing conditions.

THE LAW

13. It is established law that governor's powers are amenable to judicial review in their own right: Leech v Deputy Governor of Parkhurst Prison [1988] 1 All ER 485. Leech concerned a governor's disciplinary powers but it is submitted that no distinction should be made between disciplinary and punitive powers and a governor's general discretionary powers including the power to grant independent medical examination of a prisoner.

(A) THE PRISON RULES

14. The decision whether or not to grant the Claimant access to medical examination by a doctor outside of the Prison Service is a matter purely within the Governor's discretion.

15. Rules 20–22 of the Prison Rules 1999 provide for two situations when a prisoner may be allowed to be seen by an external doctor – (a) where he has not yet been convicted (rule 20(5)), and (b) where he is a party to any legal proceedings (rule 20(6)).

16. No personal injury claim has yet been instituted on behalf of the Claimant although it is in the process of being drafted by his

new solicitor in the difficult circumstances that prevail. However, the Governor has been supplied with a copy of Dr Johnson's report: he should be aware from Mr Mallett's requests for preaction disclosure of the Claimant's medical records and other documents that proceedings are contemplated (App 3, doc 6).

17. In the interests of justice, the Governor should allow access under rule 20(6) even though no formal proceedings are under way. His obdurate reluctance to allow independent examination in the face of the critical medical circumstances attested to by Dr Johnson is unjustified. In the absence of any reasons, the only logical inference is – at worst – that he is seeking to obstruct any investigation which might expose the actions of officers at HMP Sutton. At best, he is acting capriciously with a complete disregard for the medical wellbeing of the Claimant. We state this robustly as on current information we can see no other reason why he is refusing a man basic medical treatment deemed essential by a senior doctor. This refusal comes against the historical refusal of his counterpart at HMP Full Sutton – all requests have been met by a wall of silence.

18. In these circumstances, his refusal amounts to an abuse of power. At the very least the Court is invited to conclude that his continuing refusal is patently irrational under the conventional three-fold division of Lord Diplock in Council of Civil Service Unions v Minister for the Civil Service [1985] AC 374 at 410.

HUMAN RIGHTS

19. A convicted prisoner retains all civil rights that are not taken away, either expressly or by the fact of his imprisonment: Raymond v Honey [1982] 1 All ER 756.

20. The right to life, Article 2 of the European Convention on Human Rights and Fundamental Freedoms 1950 (ECHR), is relied upon by the Claimant. It is clear from Dr Johnson's report that he is suffering a renal injury that may be life-threatening unless he receives urgent specialist medical attention. The Court's attention is further drawn to the addendum from Dr Johnson received

shortly before lodging this application (App 3, doc 7). The Governor has not indicated whether this specialist medical attention has been given to the Claimant. From the anecdotal evidence of the Claimant's wife it would seem that it has not been given. Even if it has been given, it is argued that the Claimant requires independent assessment for the reasons set out in Dr Johnson's report – namely the conflict of interest that arises where prison medical officers are asked to examine injuries caused by prison officers. The difficulties which this situation poses are vividly illuminated in Dr Johnson's report and are not rehearsed here.

21. It is submitted that any decision to refuse such examination can only be exercised in exceptional circumstances and to the extent that it does not breach a prisoner s rights under Article 2. It is difficult to think of circumstances that would trump the Claimant's right to be seen bearing in mind the extent of his current injuries which may (in the case of the renal damage) be a life-threatening condition. His condition demands that reasons be given for the refusal at the earliest opportunity and yet none have been forthcoming. The more substantial the interference with fundamental rights the more the courts will require by way of justification before it can be satisfied that the interference is reasonable in a public law sense: Regina v MOD exparte Smith [1996] 1 All ER 257.

22. Further, Article 3 of the ECHR is relied upon. The denial of access to medical examination and treatment is causing the Claimant to endure considerable pain and suffering as a result of his injuries. This amounts to inhuman and degrading treatment under Article 3.

23. It is unlawful for a public authority to act in a way which is incompatible with a Convention right: section 6 Human Rights Act 1998. It is contended that the Governor's refusal amounts to a breach Article 2 in that it is potentially endangering the Claimant's life and it amounts to a breach of Article 3 for the reasons stated above.

JUDICIAL RELIEF SOUGHT

CHRONOLOGY OF EVENTS

1. Peter Boddy Solicitors (PB) indicates to HMP Wakefield that AA assaulted by prison officer (stamping on ankle) and requests CCTV footage and record of injuries.

2. HMP Wakefield confirms no medical record as AA 'refused to see doctor and have X-ray'.

3. HMP Wakefield confirms no CCTV footage.

4. Dec 2002/Jan 2003 – AA transferred from HMP Wakefield to HMP Full Sutton.

5. 9 January AA assaulted in Segregation Block HMP Full Sutton. HMP Sutton informs solicitor that visits still to be closed visits; no explanation given.

6. PB indicates to HMP Sutton that AA assaulted by prison officers. Injuries are serious. Requests immediate attendance of doctor and photos to be taken of injuries.

7. PB attends GB and takes instructions re allegations of assault.

8. 16 January Humberside Police instructed re assault on AA.

9. 6 February – Dr Bob Johnson attends AA after threatened High Court proceedings force Governor to grant him access.

10. 15 February – Further assault on AA at HMP Full Sutton, injuries to back and neck, incident on CCTV. Video requested but not granted. Injuries arising from this assault have not been seen by anyone external to the Prison medical team.

11. 17 February – Letter from PB to Governor of HMP Sutton stating AA should immediately be seen by: I. ENT specialist re ear II. Renal expert re Kidney. No response received to letter.

12. 19 February – Henry Joseph (of counsel) instructed to consider generally bringing civil action against prison officers/Governor and/or judicial review of decision to operate 'closed visits' policy.

13. 21 February – PB writes to 9 potential witnesses of 15 February assault. PB informed CCTV video of 15 February incident sent to Directorate of High-Security Prisons at Prison Service Headquarters.

14. 24 February – PB withdraws from case.

15. AA transferred to Whitemoor (precise date not known).

16. 3 March – PB writes to Court of Appeal and confirms conflict

has arisen and Malletts Solicitors now acting.

17. 7 March – RIM attends HMP Whitemoor to be informed attendance to be on 'closed visit' basis, AA refuses to see RM in those conditions.

18. 11 March – Letter before Claim faxed to Governor, cc'd to Treasury Solicitors requesting response within 48 hours. No response received.

19. 12 March – Letter faxed to the Prison Directorate requesting response within 48 hours. No response received.

20. 13 March – Judicial Review application drafted.

21. 14 March – Judicial Review Application lodged.

WORLD'S WORST, OLDEST, HARDEST AND MOST INFAMOUS

I start with the worst, but I don't believe it to be the worst in the world. It was voted, though, along with Holloway, Brixton and Walton Prisons, as being one of the worst jails in England and Wales.

WORST:
HM PRISON DARTMOOR

Location: Yelverton, Devon, England.
Capacity: 700 beds
Category at present: Closed 'B' – Male.
Opened: 1809.
History: The architect Daniel Alexander, who also designed the London Docks, designed the prison. Dartmoor Prison was originally built some 1,500ft above sea level, supposedly using local labour, at Princetown, in Devon, between 1806 and 1809 solely to house French captives during the Napoleonic Wars (1803–15). Claims have been made that French prisoners also helped build the heavily fortified prison with its dungeons and solid 14ft-high stone walls.

The walls formed a half moon, with three separate yards containing

Dartmoor Prison, known as the most brutal and highest-security prison of its time.

seven mossy stone buildings, capable of holding from 1,500–1,800 men each; these buildings were located on the slope of a hill, fronting the east, each three storeys high, with a flight of stone steps at each end. The centre one was exclusively for black or 'coloured' prisoners. Even to this day, there is racism amongst the screws. Some 600 soldiers guarded the prison, as this was a military prison.

During the American War of 1812, many American sailors and soldiers were also imprisoned here. By 1812, the prison that was designed to hold some 5,000 prisoners was already overcrowded, and held 9,000 prisoners. Between 1812 and 1816, out of some 5,000 prisoners held there, about 1,500 American and French prisoners died in Dartmoor Prison and were buried in a field beyond the prison walls. This was the Auschwitz of English prisons!

As well as French and American prisoners being held here, it also housed some 200 who came there from the British Navy.

After the war, the brutal mistreatment of American prisoners of war was investigated by an Anglo–American commission, which awarded compensation to the families of those who had died there.

Dartmoor Prison closed around 1816 and remained unoccupied for more than thirty years, before it was reopened in 1850 as a civilian prison for convicts sentenced to long terms of imprisonment, or to hard labour; it has remained in use ever since.

A prison mutiny in 1932 resulted in the prison administration block being burnt out and most of the records up to that date were destroyed when police from all over the county were called into action. A surgeon, Cyril Sprance, who used to call on Dartmoor Prison to tend the prisoners prior to the mutiny, in his own words, is able to describe what it was like during the mutiny: 'I drove into the prison and got to the hospital. Prisoners were all round the hospital making a tremendous noise. They didn't attack us although we expected them to do so. Then Colonel Wilson arrived and I saw him lead a little over a score of men against the convicts.'

In 1959, a government White Paper declared that it was near the 'end of its serviceable life'.

In 1961, when Albany Prison on the Isle of Wight was commissioned, it was intended as a replacement; however, Dartmoor remained open.

As long ago as 1979, Lord Justice May (May Committee) commented that Dartmoor Prison was '... simply against nature'.

The prison remained in use and, following the wave of revolt which swept through British prisons in 1990, this attracted another Law Lord's dismay at the prison when Lord Justice Woolf deemed that the prison should either be closed or undergo radical changes quickly. The Woolf Report said that Dartmoor should be given a 'last chance'.

A year later, a Chief Inspector's report called Dartmoor a 'dustbin', but again said that it should be given a 'final chance'. As that report was issued, police were investigating a racket whereby desperate prisoners were allegedly paying £250 to prison officers to arrange transfers to other prisons!

Dartmoor Prison front complete with fitments

In 1991, the Prison Reform Trust, usually known for the mildness of its criticisms, called for Dartmoor to be closed: 'It is isolated and rundown and for 200 years has been dominated by a culture of barbarity and punishment. That culture is all pervasive and repeated attempts to change it have produced nothing but failure.'

In 2001, Prisons Inspector, Anne Owers said: 'Dartmoor needs to find a positive role supported by a new culture ... It needs to be part of a regional and national strategy for the dignified and decent treatment and resettlement of prisoners.'

Of course, all of this fell on deaf ears ... as usual! Dartmoor currently operates the Extended Sex Offender Treatment Programme.

Dartmoor was the setting as the site of the fictional Baskerville Hall from the *Hound of the Baskervilles* in the Sherlock Holmes series of books and films.

I have selected Dartmoor Prison for a number of reasons, but mainly because of its most notorious prisoner ever held there – Frank Mitchell ... a legend! Although Dartmoor was a place where inmates were routinely abused and degraded by prison officers, this wasn't the case with our Frank ... he did the abusing.

In jail, Frank was a feared figure and he would easily get his own way with prison staff, although he was once flogged for beating a prison officer senseless.

In 1955, being declared mentally defective, he was sent to Rampton. After escaping from Rampton in 1957, he broke into a house and used an iron bar to attack the owner.

During the police operation to capture Frank, he used a pair of meat cleavers to resist arrest; this led to him being sent to Broadmoor. Soon after this, he escaped, broke into another house and was said to have attacked the occupants with an axe, but in reality he did little more than break into an old couple's house and held them captive with an axe he found in their garden shed, and doing nothing more than forcing them to watch television with him while he drank tea with the axe neatly

Frank Mitchell

balanced across his knees. This led to the life sentence being imposed on him and the newspapers labelling him the 'Mad Axeman'.

For some reason, Frank was deemed mentally stable and was sent to Dartmoor, where his behaviour took a turn for the better. While at Dartmoor, Frank started breeding budgerigars, which could have resulted in him being called the 'Birdman of Dartmoor', but it wouldn't have sounded as good as the Mad Axeman!

By September 1966, this marked improvement in Frank's behaviour led to him being allowed to work on the outside of the prison in what was called an 'Honour Party'.

While working outside the prison, Frank would take advantage of the low security applied to him and traipse off to local pubs, always returning back to prison for the end of work; as long as he was back in time for the evening role call he was left to his own devices.

The Home Office had not issued Frank with a release date from his life sentence and he became disgruntled and word of this soon reached the Kray gang in London. On 12 December 1966, Frank was helped to escape from Dartmoor Prison by members of the notorious Kray gang and whisked away to a flat prepared for him in Barking Road, East Ham, London.

The friendship Frank had with Ronnie and Reggie Kray had started years before in Wandsworth Prison. Frank kept up this relationship and often wrote to Ron telling him of his frustration at not being given a review date for his case.

Not surprisingly, the escape made headlines and sparked the biggest manhunt in British criminal history. Exactly why Frank was sprung from the clink is not clear, but such a powerful man could only add to the dimension of the Kray gang. One theory as to why the Kray gang broke Frank was purely to highlight the fact that he hadn't been given a release date and that if they could keep him out long enough without him getting into trouble, then the Home Office would have to consider his case.

Being cooped up in a small flat led to Frank becoming agitated. The Krays brought in blonde nightclub hostess Lisa to keep Frank from becoming bored. Soon after this, Frank told some of the Kray minders that he was going to marry Lisa.

The springing of Frank seemed to have brought problems when, within days of Frank escaping (although these days it would be called 'absconding'), two letters landed at the *Times* and the *Daily Mirror* newspapers asking the Home Secretary for a release date for Frank

Mitchell. In order to confirm that it was Frank who had written the letters, his thumbprint was embossed at the bottom of each letter.

This prompted the Home Secretary to appear on national TV advising Mitchell to hand himself in. Fear started to spread amid the Kray gang that Mitchell was becoming a liability and that, if he was caught, he might talk and give the game away as to who it was who had freed him! As well as this, Frank was making more and more threats saying that if the Twins didn't come to see him then he would go to them; a solution to the problem had to be sought.

A plan was hatched to kill Frank and he was given the story by the Kray gang that he was being moved to a place in the country. The next day, 22 or 23 September 1966, a van arrived that was supposed to transport Frank to safety. As Frank stepped out to get in the van, three shots rang out, and these were followed by a further two shots.

Lisa dashed out and confronted Ronnie Kray, shouting, 'They've shot him. Oh, God, they've shot him.'

Ronnie Kray later told another gang member, 'He's fucking dead. We had to get rid of him; he would have got us all nicked. We made a mistake getting the bastard out in the first place.'

Although Frank was a fanatical bodybuilder and weightlifter, his

The desolate landscape of Dartmoor where Frank Mitchell used to roam freely brainpower did not match his size or strength. He could be lured into anything if the reward fitted what he desired. Although Frank was described as a violent and brutal psychopath, in reality he was as far removed from that description as he could possibly be. Anecdotal evidence points to Frank being nothing more than a gentle giant.

Three years later, the Kray twins, Freddie Foreman and several other associates stood accused of murdering Frank; they were found not guilty. At a later trial, Reg Kray received five years' imprisonment for freeing Frank Mitchell from Dartmoor and another nine months for harbouring him, to run concurrently with his other sentences.

Debate has continued as to where the body of Frank Mitchell was disposed of; these places range from in the concrete of the Bow Road flyover, in the heating boilers of the local baths, in the boilers of Southwark power station, in the sea off Newhaven Harbour or it was cremated by one of the firm who was also a crematorium worker.

Following the escape of George Blake and Frank Mitchell in 1966, the developments in the treatment of offenders were inevitably held back when the Prison Department found itself involved in a heavy programme of tightening up security in the wake of the report on prison security by Earl Mountbatten.

It was rumoured that on hearing of Frank Mitchell's death that Reggie cried. Many years later, a Kray gang associate, Freddie Foreman, accepted the role of being the gunman, although this is thought to have been a role belonging to another Kray associate. Frank Mitchell – RIP.

HMP Dartmoor, by all accounts, is a soul-destroying place. The segregation unit is large and is built in a forbidding, medieval, granite-walled wing. The exercise regime in the seg unit was one where you were locked inside what was described by the screws as a 'pen'. Although this was supposed to be shut down, it was still used for some time after this order was given.

This is a prison where excessive use of control and restraint has been the norm, were feigned concern from senior Prison Service bureaucrats is followed by standard denials from the Prison Officers' Association.

Disturbed and suicidal prisoners were caged like animals, which raises an even more fundamental question about who was running Dartmoor and who had the final say as to how prisoners were treated ... was it the Governor or the screws? There are parallels here with Wormwood Scrubs Prison, where prisoners were routinely beaten in the segregation unit, and all levels of staff conspired and colluded to keep the lid on it. Quite obviously, Dartmoor has always been designated as a punishment prison for difficult and awkward prisoners.

Dartmoor has experienced some changes but has a long way to go before it can become anywhere near an acceptable place to house prisoners, in particular the way that allegations of racist behaviour by the staff had almost doubled between 2001 and 2002. Dartmoor is one of the worst – give it a miss!

For those of you interested, there is a nearby place of interest – Dartmoor Prison Museum. The museum has a display on prison history and sells gifts and garden products, made by the prisoners. Would you believe that a whole industry has sprung up based on the sale of prison memorabilia?

A Dartmoor Prison walking stick ornament depicting the front of HMP Dartmoor

Worst:
HMP MAIDSTONE

Location: Maidstone, Kent, England.

Capacity: 650 beds.

Category at present: Closed 'B' and 'C' – Male.

Opened: 1819.

History: Going back to the times when the so called 'mad priest' of Kent, John Ball, was released in 1381 by the leader of the Peasants' Revolt from the dungeons, a massively buttressed fourteenth-century building. You would think that this is enough to catapult Maidstone Prison to the front of the queue when it comes to the oldest of the prisons ... not so. For this event in 1381 didn't take place at or on the actual prison site that exists today, although it did take place in Maidstone.

Work on the prison began in 1811 and was finally completed in 1818 at a cost of £200,000. You might be able to see from the older aerial shot of the prison the four-storey Roundhouse that dominates the view.

This was a hanging prison that simply carried on the accepted mode of dispatching the condemned. Prior to such a 'humane' method of execution, it was common to be burned at the stake!

Prior to executions taking place at Maidstone Prison from 1831, previously most executions had been carried out at Penenden Heath, where the gallows stood at a crossroads. The last executions performed at Penenden Heath were carried out on Christmas Eve 1830 – a treble hanging. Rumour has it that if you stood at those crossroads on the night of a full moon, you would be able to communicate with the devil.

A spoon (Old Melbourne Gaol) depicting a hanging, such is the interest in collecting this type of memorabilia

Although Maidstone Prison was a hanging prison, it was not as prolific as some of the others previously mentioned in this book. From its inception, a total of fifty-eight executions took place at Maidstone Prison, including three women, although only twenty-eight of these executions took place in public, outside the main gate, between 1831 and 1868.

The modern-day case of the child-killer Mary Bell struck a chord when she was one of the youngest child-killers around at the age of eleven when she was given a life sentence in 1968 after being found guilty of the manslaughter of four-year-old Martin Brown, and Brian Howe, 3, on the grounds of diminished responsibility.

In 1980, Mary Bell was released and she started a new life for herself under a different name. In 1984, she gave birth to a daughter. An injunction prevents their identities from being disclosed.

But going back to 1831, the youngest person to be executed at Maidstone Prison was the namesake of Mary Bell, John Bell, fourteen, who was hanged in front of the prison on 1 August 1831 with a crowd of 5,000 onlookers.

Had Mary Bell been convicted back in that time then she might have been assured a swift hanging, but she escaped, as did the eleven-year-old brother of John Bell, James, who was involved in the crime but turned against his brother and became a witness for the prosecution (Queen's Evidence).

Both James and John Bell attacked thirteen-year-old Richard Taylor and robbed him of the sum of 9s when he walked through a wood in Chatham. John Bell was executed by hanging on 29 July 1831.

Maidstone Prison holds the record for the last public hanging in Britain when, at midday on Thursday, 2 April 1868, 2,000 people watched as Frances Kidder, twenty-five, was hanged for the murder of her eleven-year-old stepdaughter, Louisa Kidder-Staples.

As if holding that record wasn't bad enough, Maidstone Prison also holds the record for the last man to be hanged in public in Britain some twenty-eight days after the last woman was hanged in public. On 30 April 1868, Richard John Bishop was hanged for murder. A minor argument had turned nasty, and when Bishop was being led away to the local police station, he stabbed and killed the man he had been arguing with who had also been arrested with him.

As if holding these two records wasn't enough, Maidstone also holds the record for having carried out the first hanging under the Capital Punishment within Prisons Bill passed on 29 May 1868, which brought an end to public hangings.

Under the new law, the first ever hanging took place inside Maidstone Prison when a minor, eighteen-year-old Thomas Wells, was hanged on the 13 August 1868 for shooting his boss. The execution took place in a makeshift execution shed, which was the former timber yard within the prison grounds.

Anyone remember the case of the 'Brides in the Bath' serial murderer, George Joseph Smith? All of Smith's new brides seemed to drown mysteriously in the bath and he went on to become quite wealthy. Nowadays, such a case would be splashed all over the newspapers and make headline news for weeks and weeks, right down to the man selling Smith the wedding dress ... and it did back then.

The first charge to be put to Smith was a one of bigamy and then the drownings were fully investigated ... and the rest is history. Smith was charged with three murders which were proven by an eminent pathologist to be non-accidental. The victims were proven to have been drowned by having their legs pulled down by lifting up the knees with one hand while having their heads pushed down with the other. Aptly, on Friday, 13 August 1915, Smith was hanged.

The last judicial hanging in Maidstone Prison was rather earlier than the last judicial hanging in Britain when, on 8 of April 1930, Sidney Fox,

31, was hanged for murdering his mother ... so no records broken there. The hangings continued, but were transferred from the remit of Maidstone to that of Wandsworth Prison.

I have never been to HMP Maidstone, so why have I given it a mention? This prison was responsible for hanging a fourteen-year-old boy! That makes it a bad place, no matter how long ago it was.

I also thought that it is a bit odd that, as one of the main prisons in and around London that I would like to have visited while on my tour of prisons, why have I never been parked up there? I'm a bit of a fan on the statistics of hanging and when I found that Maidstone held some records in this department, I wanted it listed in my book.

Oldest Working Prisons:
HM PRISON LANCASTER

Location: The Castle, Lancaster, England.
Capacity: 220 beds.
Category at present: 'C' – Male.
Opened: 1458.
History: This is the oldest working prison in Europe. The foundations of the castle are that of a Roman Hill Fort dating back to AD 95. Some of the walls in places are over 5ft thick. No tunnelling out of this place.

You don't get a meaner-looking place than this! This is how I imagined in my worst nightmares what a prison would look like; it even puts Colditz to shame, but I have been fair and listed it amongst the oldest.

Oldest Working Prisons:
HM PRISON SHEPTON MALLET

Location: Shepton Mallet, Somerset, England.
Capacity: 220 beds.
Category at present: 'C' – Male.
Opened: 1610.
History: This is the oldest and grimmest-looking working prison in England, apart from Lancaster Castle, which has been classified as

Europe's oldest working prison. The place is awash with history; it even housed the Magna Carta, the logs of Nelson's Flagship, HMS Victory, and a copy of the Domesday Book for protection during World War II.

During the Second World War, part of the prison was taken over by the American government. As well as serving the USA as a military prison, it also served as a place to execute American servicemen convicted under the provisions of the Visiting Forces Act (1942), which allowed for American Military justice to be enacted on British soil.

The US method of hanging was outlawed in the UK, as it was a fair bit more barbaric than the British way, they did not have a calculated drop based on the condemned person's height and weight, they just had a standard drop and the noose was just left coiled on the gallows floor.

Oldest Prisons:
BISHOP'S PRISON, 1080

Now this place will take some beating for age! This is the nearest thing you will get to see what the 'Clink' prison cells must have looked like. This prison can be seen in Durham Cathedral, England, where it was used to house bad monks. Yeah, a corrective holding cell for way-out mad monks. And it's no longer in use!

Oldest Prisons:
CLINK PRISON, 1127–1780

Many claims to the title of the oldest prison in England have been made, but I reckon the original 'Clink' gaol, which was in the London borough of Southwark, was certainly one of the oldest prisons in England, although the first mention of a secular prison is made in *The Laws of King Athelstan* (925-39), which stated that a 'thief can spend up to 40 days in prison'.

The use of the saying 'in the clink' stems from this prison, which was a franchise of the Bishops of Winchester ... so long before Group

4 came along to run privatised prisons, these Bishops had a hand in running them.

The prison may well have been up and running as early as 1127 when Bishop Gifford had completed his palace when bawds and whores were to be committed to the bishop's prison.

The Clink Prison Museum is on the site of the original Clink Prison, which held prisoners from the early Tudor years until 1780. Shakespeare allegedly visited an old schoolfriend at the prison. The museum is located at 1, Clink Street, London SE1 9DG, England.

Oldest Prisons:
HEXHAM TOWN PRISON, 1330

This prison was the first purpose-built prison in England and was used to imprison convicted Reivers. This area is bathed in history and there is mention of St Wilfrid (634–709AD) coming into conflict with the

King of Northumbria, who threw him into prison for nine months. This indicates that a prison within Northumbria existed much earlier than the one in Hexham town. On release from prison, Wilfrid was banished from Northumbria and he fled to Sussex. While in Sussex, he played a very important part in converting the South Saxons to Christianity.

Currently, the old jail is a museum and concentrates on the history of the Reivers with reconstructions, artefacts and interpretation. The museum is open all year, 10.00am to 4.30pm daily from April–October and Saturday, Mondays and Tuesdays throughout the rest of the year. Tel: +44 (0) 1434 652349.

Oldest Prisons:
NEWGATE PRISON, 1188–1902

Not quite the oldest, but it is always laying claim to this title. In 1188, Henry II ordered that a piece of land adjoining Newgate be bought and that a prison be erected on it and, from that, Newgate Prison was built by two carpenters and one smith for the cost of £3 6s 8d!

I have mentioned the worst prisons, but this prison was built for the worst prisoners. Good job it's closed down. The whole grisly bunch of prisoners were known as 'Newgaters'.

Along came Henry III, and the prison was then enlarged; no one ever comes along to make a prison smaller! But by the 1500s it was in poor shape and had to be given a further facelift, but the Great Fire of London in 1666 came along and burned the place down ... what a shame!

Soon after, the place was rebuilt in 1672, but, by all accounts, it was still a dog of a place. Not much different to many of the places I've been incarcerated in – poor lighting, poor ventilation, poor hygiene facilities and a poor water supply ... what's changed?

Every such prison like this has a dungeon below ground. I've been slammed into many such dungeons in what are called 'modern-day' prisons; how nice! At Newgate Prison, they had such a place below ground called a 'stone hold' where certain prisoners were segregated. These places had no beds; you lay on the stinking ground, like I have had to on many occasions. Historians damn these places, yet they overlook modern prisons! Are they blind?

By 1778, the prison was demolished and a new one built on the old site, but along came rioters from the 'Gordon Riots' and the place was wrecked. Reminds me of the Strangeways Riot, only, in the Gordon Riots, some 300 prisoners escaped from Newgate Prison.

Between 1780 and 1783, the prison was rebuilt ... can't blame them for not trying! The place was now a hanging prison and many a condemned person was hanged from the gibbet at the front of the place. This was a regular entertainment event and people would pay to get the best seats.

In 1868, in accordance with new laws, hangings were carried out behind the prison walls.

In 1902, the place was finally demolished in order to make way for the central criminal court.

Hardest:

HM PRISON PORTLAND

Location: Portland, Dorset, England.
Capacity: 600 beds.
Category at present: Closed 'YOI' – Male.
Opened: 1848.
History: The decision to site such a prison in this location was based upon the presence of quarries where the convicts could labour, and its dominant coastal position, which was convenient for the disciplining of convicts prior to their transportation.

The conditions within the prison back in the 1800s were cruel and its quarries were a major catalyst in bringing about penal reform in this country.

The quarries were the scenes of many a convict death; the stone hewn from the quarry by the convicts was used to build Portland's naval breakwater.

During the 1870s, the mortality rate among prisoners was high with nearly one prisoner dying every week. With floggings still being a part of the daily punishment and poor working conditions, it meant that many a prisoner's scream could be heard in the nearby homes of civilians. This was the hardest of prisons by far, and a far cry from the cushy lifestyle the young offenders have know ... they only get beaten once a week!

Top: Prisoners making boots a rather long time ago in HMP Portland. Look at the screw in the background ... looks like a Keystone cop.

Middle: A very old photo showing prisoners being frisked by prison officers at HMP Portland. Note the arrows on the prisoners' clothes.

Left: These Wade prisoner figures have the same arrows.

One of the most famous of prisoners to come out of Portland Prison was a man called John 'Babbacombe' Lee. They tried to hang him three times and failed, so he became world-famous as the man they could not hang.

The history of John Lee was that he had been a servant since leaving school, but in 1879 he had joined the Navy but was invalided out after three years. Eventually, he found work as a boot boy at the Royal Dart Hotel in Kingswear.

After a short while, he then went back to Torquay and worked as a porter at Torre Railway Station and then as a footman at a large villa in the Warberries.

In 1883, he was convicted of stealing from his employer and sentenced to six months' imprisonment. In January 1884, he was taken on in the employ of his half-sister, Elizabeth Harris, who had spoken for Lee.

On 14 November 1884, in the early hours of the morning, the usual quiet of Babbacombe was greatly unhinged when a servant at The Glen discovered some very large fires and she rushed to get help.

After the fires were extinguished, the body of Miss Keyse was

The fitters shop at HMP Portland, looks about 100 years or so ago!

discovered lying on the dining room floor ... her throat had been cut and she had three wounds to her head. The killer had tried to cover his tracks by setting fire to the place in the hope that the body would have been burned and so, with it, any evidence of foul play.

Nothing had been stolen, but John Lee, 20, was the only male in the house and he had a cut to his arm and could not account for the injury or give an account of his movements at the time of the murder.

At Exeter Assizes on 5 February 1885, Lee was found guilty of murder and sentenced to hang. The evidence against Lee was only circumstantial, and he pleaded his innocence prior, during and after the trial. After being sentenced, Lee said to the judge, 'The reason I am so calm is that I trust in the Lord and he knows I am innocent.'

Come the day of the execution, the man in black doing the hanging was James Berry, an experienced executioner. The condemned man stood on the trap door, the lever was pulled ... and nothing happened! Three times this was carried out and each time the trap door was tested and, although the trap on the scaffold opened successfully every time it was tested, it failed to open when John Lee stood on it with the noose around his neck.

The execution was cancelled and the Home Secretary commuted the death sentence to penal servitude for life.

After serving twenty-three years behind bars, on 18 December 1907, John Lee was released from prison. Rumours abound about what happened to him after his release, but in 1909 he is said to have married a girl called Jessica Bulled in Newton Abbot. By 1911, he and his wife and two children were said to be in London, but Lee deserted his family and possibly went to America or Canada, but it may even have been Australia. Nobody really knows.

Most Infamous:
ALCATRAZ

Location: San Francisco, USA.

Capacity: 336 beds.

Category at present: None.

Opened: 1934 as a prison for criminals.

History: In 1934, the old military prison on Alcatraz was given a face-lift along with a variety of security upgrades. The type of prisoner being housed here was originally intended as the most dangerous, but time would see unruly prisoners who fought against the establishment making their homes here.

The place even had tear gas canisters permanently installed in the dining room ceiling and guards and guard stations were strategically placed to further heighten security. Dubbed 'The Rock' due to its location on an island, it was used for twenty-nine years to house the USA's worst criminals, and earned its reputation as 'Uncle Sam's Devil's Island'.

The federal government wanted to prove to the American public that it was tough on crime, just as the former Home Secretary Jack Straw

The Rock – Alcatraz, the prisoners' prison!

tried to prove so in England. The Great Depression of the 1920s in the USA brought about a massive rise in serious crime, and organised crime was fast becoming a problem.

The Prohibition law outlawing booze resulted in major gangster activity and public pressure prompted the decision to open a maximum-security prison to house some of the worst offenders.

The conditions on Alcatraz were never overcrowded due to the prison never running to full capacity – the one-man-to-a-cell living conditions actually made it a more desirable place to be incarcerated than in other prisons.

Although Alcatraz was a humane place, there were still strict rules in place: inmates weren't allowed to speak to each other except during meals and recreation periods. Escape from The Rock, with its cold waters surrounding the prison, was difficult and the winds blowing in from the water made the prison itself an unpleasantly cold place.

Although physical punish-ment was limited, torture to inmates on emotional and physiological levels could be promoted by putting them into cells with such aptly titled names such as the 'strip cell' or the 'hole'.

By August 1934, the first batches of inmates were selected from the penitentiaries of the USA when prison wardens were polled on whom they would like to send from their own establishment to Alcatraz. Among the first batch were the likes of Al Capone, Robert 'Birdman of Alcatraz' Stroud and Floyd Hamilton (Bonnie and Clyde gang driver).

By the time Alcatraz closed down, some 1,742 unruly and dangerous prisoners had passed through the place, but not all of them were gangsters, but just prisoners who had refused to follow rules, who were considered dangerous, or who required closer supervision to prevent escape.

Robert Stroud, the Birdman of Alcatraz.

PRISON MUSEUMS

These collectable Wade figures illustrate the kind of industry there is in law and order memorabilia.

BEAUMARIS GAOL

The prison was built in 1787 and enlarged by the Victorians. Many prisoners here were deported to Australia and many more were executed on the ramparts. The prison chapel is fascinating in its sadistic design – rows of cubicles were built so that felons could see the preacher but not their fellow inmates. Beaumaris Gaol, Steeple Lane, Beaumaris, Anglesey, LL58 8EP, North Wales. Opening hours: Easter–September 10.30am–5.00pm or at other times by appointment. Educational groups and parties welcome. Tel: 01248 810921. Anglesey Heritage Gallery: Tel: 01248 724444.

DERBY GAOL

Derby Gaol is situated in the basement of 50/51 Friar Gate. Derby is a working museum where you can go and see the actual cells where prisoners were housed. The prison first opened in 1756 and closed down in 1828, but has now been restored to its former condition. The museum is normally open on Saturdays from 11.00am–3.00pm where you can even have parties in the cells ... we have them in prison so you might as well have them in a prison, too! Derby Gaol, 51/55 Friar Gate, Derby, England.

INVERARAY GAOL

Since opening in 1989, Inveraray Gaol has established itself as one of Scotland's most exciting heritage attractions. Visit the magnificently restored 1820 Courtroom where you can sit and listen to excerpts from trials of the past. Then pass on to the prisons below, and meet with Warders, Matron and Prisoners in period costumes. See the airing yards, furnished cells and experience prison sounds and smells. Ask the 'Prisoner' how to pick Oakum. Turn the handle of an original crank machine, take forty winks in a hammock or listen to Matron's tales of daily life as she keeps one eye on the nursing mother, barefoot thieves and the lunatic in her care. Church Square, Inveraray, Argyll, PA32 8TX, Scotland. Tel: +44 (0) 1499 302 381. Fax: +44 (0) 1499 302 195. Website: www.inverarayjail.co.uk

JEDBURGH CASTLE GAOL

The Castle Gaol, with a commanding view over the town, was built as a reform jail in 1820 on the site of the original Jethart Castle, which was demolished in 1409 to keep it out of the hands of the English. The jail now houses a museum of social history, re-opening in 1996 following major refurbishment of its displays. The displays in the cell blocks tell the story of the Howard Reform Prison, using costumed figures and period rooms. Jedburgh Castle Gaol, Castlegate, Scottish Borders. Tel: +44 (0) 1835 863254. Open: Easter to end October.

KILMAINHAM GAOL

Kilmainham Gaol is where you need to go to learn about the origins of the modern Irish State. It was here that the rebels of the last 150 years of British rule were held and it was here that the leaders of the 1916 Uprising were executed. No other single event propelled Ireland to independence.

The Gaol was much neglected since Eamon De Valera left it as the last prisoner in 1924 and, although it has undergone much renovation since, the terrible character of the place is undiminished. The struggle for independence is very well charted and a guided tour and video show fills out the details.

It is believed to be the largest unused prison in Europe and over its existence housed many criminals as well as political prisoners. You can only imagine the suffering that went on here. Kilmainham Gaol, Dublin, Eire. Opening Hours: April–Sept: 9.30am–4.45pm daily. Oct–March: Monday–Friday 9.30am–4.00pm, closed Saturdays. Sundays 10.00am–4.45pm.

STIRLING OLD TOLLBOOTH GAOL

For 400 years, Stirling's prisoners were kept in the old Tollbooth Jail. It was a stinking, overcrowded place. There came pressure for improvement and prison reform so the new purpose-built Stirling Old Town Jail was opened in 1847. Designed by Thomas Brown and opened as a County Jail, the building was used as the only military prison in Scotland from 1888 until 1935. Restoration to its current use began in the early 1990s. Stirling, St John Street, Stirling Old Town, Scotland. Tel: +44 (0) 1786 450050. Site open daily all year round.

Yorkshire Law and Order Museum
For details about the museums attractions, access the website: www.ripon.co.uk/museums

TIEPINS, QUOTES
AND GHOSTS

The prison industry has become big business – book sales, newspaper sales, employment and the media ... all big bucks. Talk about prisoners exploiting the system, what about the others milking it? People talk about the 'victim' as if it were a crime to make a penny from the crimes one commits, but the bigger fish are riding on the backs of those committing the crimes. For one, cut crime down to zero and you'd make a billion people lose their jobs. Don't knock us criminals; we're keeping one billion people in their jobs, and helping many of them get rich.

A tiepin badge promoting the former Maze Prison (Northern Ireland) Rugby Football Club

Any of you a fan of Lynda La Plante? Did you know that her production company used my character in their *The Governor* TV series? I include copy of her letters below:

La Plante Productions Limited
Paramount House

1st May 1996

Dear Charlie

Thank you for your letters and especially thank you for your wonderful cartoon book. The drawings made me laugh and cry. They also impressed me because you are still able to joke about your situation. Sometimes when I read what you have written in your letters I have to stop and look away from the page. Thirty years behind bars is hard to comprehend, making your jokes and wit even more poignant.

I've just spent a long time in America, but I think Alice wrote and told you I was away. I was actually on a book tour, crossing the United States from New York to LA with seven stops between. Jet-lag is a strange feeling, a little bit like you've woken up and are not sure where you are, what time it is, or what day or month for that matter.

I have been told that you are to be the subject of a Panorama. *So, your story, your life, will unfold for many people who I don't think truly believed that* The Governor *depicted prison life as it is today. The actor who portrayed the character called Tarzan is called Terry O'Neill. I will pass on your best wishes to him as he will be pleased that you approved of his performance.*

Terry is very famous as a karate seventh Dan black belt, and three times world champion. He writes and edits his own magazine called Fighting Arts International. *He is a man I respect greatly; very kind and thoughtful, and physically a very strong man. I shall pass on your letter and perhaps he will write to you, or you could write to him. I will also ask him to send you some magazines if they are allowed to be handed over to you.*

You must understand though, Charlie, that Tarzan is only based on you and some of your background. When writing a drama I cannot ever state categorically that the character is someone in particular and your name is never mentioned. The Governor is not a documentary but a drama series. And therefore sometimes I have to take a certain amount of dramatic licence. I have not put in anything that Lorraine did not approve of. Also, Tarzan does return to the wing and he does prove himself to be a highly intelligent individual. But, you must understand that what I have depicted is probably two to three years ago and all past. Whatever happens to you now is your future. And I hope it will be one with a possible release for you, so that you may care for your father.

I am very excited about your forthcoming book and I think your title Concrete Coffin *is a good one. I also hope, Charlie, that because of your talent as a writer it will help you become more settled as a person. And you do have such a talent and you must try not lose it due to anger or bitterness. Writing is a special gift, it will open doors of freedom, if not physically then mentally, and you will, and can, go any place you choose. That is why writing means so much to me. Sometimes I lose myself in words, lose any hurt or pain I feel. I just put it all down and it eases me, as I hope your work will begin to ease you, and calm you.*

Thank you for your letters which I appreciate. Thank you also for allowing the character of Tarzan to exist, he really made a great impact on the series. I do not know if I will get another series going as I have not heard from the ITV network yet. I hope so as I feel the series teaches the public about prison life. I also hope it will act as a deterrent for young men watching who might foolishly think that a life behind bars and a prison sentence is something they can misguidedly be proud of.

I think you have a lovely soul sister in Lorraine. She really is a nice lady and we keep in touch. I will write to you again soon but in the meantime I want to ask you to do something for me. I know perhaps you have felt great animosity, anger, and hatred towards Prison Officers, but I also met some truly caring men who want nothing more than to help prisoners. These men have a job to do, whether you like them or not. They have to do their job, Charlie.

They have to earn a living and provide for their families. So, I am asking you to stay calm, concentrate on your writing, and not think crazy thoughts.

My grandfather used to have these words printed on a card by his bed and I think of them often. I want you to think of them, too.

Think big and your dreams will grow
Think small and you will fall behind
Think that you can and you will
It is all in a state mind.

Goodbye for now.

Lynda La Plante

Look at some of the projects to emerge using prison and crime themes:

FILMS
The Birdman of Alcatraz
Buster
Face-Off
The General
The Great Escape
The Green Mile
Hannibal
Harry Potter and the Prisoner of Azkaban
The Hurricane
Lock-Up
The Mean Machine
Reservoir Dogs
Scum
The Shawshank Redemption
Tango and Cash

TELEVISION
Bad Girls

Bergerac
The Bill
Carry On the Prisoner of Spenda
Cracker
Crimewatch UK
Columbo
Shoestring
Frost
The Governor
Inspector Morse
McCloud
Midsomer Murders
Murder She Wrote
Prime Suspect
Porridge
Prisoner Cell Block H
The Prisoner
The Sweency
Z Cars
The list is endless ...

BOOKS
The Godfather by Mario Puzzo
The Prisoner in the Mask
The Prisoner of Zenda by Anthony Hope

PC GAMES
Alcatraz – Prison Escape

CONSTRUCTION GAMES
Lego's Pirate Jail

PLAYSTATION
Prisoner of War

BOARD GAMES
Monopoly

THE GOOD PRISON GUIDE

HENRY BRACTON
(Priest and Jurist) died 1268

(carcer ad continendos et non ad puniendes habere debeat)
'These private prisons developed according to the foibles and
idiosyncrasies and the financial and political fluctuations in power,
of the grantees, creating a multitude of abuses which of
themselves constituted actual punishment.'

ANGELA DAVIES
(Activist)

'Jails and prisons are designed to break human beings,
to convert the population into specimens in a zoo –
obedient to our keepers, but dangerous to each other.'

LORD DENNING
(Then head of the Court of Appeal (Civil Division),
in the case of Becker v Home Office 1972)

Lord Denning ruled that the Prison Rules did not give prisoners
any rights at all and, as a consequence, even if the prison Governor
drove a coach and horses through them, that did not of itself give
any prisoner the right to complain to the courts.

DWIGHT D EISENHOWER

'Americans, indeed all freemen, remember that, in the final choice,
a soldier's pack is not so heavy a burden as a prisoner's chains.

JIMMY HOFFA

'I can tell you this on a stack of Bibles: prisons are archaic, brutal, unregenerative, overcrowded hell holes where the inmates are treated like animals with absolutely not one humane thought given to what they are going to do once they are released. You're an animal in a cage and you're treated like one.'

HUBERT H HUMPHREY
(1911–1978)

'There are not enough jails, not enough police, not enough courts to enforce a law not supported by the people.'

ROBERT KENNEDY

'Every society gets the kind of criminal it deserves. What is equally true is that every community gets the kind of law enforcement it insists on.'

ROBERT MITCHUM

'The only difference between me and my fellow actors is that I've spent more time in jail.'

FRANKLIN D ROOSEVELT
(1882–1945)

'Men are not prisoners of fate, but only prisoners of their own minds.'

'No man is above the law, every man is below it, and we need ask no man's permission when we require him to obey it.'

JOHN RUSKIN

'Let us reform our schools,
and we shall find little reform needed in our prisons.'

GEORGE BERNARD SHAW

'It is the deed that teaches, not the name we give it.
Murder and capital punishment are not opposites that cancel one
another, but similars that breed their own kind.'

ALEXANDER SOLZHENITSYN

'The thoughts of a prisoner – they're not free either.
They keep returning to the same things.'

MOTHER TERESA

'What you do to these men, you do to God!'

MARK TWAIN

'There was a proposition in a township there to discontinue
public schools because they were too expensive. An old farmer
spoke up and said if they stopped the schools, they would not save
anything, because every time a school was closed a jail had to
be built. It's like feeding a dog on his own tail. He'll never get fat.
I believe it is better to support schools than jails.'

OSCAR WILDE

The vilest deeds like poison weeds
Bloom well in prison air;
It is only what is good in man
That wastes and withers there.

HMP BROCKHILL

Location: Redditch, Worcestershire.
Capacity: 170 beds.
Category at present: Female Local.
Opened: 1965.
History: This prison was originally a remand centre for male and females serving HMP Winson Green in Birmingham. After two years, all of this changed and the place became a YOI Remand Centre and then it was earmarked for closure in the early nineties. But, as always, these decisions, based on cost, are often overruled, and the place became an all-male Cat 'C' training prison. All change! Again, the place changed status and became, due to female overcrowding in the penal system, an all-female local prison, which it remains at the time of writing.

After reports that a ghostly monk was walking through walls at this prison, inmates were offered counselling. Even some of the prison officers also reported feeling uneasy after spotting ghostly goings on while on their night shifts.

The jail, with a small population of less than 170 prisoners, stands in the grounds of Hewell Grange Estate, a former manor house owned by the Earl of Plymouth. There is also a male open prison nearby.

Such a sighting of a monk could be due to the past history of the estate and the fact that it is near Bordesley Abbey in Redditch, which would account for the apparition being a monk. On seeing the apparition, both staff and inmates admit to having had strange sensations. Sleep well, girls!

HM PRISON DURHAM

All old jails have to have a ghost or two. Durham Prison also, apparently, has its own ghost. The story goes that in December 1947, an inmate stabbed a fellow prisoner to death with a table knife. Then, a few days later, another prisoner was put into this same cell and, the next morning, was found in the corner of the cell in a huddled up state of fear. What he told the screws sent chills of fear down their spines; he had seen the murder re-enacted. Eventually, the cell was converted into a storeroom due to prisoners refusing to be put into it.

HM PRISON OXFORD

Although I didn't stay at Oxford for more than the blink of an eye, I did follow up my stay there by digging around into its past. Well, what is a man to do in his cell all day but read and exercise? There have been many ghostly happenings at Oxford Prison, and I do a like a ghost story or two.

As I've already said earlier on, you surely can't escape hauntings by those who have passed on inside prison. What about all those people executed behind the walls of pain and suffering? What about executing a woman by hanging, isn't that an evil thing to do, unless it's Rose West or the like?

Back in the 1700s, they were hanging women like it was going out of fashion. One particular woman to receive the neck bungee jump was Mary Blandy; she was executed in 1752 for the alleged murder of her father. Her ghost is said to haunt the area and has been seen darting across the top of the Castle Mound.

As the prison drew to the end of its life, a group of prisoners held a séance in their cell. Afterwards, it is said, they experienced poltergeist activity. From what I read, a priest was called in to perform an exorcism.

Back in the late 1980s, two security guards were on duty one night, sitting in A Wing offices overlooking the stairs to the basement. As they sat there, they saw a white misty shape rise up the steps towards them before fading away.

A Wing seems to be the most haunted of places in Oxford Prison; this is confirmed from an incident that took place in September 1998.

His dog growling and snarling, as if in pain, alerted a security guard on patrol outside the entrance to A Wing. The guard spotted a pair of black figures; they turned in his direction. These 'intruders' seemed to lack arms and legs, and they were hovering above the ground!

Now, I've never read about ghosts being able to talk, but the guard swore that he heard the figures say, 'We live here, why are you here?'

After running to his van and making for the gate, the figures were in front of him.

The following morning, his wife found him sitting in shock in his van outside their house. The guard couldn't remember anything between leaving the prison and the morning. In a bizarre follow-up, his guard dog died a few days later.

In another A Wing incident, two members of the cleaning staff were cleaning A Wing when they heard a voice screaming, 'Help, let me out!' The voice was coming from the cell area, but when they went to investigate, the voice was coming from the area they had just left.

Another incident experienced by a cleaner who was cleaning a ground-floor cell in A Wing happened when she sensed someone enter the room. Turning around, she expected to see one of the other two cleaners in the block, but later on found them both to be on the third floor.

Other ghostly happenings in or near A Wing include a cleaner's bucket tipping and spinning by itself, a full binbag lift itself at least 3ft into the air and the sound of a stick being dragged along the nearby railings. Other strange happenings include voices being heard to shout from empty cells, and physical damage to items stored in the empty prison.

One of the other wings reported to be haunted is C Wing's recess, so no slopping out now!

HM PRISON STRANGEWAYS

The set of ghost stories wouldn't be complete without old Strangeways Prison having a story to tell. Night duty staff have often seen a mysterious man in a dark suit carrying a small briefcase scurrying about the place, walking along B Wing from just outside the old condemned cell towards the central control area. Some of the staff gave chase to the sinister-looking figure, but as the figure got to the old iron staircase leading up to the main office, he vanished into thin air. Some say that this apparition is John Ellis who committed suicide in 1932.

LAST MAN/WOMAN HANGING

And now we get to the moment when the violin starts to play and you get your handkerchief out to wipe the tears away. But I don't want any of that. I will just give you facts, thousands of them ... all dead!

Prison is no holiday camp, regardless of what these politicians tell you ... look at how they lied about the Iraq situation and saying we were all going to be fizzed out by chemical weapons ... bollocks! And so the same is true of our penal system!

I would hope that you now have a grasp of what it's like being a prisoner. Even if it's just being an armchair prisoner, then you will have learned something.

A life of hard labour was imposed on prisoners when they were given such tasks as turning the crank machine, shot drill or climbing the treadmill. Man has always taken delight in imposing such punishments on his fellow human beings. These useless and exhausting activities were thought to act as a deterrent and discourage prisoners from committing further crimes on their release ... as well as giving great pleasure to those imposing such punishments. Haven't you heard of masochists?

Samson in Prison from the painting by E Armitage which was housed in the Bristol Museum and Art gallery

It was common to impose such brutal punishments as every prisoner being expected to walk six hours a day on a treadmill in twenty-nine-minute increments with five-minute breaks, covering the equivalent of a 6,000ft incline. The tread wheel was rather like the elongated wheel of a paddle steamer with twenty-four steps instead of paddles. Prisoners stood, hanging on to a bar or strap, in individual compartments over these steps. The wheel turned under their weight. Prisoners had to keep climbing or fall off. Though they were widely used in English prisons, few tread wheels were built in Scotland and all were removed by the 1840s. Nowadays, these brutal punishments are outlawed in the UK.

Such punishments as the illustrious crank machine formed part of a useless labour regime that was introduced in the middle of the nineteenth century to make prison life tougher for those prisoners sentenced to hard labour. As I mentioned earlier, the prisoner (male) had to turn the handle some 14,400 times a day forcing four large cups or ladles through sand inside a drum. The number of revolutions was registered on a dial, so no one could cheat. The warder could, and usually would, make the task harder by tightening a screw – hence the slang word for prison warder. In Inveraray Jail, there was only one crank machine and little evidence that it was, in fact, used.

Another form of hard labour was the shot drill, which was practised in certain English prisons. The drill consisted of stooping down without bending the knees, picking up a heavy cannon-ball (much like the Atlas stones used in the TV competition *The World's Strongest Man*) bringing it up slowly until it is level with your chest, then taking three steps to the right, replacing it on the ground and then stepping back three paces ... and then starting the whole mundane procedure all over again. All of this was done while the screws shouted and bawled at you!

Moving away from the self-inflicted punishment of the treadmill and other highly exciting machinery, what about when screws dish out the punishments? Screws assaulting us cons? Nah, that can't be true! Well, here is some proof for you; a prison officer from Barnet was jailed for three-and-a-half years for his part in beating up a convict for his own 'bizarre and sadistic entertainment'.

You are going to say that I'm making this one up ... wrong. The screw's name is Darren Fryer, of Barnet; he was sentenced with two other screws for assaulting Steven Banks, an inmate of Wormwood Scrubs Prison, in March 1998. You've read about my claims of prison brutality in HMP Wormwood Scrubs; well, here is the proof.

The court heard how Fryer, Robert Lawrie and senior officer John Nicol, who both received sentences of four years, subjected inmate Steven Banks to a beating, crying, 'There's going to be a death in custody tonight!' With that, the three screws then smashed the con head-first against a wall before repeatedly punching and kicking him.

Passing sentence at Blackfriars Crown Court, Judge Charles Byers, said, 'You three men are guilty of not only an appalling assault but also of the grossest breach of that authority, responsibility and trust.'

The screws, as usual, claimed that Banks had attacked them with a mop handle! This is the normal ploy used by bent screws, but the jury rejected this and convicted them of assault and actual bodily harm.

At the end of the trial, The judge added, 'Not only did you commit the assault, you sought to cover the matter by charging him with assault on you, and saw to it his record was endorsed as a violent prisoner, particularly violent to prison officers. I can only conclude this episode was done for your own bizarre and sadistic entertainment.' So there was also proof that these screws were falsifying inmates' records and putting them down as 'violent'.

The court cases involving twenty-seven prison officers from Wormwood Scrubs who were accused of assaulting inmates took fourteen months to conclude. Only three others were found guilty with the twenty-one remaining officers being acquitted. Why wasn't my case put in with the multi-party action against the Home Office?

DEATHS IN POLICE CUSTODY TO 2001

1990	1991	1992	1993	1994	1995
59	60	47	36	52	48
1996	1997	1998	1999	2000	2001
53	58	65	44	35	34

A total of ninety-four prisoners took their own lives in Britain in 2002, compared with seventy-three the previous year, a rise of 29 per cent. Many more prisoners across the world have died in uprisings and fires caused by overcrowding.

DEATHS IN PRISON 1990 – MARCH 2002
(ENGLAND AND WALES)
Source: Inquest monitoring – Figures to 26 February 2002

Classification	1990	1991	1992	1993	1994	1995	1996	1997	1998	1999	2000	2001	2002	Total
Self-inflicted	52	42	41	48	59	60	64	69	83	91	81	72	12	774
(of which on remand)	24	16	18	27	24	24	33	30	31	30	37	27	5	325
Non Self-Inflicted	na	na	na	2	5	7	53	46	45	55	57	50	16	337
(of which on remand)	na	na	na	1	2	1	1	4	4	4	4	2	1	23
Homicide	na	na	na	1	2	2	2	2	6	0	3	1	0	19
(of which on remand)	na	na	na	0	1	1	1	1	0	0	2	1	0	7
Control & Restraint	na	1	na	0	1	3	0	0	0	0	0	0	0	5
(of which on remand)	na	1	na	0	0	1	0	0	0	0	0	0	0	2
Not Yet Classified	0	0	0	0	0	0	0	0	0	0	1	1	1	3
Black Deaths in Prison														
Self-inflicted	3	3	7	3	3	8	3	6	9	7	8	5	1	67
(of which on remand)	3	0	3	2	2	3	1	3	4	3	5	2	0	31
Non Self-inflicted	na	na	1	1	1	0	5	6	5	10	1	2	0	32
(of which on remand)	0	0	0	1	1	0	0	0	2	1	0	0	0	5
Homicide	0	0	0	0	1	0	1	0	0	0	1	0	0	3
(of which on remand)	0	0	0	0	0	0	1	0	0	0	0	0	0	1
Control & restraint	0	1	0	0	0	3	0	0	0	0	0	0	0	4
(of which on remand)	0	1	0	0	0	2	0	0	0	0	0	0	0	3
Deaths of Women in Prison														
Self-Inflicted	1	3	1	1	1	2	2	3	4	5	8	6	2	38
(of which on remand)	0	0	1	1	0	1	1	0	0	0	3	2	2	11
Non Self-inflicted	0	0	0	1	0	0	2	1	1	4	1	1	1	12
(of which on remand)	0	0	0	0	0	0	0	0	0	0	0	0	0	0
Youth Deaths in Prison														
Self-Inflicted	10	5	10	3	12	12	14	16	15	19	18	15	3	152
(of which on remand)	6	1	6	0	7	4	10	4	4	5	7	4	2	60
Non Self-inflicted	na	na	na	0	2	0	3	1	3	1	0	0	1	11
(of which on remand)	na	na	na	0	0	0	0	0	0	0	0	0	1	1
Homicide	na	na	na	0	0	0	0	2	1	0	2	0	0	5

OVERCROWDING KILLS PRISONERS

As the prison population increases then so will the suicide rate among prisoners rise.

In an uprising against overcrowding in Lincoln Prison, one prisoner, Lee Blake, died. At the current rate, the British prison population is set to reach close to 100,000 by 2009. In a survey conducted by the London School of Medicine, it is revealed that black people are six times more likely to be sent to prison than white people.

The current Chief Inspector of Prisons, Anne Owers, has noted the situation of having inmates locked in cells for twenty-three hours a day, and states that 'prison overcrowding threatens all four of the Inspectorate's tests of a healthy prison – safety, respect, purposeful activity and resettlement.'

Believe it or not, Scotland only has one women's prison, Corton Vale. You would think all would be cosy at such a place, but it has seen three suicides since May 2001 and it only has 290 inmates. The population in Corton Vale in 1996 was only 180; maybe now you can see the correlation between the increases in population and the suicide rate. Former Chief Inspector of Prisons, Clive Fairweather, has said that overcrowding contributes to a 'recipe for disaster ... a large proportion of the women at Corton Vale are more of a danger to themselves than they are to the public.'

Take a moment to think about Richard Jones, a remand prisoner who hanged himself in Gloucester Prison, the third suicide in the prison in two years. A report on Gloucester Prison from the Prison Service said overcrowding there was creating unacceptable living conditions.

DEATHS OF BLACKS, ASIANS AND MIXED-RACE PRISONERS
1969 to November 2001

Key
Po: Police
Pr: Prisons, Young Offenders Institutes, Remand Centres
Ps: Psychiatric Hospitals

No.	Date of Death	Name	Age	Circumstances surrounding death/Inquest verdict	*
1	18/04/69	David Oluwale	38	Found drowned in the River Aire, Leeds	Po
2	29/04/71	Andre Savvas		Died from fractured skull in Hornsey Police Station	Po
3	13/05/71	Aseta Simms		Died in Stoke Newington Police Station; death by misadventure	Po
4	1972	Lil' Douza	17	Died in Oxford Detention Centre; Pneumonia virus	Pr
5	26/11/73	Horace Bailey		Found hanged in Ashford Remand Centre	Pr
6	05/02/74	Stephen Bernard	33	Died 15 hours after being released from Ladywell Police Station; acute bronchitis	Po
7	20/02/74	Joseph Lawrence		Found dead in Brixton Prison; natural causes	Pr
8	26/05/74	John Lamaletie		Died nine days after being arrested by police officers from Hornsey; accidental death	Po
9	17/01/77	A Neelayya	32	Died in Chatham Police Station	Po
10	09/11/77	Basil Brown	25	Found dead in Albany Prison, his family were suspicious about his death	Pr
11	10/12/78	Michael Ferreira	19	Died in Stoke Newington Police Station after being stabbed in a racist attack	Po
12	02/08/79	S Singh Grewal	40	Died in Southall Police Station	Po
13	23/08/79	Henry Floyd	26	Found hanged in cell of West End Central Police Station; suicide	Po
14	24/10/79	John Eshiett	26	Died in Brixton Prison while awaiting trial	Pr
15	31/03/80	Richard Campbell	19	Died of dehydration after being force fed large quantities of drugs in Ashford Remand Centre; death by self-neglect because of inadequate medical facilities	Pr
16	Aug 1980	Leroy Gordon	20	Died in Pershore Police Station after crowd suspecting him of robbery sat on him; asphyxiation due to compression of the neck	Po

No.	Date of Death	Name	Age	Circumstances surrounding death/Inquest verdict	*
17	13/07/81	Winston Rose	27	Died in police van after being restrained by police officers taking him to psychiatric hospital; unlawful killing at the hands of the police	Po
18	06/11/81	Shohik Meah	43	Died in Thornhill Road Police Station, Birmingham	Po
19	12/01/82	Paul Worrell	21	A suicide risk; was found hanged in Brixton Prison after obtaining the materials to kill himself; open verdict	Pr
20	25/03/82	Changa Singh	60	Died of alcoholic poisoning in Cathay Park Police Station; misadventure	Po
21	September 1982	Franklyn Lee	20	According to the police died of injuries sustained during a burglary	Po
22	10/12/82	Simeon Collins	17	Died of acute injuries to liver and spleen, day after being arrested by City Road Police; accidental death	Po
23	12/01/83	Colin Roach		Died of gunshot wound sustained while he was in Stoke Newington Police Station; suicide	Po
24	14/02/83	James Ruddock	44	Died after being denied treatment for diabetes and sickle cell for 12 hours in Kensington Police Station; natural causes attributed to self-neglect	Po
25	06/05/83	Nicholas Ofusu	31	Death by misadventure	Po
26	06/05/83	Mathew Paul	19	Found hanged in Leman Street Police Station; suicide due to lack of care	Po
27	06/12/83	Leslie George Singh		Fell from 4th floor of Hammersmith Hospital after being transferred from Wormwood Scrubs	Pr
28	06/07/84	Michael Dean Martin		Accidental death aggravated by lack of care	
29	21/10/84	Curtis Marsh	27	A suicide risk who hanged himself inside Brixton Prison; suicide	Pr
30	02/01/85	Chittaranjan Joshi		Found hanged in his cell while on remand in Pentonville; suicide	Pr
31	11/03/85	Harold Roberts		Suicide	Ps
32	30/03/85	James Hall			Po
33	15/07/85	John Mikkelson	34	Unlawful killing, after police appeal IV changed to death by misadventure	Po
34	06/10/85	Cynthia Jarrett		Accidental death	Po

No.	Date of Death	Name	Age	Circumstances surrounding death/Inquest verdict	*
35	1986	Keith Hicks	34	A schizophrenic epileptic who died in Brixton Prison; misadventure	Pr
36	Feb 1986	Anthony Lloyd Powell	18	A schizophrenic, died after being given an injection of Modecate; open verdict	Ps
37	12/08/86	Stephen Bogle	27	Natural causes aggravated by lack of care	Po
38	11/09/86	Donald Chambers	29	Death by misadventure	Ps
39	06/10/86	Anwar Kureshi		An obvious suicide risk, managed to hang himself in Brixton Prison while on remand; suicide	Pr
40	08/10/86	Caiphas Lemard		Non-dependent drug abuse aggravated by lack of care	Po
41	27/01/87	Akhtar Moghul	47	Died in Holloway Prison while on remand, spoke no English and was allegedly denied medical treatment for a heart condition; natural causes aggravated by lack of care	Pr
42	20/02/87	Clinton McCurbin		Death by misadventure	Po
43	23/03/87	Ahmed Katangole	24	A suicide risk was found hanged in his cell at Pentonville; suicide aggravated by official indifference and lack of care	Pr
44	23/04/87	Jasbir Singh Rai	32	Found hanged in Wakefield Prison	Pr
45	24/04/87	Nenneh Jalloh		Death by misadventure	Po
46	01/05/87	Mohammed Parkit	50	Open verdict	Po
47	18/05/87	Anachu Osita	28	Natural causes aggravated by lack of care	Pr
48	26/06/87	Tunay Hassan	25	Drug dependency aggravated by lack of care	Po
49	July 1987	John Ryan	24	Died in Winson Green hospital, 3 days after being admitted suffering from dehydration, had been seen drinking his own urine; death by lack of care	Pr
50	Aug 1987	Terence Brown	35	Open verdict	Ps
51	19/08/87	Anthony Mahony	24	Died almost naked in a strip cell in Brixton Prison, had a history of mental illness; natural causes aggravated by lack of care	Pr
52	24/09/87	Mark Ventour		Asphyxia caused by chewing gum in throat	Po

No.	Date of Death	Name	Age	Circumstances surrounding death/Inquest verdict	•
53	Oct 1987	Joseph Palombella	40		Po
54	Feb 1988	Femi Adelaja	36	Died of a heart condition in a cell at Old Bailey, was denied treatment for sarcoidosis of the heart	Pr
55	05/02/88	Samuel Carew	22	Killed himself in Brixton Prison's hospital wing; suicide	Pr
56	16/03/88	Armando Belonia		Died of pneumonia in locked hospital wing of Wandsworth Prison; natural causes aggravated by lack of care	Pr
57	13/05/88	Bahader Singh	26	Died in India, hours after leaving Barlinnie Jail, where he had suffered physical and racial abuse	Pr
58	June 1988	Oakley Ramsey	25		Po
59	20/06/88	Kelroy Briscoe	32	Hanged himself in Wormwood Scrubs	Pr
60	23/08/88	Joseph Watts	30	Accidental death	Ps
61	04/09/88	Derek Buchanan	19	Drowning	Po
62	04/09/88	Sajjan Atwal	36	Hanged himself in Winson Green, was a suicide risk and had made other attempts on his life; lack of care, verdict was quashed and suicide due to lack of care verdict recorded	Pr
63	04/12/88	Martin Richmond	30	Found hanged in Brixton Prison; open verdict	Pr
64	Dec 1988	Wayne Tombison		Found hanged in Wandsworth Prison	Pr
65	Feb 1989	David 'Duke' Daley	44	Open verdict	Po
66	March 1989	Nicholas Bramble	17	Accidental death	Po
67	July 1989	Vincent Graham	40		Po
68	02/07/89	Jamie Stewart	22	Death by misadventure due to excessive overdose of cocaine	Po
69	12/07/89	Edwin Carr	39		Po
70	Oct 1989	Mr Romany		Found dead in Chanings Wood Prison; other prisoners said his screaming for a day and a night had been ignored	Pr
71	05/10/89	Siho Iyugiven	27	Kurdish asylum seeker set himself alight in Harmondsworth Detention Centre after being refused asylum; misadventure	Pr

No.	Date of Death	Name	Age	Circumstances surrounding death/Inquest verdict	•
72	06/12/89	Germain Alexander		Died after being removed to strip cell in Brixton, had bruising all over his body; natural causes aggravated by lack of care	Pr
73	15/06/90	Kimpua Nsimba	24	Zairean asylum-seeker found hanged in Harmondsworth Detention Centre, no one had spoken to him in over four days; suicide	Pr
74	24/07/90	Oliver Pryce	30	Unlawful killing	Po
75	12/10/90	Aslam Khan	29	Hanged himself while on remand in Brixton	Pr
76	30/11/90	Edwin Robinson	28	A suicide risk, with a psychotic illness hanged himself in Brixton Prison; killed himself because of lack of care	Pr
77	19/01/91	Delroy McKnight	29	Cut his own throat with glass from cell window and bled to death in Wandsworth Prison; killed himself while the balance of his mind was disturbed and death was contributed to by lack of care	Pr
78	29/04/91	Vandana Patel	21	Died after being stabbed in DVU in Stoke Newington Police Station	Po
79	13/06/91	Kwaku Ohene	30	Had mental problems and committed suicide in hospital wing of Swaleside; death aggravated by lack of care	Pr
80	12/08/91	Ian Gordon	24	Psychiatric patient shot dead by Telford Police; lawful killing	Po
81	28/08/91	Orville Blackwood	31	Died after being given injection of 'calming' drugs in secure unit at Broadmoor; accidental death; on appeal to High Court by Orville's family, verdict quashed and a verdict of accidental death recorded again	Ps
82	08/10/91	Omasase Lumumba	32	Died of a 'heart attack' while being 'controlled and restrained' by six guards in Pentonville; unlawfully killed using improper methods and excessive force in the process of control and restraint	Pr
83	1992	Arthur Allison	50	Died four days after being arrested by Leicester Police	Po
84	03/01/92	Melita Crawford	24	Had mental problems and was found dead while on remand at Risley; misadventure	Pr
85	08/01/92	Mark Fletcher	21	Detained under the Mental Health Act, died in All Saints Psychiatric Hospital after being given an injection in his spine; cardiac arrest	Ps
86	June 1992	Munir Yusef Mojothi	26	Died of an OD in Clifton Hospital after being given injections of Droperidol; lack of care	Ps
87	23/06/92	Jerome Scott	27	Collapsed and died on the way to hospital in a police van after being given two injections; therapeutic misadventure;	Ps

No.	Date of Death	Name	Age	Circumstances surrounding death/Inquest verdict	*
88	03/07/92	Errol Commock	24	A known suicide risk committed suicide in hospital wing of Winson Green; suicide	Pr
89	28/08/92	James Segawa	28	HIV+ asylum-seeker died in Belmarsh after officials refused to believe he was ill	Pr
90	05/09/92	Ian Francis	28	Died of blood poisoning 12 days after injuring himself at Send Prison; death by natural causes	Pr
91	21/11/92	Leon Patterson	32	Died while on remand at Stockport Police Station; unlawful killing – overturned in 1994; misadventure to which neglect contributed	Po
92	04/12/92	Nadeem Younus	21	Died of an overdose in Little Hay Prison after obtaining paracetamol tablets from the hospital; open verdict	Pr
93	19/12/92	Randhir Showpal	43	Died in Norbury Police Station after being detained under the Mental Health Act; misadventure	Po
94	01/01/93	Warren Jones	26	Found hanged in Leicester Prison; suicide;	Pr
95	10/03/93	Adejare Akinbiyi	30	Died after suffering a succession of severe asthma attacks in Belmarsh; accidental death brought about by lack of care;	Pr
96	16/03/93	Turan Pekoz	43	Died after setting himself alight in Quest House Immigration Centre, Croydon; misadventure	Pr
97	01/08/93	Joy Gardner	40	Died after being arrested by 'specialist' officers from the Extradition Unit of the Met, was gagged with 13ft of tape; adjourned until trial of officers involved; officers later acquitted	Po
99	30/01/94	Rupert Marshall	29	Died in Horton Psychiatric Hospital after being injected with an anti-psychotic drug; not known	Ps
100	27/04/94	Kwanele Siziba	27	Fell 150ft to her death, attempting to flee what she believed were immigration officials; misadventure	Po
101	31/05/94	Carl Owens	22	Died while on remand of a Methadone OD in segregation unit of Brixton Prison; misadventure;	Pr
102	26/06/94	O Akinbobola,	24	Dound hanged in cell at Woodhill Prison, had protested innocence and had gone on hunger strike; suicide;	Pr
103	10/07/94	Mark Harris	31	Found hanged after arrested by Bristol police officers; open verdict;	Po
104	10/08/94	Jonathan Weekes		Died in Chase Farm hospital; natural causes – pneumonia;	Ps

No.	Date of Death	Name	Age	Circumstances surrounding death/Inquest verdict	*
105	19/09/94	Shkander Singh	37	Died in Stewart Street Police Station, Glasgow. Had been heard shouting and crying in cell but was ignored; heart failure	Po
106	29/09/94	Norman Manning	26	Stabbed to death by inmates in Long Lartin Prison; in November 1997, 41-year-old Frederick Low was convicted of Norman's murder	Pr
107	23/10/94	Joseph Nnalue	31	Died after falling from balcony in flat in Stockwell. Police and immigration officials wee calling at his flat at the time; accidental death	Po
108	18/11/94	Tyrone Wilson	34	Died eighteen days after police were called to his flat in Ipswich; not known	Po
109	16/12/94	Oluwashiji Lapite	34	Died during a struggle with police officers from Stoke Newington Police Station; unlawful killing. In June 1998, the CPS reaffirmed its decision not to prosecute the officers involved	Po
110	14/01/95	Mark Holness,	28	Found hanged in his cell at Whitemoor Prison; not known	Pr
111	06/05/95	Lungile Simelane	27	Found hanged in her cell at Holloway Prison; not known	Pr
112	08/05/95	Brian Douglas	33	Died eight days after being restrained with new batons by Clapham Police Officers; misadventure	Po
113	05/06/95	Dajin George	26	A schizophrenic, died after falling fifteen floors from a flat in Leyton, was meant to be under supervision by hospital staff;	Ps
114	Aug 95	Mohammed Massaquoi	22	Found hanged in his cell at Highdown Prison	Pr
115	25/08/95	Muttavel Vasanthan	25	Sri Lankan asylum seeker found hanged in his cell at Norwich Prison	Pr
116	31/08/95	Peter Williams	19	Found hanged in his cell at Aylesbury YOI	Pr
117	05/10/95	Raja Khan	24	Found hanged in his cell at Mount Prison	Pr
118	18/10/95	Denis Stevens	29	Found dead in punishment block of Dartmoor Prison, had been restrained in a body belt for 24 hours; accidental death recorded December 1997, despite appeal to Court of Appeal by family who wanted verdict of unlawful killing; coroner would not allow this; family boycotted resumed inquest	Pr
119	30/10/95	Brian Augustine		Found hanged in his cell at Pentonville Prison	Pr

No.	Date of Death	Name	Age	Circumstances surrounding death/Inquest verdict	•
120	26/11/95	Kenneth Severin	25	Found dead in his cell at Bellmarsh after being restrained face down by eight guards; open verdict	Pr
121	05/12/95	Wayne Douglas	25	Died in Brixton Police Station; accidental death	Po
122	09/12/95	Alton Manning	33	Died after being forcibly restrained by eight guards at Blakenhurst (private) Prison; unlawful killing. In March 1999, the CPS decided not to prosecute the officers involved in his death, saying that there was no realistic prospect of obtaining a conviction	Pr
123	Jan 1996	Newton White	33	Drowned in bath at Denis Hill Unit of Maudesley Hospital; open verdict	Ps
124	15/03/96	Noorjahan Begum	35	Died after falling from balcony of flat where she was living; two immigration officials were calling at the flat at the time; accidental death	Po
125	16/03/96	Ibrahima Sey	29	Died after being sprayed (while handcuffed) with CS spray in Ilford Police Station; unlawful killing. In October 1998, the CPS decided that thare was not enough evidence to prosecute the officers involved in his death	Po
126	April 1996	Ziya Bitirim	47	Died after collapsing and vomiting during his arrest; accidental death	Po
127	April 1996	Donovan Williams	36	Died after collapsing in his cell during a search in Peckham Police Station; accidental death	Po
128	22/05/96	Dominic Otoo	19	Found dead in Hindley Remand Centre; natural causes	Pr
129	13/8/96	Ahmed El Gammal	33	Died after struggling with police from Leyton Police Station; not known	Po
130	4/10/96	Fred Tokunpor Akiyemi	46	Died after falling from fifth floor of flat; Peckham police were calling at his flat at the time; not known	Po
131	Oct/Nov 1996	Veron Cowan	32	Died in secure unit of Blackberry Hill Hospital; natural causes	Ps
132	7/10/96	George Bosie Davies	36	Died in Marylebone Police Station after being arrested on suspicion of being drunk	Po
133	11/11/96	Oscar Okoye,	53	Died five months after being arrested by Streatham Police on suspicion of being drunk; natural causes	Po
134	10/01/97	Herbert Gabbidon	68	Died while in the custody of Walsall Policewho were deporting him back to Jamaica	Po

No.	Date of Death	Name	Age	Circumstances surrounding death/Inquest verdict	*
135	30/01/97	Peter Austin	30	Found hanged in Brentford Magistrates' Court; lack of care contributed to accidental death	Po
136	06/03/97	Ronnie Clarke	38	Found unconscious in cell at Wellingborough, taken to Kettering Hospital, where he died without regaining consciousness; not known	Pr
137	12/03/97	Abel Mukuna	39	Died in Greenwich Hospital, five days after being admitted from Belmarsh	Pr
138	23/03/97	Marlon Downes	20	Found hanged in cell of Harlesden Police Station; open verdict	Po
139	3/04/97	Peter San Pedro	25	Died after walking into path of lorry, hours after being arrested and sprayed with CS spray; open verdict December 1998	Po
140	1/05/97	Lytton Shannon	36	Collapsed and died after being arrested by Wolverhampton Police	Po
141	19/09/97	Jason Sebastian	23	Found hanged in Belmarsh following 4-day segregation as punishment; open verdict	Pr
142	26/02/98	Elliott Mitchell	20	Found hanged in Reading Remand Centre	Pr
143	1/04/98	Christopher Alder	37	Died after being arrested by Hull Police, dragged to the station, placed on floor face down and handcuffed. Five police officers suspended and charged with misconduct in public office; unanimous unlawful killing verdict	Po
144	31/10/98	David Bennett	38	Died after being restrained face down for over twenty minutes by at least three nurses at the Norvic Clinic, Norwich; accidental death aggravated by neglect, coroner made six recommendations	Ps
145	2/11/98	Patrick Louis		Died in the custody of Plumstead Police who arrested him for being drunk and incapable	Po
146	18/01/99	Roger Sylvester	30	Died seven days after being restrained by police in Tottenham	Po
147	24/01/99	Robert Allotey	37	Collapsed and died after being arrested by Wolverhampton Police	Po
148	3/05/99	Paul Jemmott	19	Attempted suicide by hanging at Aylesbury YOI, died five days later in hospital	Pr
149	15/07/99	Leon Marshall	24	Died in hospital two days after being arrested for drugs-related offences. Officers were aware he had swallowed drugs but failed to take him to hospital; accidental death	Po

THE GOOD PRISON GUIDE

No	Date of Death	Name	Age	Circumstances surrounding death/Inquest verdict	*
150	6/08/99	Sarah Thomas (aka Lai Hong Cheng)	34	Died in hospital two days after collapsing in Stoke Newington Police Station	Po
151	14/12/99	Ertan Uzan	25	Found hanged in his cell in Brixton Prison	Pr
152	3/1/00	Mr Benmerabet	42	Algerian Mr Benmerabet collapsed outside the Atomics nightclub in Kent. Kent Police were called to assist the ambulance service but deny restraint was used	Po
153	16/1/00	Asif Dad	26	Died in the custody of Chelmsford Police. According to the police, Asif was arrested after they were called to a disturbance in the street and he collapsed and died after a struggle	Po
154	24/1/00	Robertas Grabys		Lithuanian asylum-seeker, hanged himself at Harmondsworth Detention Centre	Pr
155	1/02/00	Keita Craig	22	Suffered with mental health problems, took his own life in Wandsworth Prison; killed himself while the balance of his mind was disturbed. February 2001: High Court orders new inquest after judicial review of the verdict. New inquest in October 2001, finds the same verdict but adds a rider that neglect was a contributory factor to the death	Pr
156	23/3/00	Zahid Mubarek	19	Victim of a racist attack in his cell at Feltham Young Offenders Institute. He was just twelve hours from being released. The attack left Zahid with massive head injuries, and he died five days later. His assailant, his cell mate, 19-year-old Robert Joseph Stewart, was jailed for life for his murder in November 2000	Pr
157	5/5/00	Edita Pommel	20	Edita Pommel was found hanged in HMP Brockhill. She had complained about racial harassment from a prison officer. Her death is now the source of an investigation being carried out by West Mercia Police	Pr
158	18/6/00	Cheryl Simone Hartman	20	Cheryl was found hanged in her cell at Holloway Prison. Cheryl had a history of mental illness and had asked to go to prison for medical help; open verdict	Pr
159	16/7/01	Derek Bennett	28	Shot dead in the street by Brixton Police, who alleged they were called by a member of the public. Derek was carrying a novelty lighter shaped like a gun	Po

No	Date of Death	Name	Age	Circumstances surrounding death/Inquest verdict	*
160	2/11/01	Michelle Allen	23	Found hanged at Barking Magistrates' Court. Securicor Custodial Services, company responsible for prisoners, refused to comment	Pr
161	22/11/01	Ricky Bishop	25	Taken to Brixton Police Station to be searched where he was restrained. Then taken to King's College Hospital where he died	Po
162	25/11/01	Jospeh Crensil		Died after falling from a third-floor window of a flat in Streatham. Two immigration and two police officers were questioning five other men at the flat. Jospeh who was hiding in the bathroom, tried to escape, and fell to his death	Po

Figures courtesy Race Relations Board

The year 2002–03 saw the highest number of suicides on record – 105.

Prison is not the answer to crime, it is a soft option. Something more radical is needed! I will end now with a quote – I can't recall who came up with it originally, but it just about says it all:

'THE ONLY PERSON WORSE THAN THE FELON WHO COMMITS A CRIME IS THE MAN WHO LOCKS HIM UP.'

For more information about my other books, access my website: www.bronsonmania.com